THE HOME FRONT: □NOTES□ FROM THE FAMILY WAR ZONE

By Louise Armstrong

MC GRAW-HILL BOOK COMPANY

New York   St. Louis   San Francisco
Toronto   Hamburg   Mexico

1 2 3 4 5 6 7 8 9   FGRFGR   8 7 6 5 4 3

ISBN 0-07-002276-3

LIBRARY OF CONGRESS CATALOGING IN PUBLICATION DATA

Armstrong, Louise.
The home front.
Includes bibliographical references and index.
1. Wife abuse—United States.   2. Family violence—
United States.   3. Child abuse—United States.   I. Title.
HV6626.A75   362.8′2   82-7788
ISBN 0-07-002276-3   AACR2

Book design by Roberta Rezk

Acknowledgments

There are so many whose previous work made this book possible—Del Martin, Mildred Pagelow, R. and R. Dobash, Florence Rush, Susan Brownmiller, Andrea Dworkin, Diane Russell, all the women who struggled against violence toward women. . . . It would be impossible to name them all.

I'd like to express my indebtedness to Debby and David Goren, to "Jan Samuels." To the work of William Ryan, Morton Schatzman, Anthony Platt, David Ferlerger . . . Here again, there are so many.

For their time and support, above and beyond their work in print, and for their discussions, suggestions, criticisms of, arguments with the work in progress, my very deepest gratitude to Florence Rush, Nicholas Kittrie, Roland Summit, Maggie Paley, Janet Fink, Joanne Schulman, Jeanine Pirro, Mildred Pagelow, Kate Phillips.

Orrie Armstrong, Tom Hawley, Alexi and Noah Hawley made the book possible in the very most profound sense.

Jonathan Dolger, my agent, flew a notable rescue mission in a distressing trouble spot. Attorney Robert Adler plotted a successful course.

A reading by Judith Plotz was most helpful. Laurie Weinstein came to the rescue in the manuscript's end-run. Jennifer Knapp did invaluable law research. Her parents, Beverly and Charles Knapp, her sister Liza, and all my friends have my promise of a vote on the next project.

EDITOR'S NOTE

All references, quote citations, and
additional notes are at the end
of the book, identified by chapter, page,
and text end-sentence or context phrase.

Contents

Preface:
Some Preliminaries

Given the variations in statistical measurements of household mayhem in this country at present, perhaps the best answer to how often physical and sexual assault occur is "a lot." Given the massive number of studies which have now been done, one can only choose to present representative findings that suggest the parameters of the issue. It is probably not necessary to present data on how many blows the average wife received per beating (allowing for error among those who passed out). Or to provide charts breaking down the percent raped vs. those hit with rocks, punched, kicked, thrown down stairs. . . .

Despite discrepancies, research numbers and estimates portray a landscape dotted with casualties. They create a picture which would alarm us were the wounded reported among our soldiers on a foreign, rather than the domestic, front.

Knowing that readers will be coming to this book with diverse degrees of prior awareness, some findings and some historical data (documenting continuity) are set down here —to be read now, scanned, or skipped, and checked later if incredulity sets in. They are presented as a preliminary crawl— the kind occasionally used to open a film: setting the scene, providing background, orienting the audience for what is to come.

According to sociologists, Murray A. Straus, Richard J. Gelles, and Suzanne K. Steinmetz, "the estimated 2 million women and children battered and beaten by family members each year are only the tip of the iceberg."

Their study showed that if you are married, the chances you will be slugged by your spouse are between one in four and one in three.

They estimate that between 3.4 and 4 million children have been kicked, bitten, or punched by a parent at some time during their childhood.

That between 1.4 and 2.3 million children have been "beaten up."

That between 900,000 and 1.8 million children between three and seventeen years of age have been threatened by a parent with a knife or gun.

A study by Professor Jeanne M. Giovannoni and Professor Rosina M. Becerra of 949 cases of reported child abuse, shows that in 459 cases the children experienced two or more kinds of abuse. At least half of the children who had been sexually assaulted had been abused in some other way.

"Intimate Victims: A Study of Violence Among Friends and Relatives" conducted by the U.S. Department of Justice, Bureau of Justice Statistics, published in January, 1980, showed that between 1973 and 1976, over 3 million incidents of violence among intimates took place. This study included *only those over the age of twelve.* In two-fifths of the cases, the results were bruises, black eyes, cuts, and scratches. One victim in every 20 was knifed or received a gunshot wound. A roughly equal proportion had bones broken or teeth knocked out, or received internal injuries, or were knocked unconscious. About 16% received burns, or had their hair pulled out.

One study by the Battered Women Research Center in Denver, Colorado, showed that 34% of the 400 battered women studied had been raped in their marriage at least once: 59% had been forced into sex, 49% more than once; 41% objected to being forced to insert objects into their vaginas, engage in group sex, have sex with animals, or play bondage games.

We know that it is often when the child gets hurt or is

discovered molested that the abused wife finally decides to get out. Where she may have been staying, "taking it" for the children's sake, discovery of their jeopardy provides the catalytic force. The Department of Justice Report tells of a case where ". . . the husband molested the younger son several times. The husband told the wife, 'if she reported him to the police, they would believe him, not the child,' because 'he was a friend of the judge, and the police can't do anything in a domestic dispute.' Her husband was a former law enforcement officer. Because of this incident and several other disputes between the husband and wife, the respondent filed for a divorce and moved out."

We know that when mothers report sexual abuse of their children by their husbands, they are themselves subject to a charge of neglect, of "unfit parent," of "depravity."

We know that in such cases, the husband is likely to receive weekend custody of the child, and the abuse continues.

We know too that divorce does not end the violence. As the Criminal Justice Report acknowledges, "the abuse usually continues until the victim either remarries or moves away."

We know that when the women try to escape, the men do not let them go free, but rather pursue them, hound them, threaten them, and victimize them with greater and sometimes deadly force. (Peculiarly human, this. One author writes: "One of the most distasteful aspects of human psychology is the fact that, once violence has begun to be used against the helpless, helplessness not only loses its capacity to inhibit, but may actually increase the use of violence. When animals of the same species engage in contests, the loser is generally allowed to go free; but men seldom let their defeated enemies escape. . . .")

We know that, although the offenders are deadly serious, their behavior sometimes borders on the ludicrous. As where the husband ". . . who had repeatedly harassed or attacked his ex-wife in order to take the children, pretended to be a maid at the motel where his ex-wife was staying. When she opened the door, he began to threaten her with a wrench."

To stay is Dickensian. To leave is Kafkaesque.

One woman

> had been separated from the batterer for two years and was divorcing him, yet he continued to harass her. He broke into her home, destroyed her property, poured acid in her car motor, attacked her at work, and bragged to others about how he was going to kill her. She repeatedly called the police for protection but they became tired of answering her calls. . . .
>
> One afternoon, minutes after she had terminated a threatening phone call from him, her estranged husband broke down the front door, shouting, "Get the gun, you bitch, 'cause I'm going to kill you and the baby." As he came at her, he saw that she had gotten the weapon from the kitchen. Still he advanced toward her, shouting, "Shoot me, shoot me." She shot and killed him, and was immediately arrested and charged with his murder.

We know, overwhelmingly, that women receive their worst beatings during pregnancy.

In one case,

> victim stated the first argument started over a pack of cigarettes. Victim stated accused (her husband) held her against the bathroom wall by the hair and continued to beat victim with his right hand.
>
> Victim is six months pregnant at this time. Victim stated accused kept telling victim, "Bitch, you are going to lose that baby"; and then accused would beat the victim in the stomach again.

Most of the women interviewed said that physical violence becomes more acute during pregnancy.

"An occurrence which appeared with great consistency was the infliction of blows to the abdominal area during pregnancy."

"Of special note was the number of reported incidents of domestic violence surrounding pregnancy. Many women reported that the first physical abuse occurred shortly after they announced their first pregnancy."

We know the violences "cut across all socioeconomic lines." Nice people do indeed do "such things."

That it should be so is entirely unremarkable.

Throughout most of history, these behaviors on the part of men toward women and children, have been overtly, publicly, legally, and religiously, *endorsed.*

It has been well-rehearsed: There was an "Age of Permitted Abuse."

For centuries, men wielded absolute power over their wives and children. The man was not just "head of household"— legally, morally, by ideation and practice, he *was* the household.

In the thirteenth century, Dominican Nicolas Byard stated, "A man may chastise his wife and beat her (*verberare*) for her correction; for she is of his household and therefore the Lord may chastise his own, as it is written in Gratian's *Decretum,* under the gloss *judicari.*" The comparison was made with the relationship of schoolmaster to schoolboy. Under Gratian's *Decretum,* "the husband is bound to chastise his wife moderately unless he be a cleric, in which case he may chastise her the harder."

Also, "Since the husband is the head of the wife, while the man's head is Christ, every wife who is not subject to her husband, that is to her head, is guilty of the same offense as the man is when he is not subject unto Christ his head."

Children, as well, were chattel of the husband. In Roman law, "The Law of the Twelve Tables" granted the father the absolute right to sell his children and the absolute power of life and death over the child. The woman would lay the infant at his feet, and he would nod or he would point. As he proposed, she disposed. This was called *patria potestas. Patria potestas* is religious in origin. "From this position as highpriest in the family worship came that life-long authority over the other members of his household bestowed by this archaic society upon the father—that authority which, known in Roman jurisprudence as Patria Potestas, is in its effects the most far-reaching subject of the early private law of Rome."

In ancient Greece, as well, the child was the father's absolute property. The positioning in importance went: father, cattle, mother, children.

Female children had no legal identity and none to look forward to: marriage was no more than a transfer of property, from father to husband. The rape of another's girl child was a matter to be settled in coin. Talmudic law decreed that betrothal and marriage could not take place before three-years-and-one-day of age.

Christian Canon law declared marriage legal at any age once copulation had taken place.

Clearly, the concept of sex with children was unremarkable.

From the 1609 edict that, "In the strictness of the law, for a husband to beat his wife was lawful," through the 1800's claim that, "For as he is to answer for her misbehavior, the law thought it reasonable to intrust him with its power of restraining her by domestic chastisement . . ." the ideation of patriarchal power and privilege held fast.

Well into the 1800's, women—for whom life unmarried was entirely a life of service without status (service to fathers, to other relatives)—could only pray for marriage, while praying their married fate would not be to be "conected [sic] with A Tyrant."

Wife-battering was condemned by statute in this country in eight states, and by judicial decision in five others, during the 1800's. But the standards were arbitrary, and in practice the statutes served only as a further weapon against the already-oppressed: immigrants and blacks.

Of 58 divorces examined between 1867 and 1887 where the woman charged cruelty, 29 were accounted for by charges of assault—ranging from "simple" physical assault to the far more brutal. One man forced his wife to beg like a dog. Another broke his wife's nose, fingers, two ribs, cut her face and lips, chewed and bit her ears and face, and wounded her head to foot. Another pounded his wife's head against the wall, forced her mouth open and spit tobacco juice down her throat. One kept a razor under the pillow and harassed his wife with it.

One took all the doors off the hinges, rolled up the carpets and left the house that way for two weeks—because his pregnant wife had failed to cook his breakfast.

Then, as now, actual wife-beating happened among proper people (although the poor, then as now, were more likely to be caught by the system). Women of note helped women of class flee from their batterers.

> The most dramatic example was the protection a battered wife and her daughter received from Susan B. Anthony and another feminist, Lydia Mott. The battered wife, a mother of three, was the sister of a U.S. Senator and the wife of a Massachusetts legislator; she had written several books and had operated an academy. When she discovered that her husband had committed an adultery, she confronted him; but he became consumed with anger, kicked her down the stairs, abused her, and *even had her committed to an insane asylum for a year and a half* [my italics]. Finally, after her release, she stayed at her brother's house; but her husband kept the children. When one of her daughters came for a visit, this mother decided to take her and flee. A Quaker family, which took in the refugees, asked Susan B. Anthony to help them escape.

She did, and they hid out for about a year. Both William Lloyd Garrison and Wendell Phillips pleaded with Anthony to return the child to her "natural" custodian, the father. Anthony, refusing, said, "You would die before you would deliver a slave to his master, and I will die before I will give up that child to this father." In the end, the daughter was kidnapped on her way to Sunday School and returned to the father.

Periodically, people noticed. Rabbi Perez, in the thirteenth century, said:

> The cry of the daughters of our people has been heard concerning the sons of Israel who raise their hands to strike their wives. Yet who has given a husband the authority to beat his wife? Is he not rather forbidden to strike any person in Israel? . . . Nevertheless have we heard of cases where Jewish women complained regard-

ing their treatment before the Communities, and no action was taken on their behalf. We have therefore decreed that any Jew may be compelled, on application of his wife or one of her near relatives to undertake a *herem* [written document] not to beat his wife in anger and cruelty or so as to disgrace her, for that is against Jewish practice. If anyone will stubbornly refuse to obey our words, the Court of the place, to which the wife or her relatives will bring complaint, shall assign her maintenance according to the custom of the place where she dwells. They shall fix her alimony as though her husband were away on a distant journey.

Truly, a better deal for the battered wife than that of today.

Again, as with Rabbi Perez, a voice rose against *The Subjection of Women* in the 1800's. John Stuart Mill wrote:

The sufferings, immoralities, evils of all sorts, produced in innumerable cases by the subjection of individual women to individual men, are far too terrible to be overlooked. . . . And it is perfectly obvious that the abuse of power cannot be very much checked while the power remains. It is a power given, or offered, not to good men, or to decently respectable men, but to all men; the most brutal and the most criminal. . . . The law of servitude in marriage is a monstrous contradiction to all the principles of the modern world. . . . It is the sole case, now that negro slavery has been abolished, in which a human being in the plenitude of every faculty is delivered up to the tender mercies of another being, in the hope forsooth that this other will use the power solely for the good of the person subjected to it. Marriage is the only actual bondage known to our law. There remain no legal slaves except the mistress of every house.

And, of course, the child of every parent.

If this book speaks only to male violences in the home, to crimes committed by men against "their" women and children, this is because those are the violences, once condoned, which we remain unwilling to seriously condemn. It is not a recital of the awfulnesses of all men.

Undeniably, women batter children, although "(t)he greater involvement of fathers and other males in physical abuse is gradually being recognized. The 1978 data from the American Humane Association showed that in 13,558 cases of 'abuse only,' 55 percent of the perpetrators were males."

However, where women behave criminally toward their children, there is little visible hesitation to seriously condemn them. The husband is not implicated in—or seen as contributory to—her behavior. He is not maligned or indicted for having failed to prevent it. Where the woman is violent toward the child, the question is, "How could she?" Where he is violent toward the child, or molests the child sexually, the question is, "How could she have let him?"

The fact that some, even many, men are brutal within the home does not implicate all men. That our response to men's household crimes is to indict women, seriously threatens to implicate all men. It diminishes all for the gross misbehaviors of some.

Enough.

Let's move on.

1
The Combat Zone

The subject of family violence is volatile. Where it comes up, the conversation crescendoes.

"Come on," a young male guest says. "You're not trying to tell me all this crazy behavior in the family is *normal.*"

Can we call something "deviant" which is both common and widespread?

"You mean you're saying it's *not* deviant?"

It has a pretty strong history of being downright legal.

"But I mean guys who molest their kids and who slug their wives are sick."

Sick?

"Sick."

If a man assaulted a pregnant friend of yours on the street and beat her until he broke her jaw, punched her repeatedly in the stomach, broke two of her ribs . . .

"Cut it out."

. . . who would you call? A psychiatrist, or a cop?

"A cop, of course."

If your six-year-old niece was forced by a stranger to perform oral-genital sex, who would you call to deal with the alleged perpetrator? A psychiatrist, or a cop?

"Cop."

Okay. If, as was reported not too long ago, a respected dentist repeatedly tied his kid to the bed—bound his wrists and ankles, refused him water while making him run in the

1

hot sun, and taught him to fall off his bicycle on command, tormented him until the kid hanged himself in the closet— what word would you use to describe the father?

"Sick. I mean that's sick."

Oh.

"Look. The way you're talking, you make it sound like half the country is beating their wives, or raping their kid, or . . ."

Or socking their elderly mothers?

"What are you saying? It's an epidemic?"

Not at all. It's the vestige of quite a—forgive me—healthy tradition.

"I don't believe it. I don't see how you can say it's not sick."

But men who batter their wives don't see they've done anything wrong. In fact, they only agree to therapy when they're seriously convinced their wives mean to leave them. Men who sexually invade their own kids don't think of themselves as child abusers. As one father said when he was caught, "I'm a decent man. I provide for my family. I don't run around on my wife, and I've never slept with anyone except my wife and my daughters." Another nice, middle-class man explained on TV, "I actually, in my own mind back then, I thought I was doing her a favor."

It's become axiomatic that the men are often pillars of the community. You might look at it, given the truth of history, that they're just inclined to have an extra-strong sense of tradition. That they're the backbone of the forefront in the movement to return to "traditional" family values. . . .

"Dinner!" comes the call up the stairs.

We go down, my young friend muttering, "Sick. It's sick, that's all." And, at the bottom step, "It's crazy."

This is not a book about family violences. It is, rather, about our response to their recent "discovery." About the effects of our decision to throw crimes in the home to the "therapeutic" state, rather than the legal state.

It's important to be clear: when I speak of crimes in the

home, I am speaking of serious (and most often often-repeated) behavior which would be criminal if directed toward a stranger. Of aggravated assault, defined as "unlawful attack by one person upon another for the purpose of inflicting severe bodily injury usually accompanied by the use of a weapon or other means likely to produce death or serious bodily harm." Of assault with intent to kill. Of rape. Of child molestation.

As the extent of these violences came to light, each "discovery" was heralded with an assumption of public moral outrage. Outrage of a kind and degree usually reserved to things we take seriously, things we seriously condemn—and declare against the law, and prosecute. Yet each, in turn, was promptly and proudly declared "de-criminalized." The criminal justice system was declared "inappropriate." The enlightened response was treatment; treatment for the whole family, which was "dysfunctional." The goal of the treatment was to keep the abusive family intact.

When C. Henry Kempe delivered his research findings on child battering in the early 1960's, he named the issue The Battered Child Syndrome. Not—it might be noted—The Battering Parent Syndrome. The medical aspects were emphasized. The legal aspects were played down. Liability was evaded. The focus was on the need for treatment intervention.

Within a few years, abuse had taken a back seat as only one of a panoply of justifications for intervention by the state. There was concern over neglect, emotional neglect, even moral and religious neglect. There were justifications for *preventive* intervention; justifications for seeking out *potential* neglect— a kind of moral ambulance-chasing. Intrusions which could not be accomplished under the legal system—with its safeguards of due process, representation—were effected, with medical/ therapeutic auspices, under an extended quasi-legal system: the "therapeutic" state.

In 1977, the federal Law Enforcement Assistance Administration, alerted to the prevalence of wife assault, proposed a program to assist the victims of "crimes in the home." That phrase was quickly scratched. In its place went "family violence" and "domestic violence." A few programs took a criminal justice approach, but that was far from the mainstream response. Apart from grassroots feminist organizing of hotlines, shelters, safe homes, etc., the major response was counseling (often couples counseling). Further medicalized, The Battered Woman Syndrome is now recognized in the International Classification of Diseases.

Incest, that recent monolithic bugaboo—of which we allegedly had some primordial dread—fell under the medical aegis. Here, too, we had no offender and victim. In jig-time, incest was diagnosed as no more than a symptom of "family dysfunction."

The goal of most treatment, in cases of all these violences, was to "preserve the family."

Peculiar. With our escalating divorce rate, statistically, at least, one divorce in each life is "normal." For, say, incompatibility. Yet our response to homes where crimes were taking place was therapeutic, often coercively therapeutic, aimed at keeping *those* families intact.

In most states parents can presently dump their children into the system—as incorrigible, beyond control, in need of supervision, or diagnosed as having something vaguely labeled "adjustment reaction to childhood." Yet where a crime by a parent against a child is discovered, the goal is to keep that family together.

This was billed as new and improved, an enlightened response. New and improved over what? Allusions—at odds with all evidence—were made to some bad old days when our reaction was said to have been primitive and vengeful, the seeking of retribution: criminal prosecution.

Progress, we were told, meant that the greater the evidence that one household member was committing criminal offenses against another, the greater the emphasis that should be placed on them—not as offender and victim—but as inseparable parts of a unit.

A letter is written to *The New York Times* by a New York State Family Court Judge—as if to me:

> Those who want to throw all these conflicts (crimes in the family) into the criminal court ask, Why should charges of disorderly conduct, harassment or assault *between* family members—usually with the husband the aggressor and the wife the victim—be treated any differently from a crime committed by a stranger?
>
> The answer begins with the fact that the men in many of these cases have *no criminal records* or histories of aggression *against anyone except the complainant.* The question of how to prevent further offenses and to protect the victim therefore differs greatly from the prevention and protection problem in cases of *criminals who attack strangers. The motive lies in the personal relationship: it is not robbery* [my italics].

While this letter by no means bears all of the arguments for treating such crimes as quasi-legal, it bears some of the underlying assumptions which regularly tend to arise, whether the crime is against a wife or a child.

It is well known that most cases of wife-assault which come to light are the culmination of years of prior repeated assault. The pattern is one of systematic and increasingly violent abuse.

If 80% of battering husbands are, as one study shows, nonviolent in all other social situations, you have, not a first offender, but a man who specializes in a single victim; in what has been called an "appropriate" victim. However, if, as the same researcher's later research suggested, "71% of the batterers had been arrested and 44% of those arrested had been convicted for various offenses . . ." (and that 53% of them were additionally abusing the children)—then the family court judge's argument simply falls through the ice.

Nonetheless, the preponderance of data seems to support the former. And if no prior conviction for *outside* anti-social behavior is a reason why this is not equivalent to a "criminal who attacks strangers," then what is being said is that a wife is a system-endorsed safety-valve for males, who might otherwise pose a threat to regular people.

To say "(t)he motive lies in the personal relationship; it is not robbery . . ." is to imply, unpleasantly, that the aggressor was "motivated" by his victim. Knowing that many instances of wife-assault begin without even an argument makes this particularly insidious. But certainly, if it is acceptable to us that she is there to domesticate his violence, if in doing so she is a soldier enlisted for *society's protection*—then it seems unkind in the extreme to disown her, wounded.

Surely she deserves—more than a divorce—an honorable discharge?

A G.I. Bill?

A 10% leg-up on a civil service exam?

What is true is not that the motive lies in the personal relationship, but that the *permission* lies there. Knowing that, where there is a "motive" in the assault, it is dinner served too hot or too cold, too early, or too late, a light bulb unchanged—surely makes the fact that the motive was "not robbery" more, not less, appalling.

Historically, men have been violent within the home with societal permission—not in spite of societal proscription. Yet historical evidence—that people behaved this way not despite the fact they knew it was wrong, but because they believed it was right, or at least *justifiable*—seemed to make no difference. Documentation that these violences had been OK'd in the past lives side by side with assertions that they are caused by violence on TV.

Evidence continued to mount that our newly revealed wife-batterers and child-molesters were normal. Often the pillars of the community. Some researchers, unwilling to look to the victim's pathology, fell to charting the course of the "disease." One theory described the violence as cyclical, so that in Phase I there is normalcy with a gradual building of tension. In Phase II, uncontrollable violence erupts, a hideous hitting out. In Phase III, there is total and winning contrition.

Reading of this, I was reminded of Another Social Group.

If we turn to this Other Social Group, we find that our typical member "has to do a great deal of intermediating between his contrary impulses. . . . His action system likewise is a two-way system, with almost equally inviting alternatives, because he is so immature. His equilibrium is unstably balanced because his inhibitory mechanisms are very incomplete. . . .

> He is so conservative that he combats innovation. He wants to have things done the accustomed way. Sometimes he is actually a ritualist, particularly at home, and insists on having things *just so*. On these occasions he may be so insistent that he seems positively imperious. His "imperiousness" is not really tyrannical: it is simply an unmodulated intensity—the same kind of uninhibited propulsive release that he shows when handling objects. Even so, it is best to take this fictitious domineering with a grain of humor and let him be King within manageable bounds . . .

The major difference between the battering husband and this Other Social Group is that Gesell assures us that "the TWO-AND-A-HALF YEAR OLD is finding his way. His adhesiveness, his vacillation, his oscillations between extremes are temporary. By the age of three he will amaze us with his conformance, his desire to please . . ."

Most experts, however, mined the more traditional field, doing psychological autopsies on living victims. Since everything about them was seen as pertaining to their victimization, they were then inextricably bound to their victimizer by the term "family dysfunction."

This was far more than a case of "to understand is to forgive." It was that to understand her role in his offense is to forgive *him*. The finding of pathology in the victim lent credibility to the diagnosis of a "deviant family unit." It very conveniently avoided the question of why normal men battered wives, and whether it was in society's contract with its citizens to seriously stop such assault. In quasi-condemning the behavior—in applying a specious kind of "understanding"—it quasi-condoned it.

It has been said that "a community that is too ready to forgive the wrongdoer may end up condoning the crime." Certainly, the concept of individualized or family "deviance" trivialized the crimes. Nor does the fact that there are largely unenforced laws sitting around do much for us. "(T)he aim . . . of criminal justice legislation is indeed to denounce certain types of conduct as something not to be practiced. It is . . . neither retributive nor reformative; the goal in denouncing theft is neither to punish nor to reform thieves—it is to declare that stealing is forbidden."

But if that were the case, that criminal legislation were sufficient, and "denouncing" were the goal, then the lawbooks would represent no more than a kind of Alice in Wonderland version of Emily Post. Laws do exist under which crimes in the home can be prosecuted—and sometimes are, in some places, in some few cases. However, this is by no means the primary response, it is the most controversial response, and it is the least emphasized response. And the double-think—which appears on the surface to suit all goals: the designating of behaviors as "crimes but not crimes"—creates a perilous no-place land: a breeding ground for (as it were) ethical bacteria.

Perhaps this can be seen most vividly in the light of our response to the "discovery" of widespread paternal child molestation.

That the distance is very short from understanding to endorsing is evident in the recent explosion of incest—from a "dread taboo" to a behavior which some experts (most with doctor before their name) are now claiming is so prevalent "as to make prohibition absurd." A behavior which can be "positive" or "beneficial."

The author of a major law paper, re-examining reasonable standards for intervention in child-neglect proceedings, does not believe that sexual abuse is "abuse." The author states, "I believe that such conduct may not always be harmful and therefore that the term 'abuse' may be inappropriate. While it will be used in this section, no condemnation of the behavior is intended." The author has assumed that the "behavior" would include oral copulation and intercourse; since the paper is entirely devoted to the subject of child abuse and neglect by parents, we know he is not talking about marriage between consenting, related adults, but is talking about sexual "abuse" of a child by a parent or guardian. However, "despite an abundance of theoretical material about the harm of sexual activity within the family, there are very few studies demonstrating the negative impact of sexual abuse. The damage, if there is any, is usually emotional and the symptoms may not be manifest."

Incest, therefore, he feels, should not be criminally prosecuted. However, making reference to what he presumes to be a general feeling of "moral condemnation" of the behavior, he recommends maintaining sexual abuse as a cause for *coercive* state intervention—a social work, casework intervention. About this, he has said earlier, "there is remarkably little evidence demonstrating the usefulness of social work intervention . . . the little existing hard data tend to indicate that providing such services, at least to unwilling clients, is not very helpful." This intervention system is, nonetheless, *not* voluntary. It is empowered to remove the child.

His estimation of the system's mending abilities certainly has been echoed elsewhere.

> For the past thirty years we have been gathering data pertaining to that set of activities which we variously call therapy, counseling, or casework, and the evidence continues to mount that such efforts, regardless of their usefulness in some individual cases, have not had any significant effect on the social problem they purport to alleviate. It is time to re-think the notion that individual or even family pathology is the prime source of the problem. Social problems are embedded in the social structure.

If there is spare evidence that this intervention works therapeutically, one must certainly wonder in what sense and for whom it does work.

That the author of the law paper, Michael Wald, elsewhere alludes to the " 'law'—as personified by judges and child welfare agencies . . ." is considerably unnerving, but very much to the point I am tracing.

Surely, involving the state—as he advocates—in a coercive intervention, is an excessive concession to an alleged "moral condemnation" of a behavior which he does not believe has been demonstrated to have a "negative impact."

Law professor and author Nicholas Kittrie writes, ". . . when no justification is available for state controls, even therapeutic controls, if compulsory, must be viewed as excessive . . ." Additionally, ". . . once public support no longer exists for criminal sanctions regarding a given behavior, it will not do to bring that conduct under the compulsory therapeutic realm."

Where support has *never* existed among that part of the public that makes up a deciding power in such matters, we should be still more suspicious of the compulsory therapeutic realm. We buy into it out of our own fears. But we do so at our own risk.

Serious questions have long been raised about the "conceptual framework of the therapeutic state and the procedural safeguards that apply to the exercise of the state's *parens patriae* powers"—that is, those powers assumed by the state, justified by its supposedly benign and protective role toward some defined segment of the citizenry. Powers separate from its police powers. Powers permitting interventions which—because they are presumed kindly and non-punitive—do not trigger due process protections for the assisted individual. Interventions which are alleged to be in the recipient's best interest, as well, of course, as in the interests of the state.

The questions raised have been about the substitution of diagnosis for factual determination, the substitution of "understanding" for civil rights, the erosion of the notion of personal responsibility, and the virtually limitless possibilities for governmental excesses inherent in the unchecked therapeutic state. "The nonpenal aim and the deviant's mental aberration continue to be asserted in opposition to the granting of procedural and substantive safeguards to the beneficiaries of therapy; and the therapeutic state's preventative ideal similarly militates against strict substantive standards limiting state intervention."

Conversations about severe violence in the home always want to pull away from the core, to spread everywhere, to leap from the brutal to the utopian—to extend themselves to emotional infractions, to "acts of omission." As the conversations go, so goes the "non-judgmental" intervention. Bottom-line ethical issues, then, get ensnarled with emotional, subjective, and (yes) judgmental ones. The literature of intervention speaks of moral neglect. And of religious neglect.

Speak of brutal child assault, speak of child rape, and a call quickly arises for every child's "moral right" and even "legal right" . . . "to receive parental love and affection, discipline and guidance, and to grow to maturity in a home environment which enables him to develop into a mature and responsible adult." Or a cry issues forth that the *state* "should assure for each child a chance to be a member of a family where he feels wanted and where he will have the opportunity, on a continuing basis, not only to receive and return affection, but also to express anger and learn to manage his aggression."

Surely the state cannot legislate love? It can only legislate behavior.

Once a system of intervention is in place, and the behavior triggering the intervention is thought to be a psychological "disease"—rather than a punishable act—the limits to the possible interventions become the dots in an open mathematical set. Where the state is the main agency of both intervention and "treatment," the possible progressions are alarming. With no bottom-line limits set on the "diseases," and with *prevention* the ideal, the categories of potential "illnesses" to be treated by the state, the number of possible families available for "help" becomes—not finite—but unlimited. Indeed, once we decide that the goal of "preserving the family" is best served by interventive prevention, what family could demonstrate that it does not qualify? What family does not merit inoculation? The limitations to intervention, then, are only those limits set by the capacities of the system.

Where fact-finding is by diagnosis, there is no appeal.

". . . the therapeutic model now offers the only system of

social control unlimited in its potential applications, for by its very aim the therapeutic state is required to look beyond the question of past misconduct and into those factors of morals, welfare, and health which might produce a present or future state of dangerousness."

Begging the question of crimes in the home; buying, unquestioned, the slogan "preserve the family" without asking which families, and in whose benefit, and at what cost—we turn our conscience over to the state, to act in its own interest. And, as this book will explore, the war on the home front—like all wars—has important ties to state and other interests.

The illness model of crimes in the home created a boomtime for diagnosticians.

Batterers had poor impulse control. Stress was stressed, almost to the breaking point. (The stress of unemployment was equaled only by the stress of employment.) Low self-esteem was commoner than colds, and more contagious. Husbands had it when they slugged their wives. Wives had it to begin with, or they wouldn't have gotten slugged. Sexually abusive fathers had it. And the abused children caught it.

Far from being the focus of this new "understanding," the offenders were all but peripheral to it, swallowed up in phrases like "family dysfunction," "family violence," "interspousal assault." The victims were swallowed up along with them—but their feet stuck out. When one listened to the diagnostic litany, it was clear that the victims, or the women who chanced to find themselves mothers of child-victims, were far more severely pelted with the language of the new understanding.

Some diagnoses were cruelly ironic. Battered women were said to have had "unrealistic expectations of marriage." They were said to have had "overly traditional views of marriage."

Some verged on epithet. The mothers of children whose fathers molested them were said to be passive, aggressive, cowardly, domineering, manipulative. They were said to have been collusive—to have "always known on some level."

And since child abuse statutes in many states now read

"commits, or allows [or permits] to be committed, a sex offense against such child," the diagnosis of collusion testified to a presumption that the mother had allowed [or permitted] it.

So the law, following the therapeutic dictate, colluded in exonerating the offender by emphasizing the role alleged to have been played by what was now called the "non-participating parent." The absorption of her into another's crime became so automatic, so quickly ingrained and reflexive, that in November, 1981, the National Legal Resource Center for Child Advocacy and Protection of the American Bar Association circulated a first-draft recommendation that statutes should "authorize protection orders to require the non-participating parent and other family members to obtain counseling." They spoke now of "intra-family child sexual abuse." And they advised that, "In deciding whether to file a petition in juvenile court against the non-participating parent or caretaker, prosecutors should consider: (1) whether such a parent knew *or should have known* of the sexual abuse," and, of course, "whether such a parent is willing to seek counseling." [my italics]

In one brief paragraph of these *legal* draft-recommendations, the word "treatment" is used three times, and the words "criminal prosecution" once—and then only to suggest "offering immunity from criminal prosecution in exchange for a stipulation of abuse in juvenile [civil] court and participation by the offender *and family* in a specialized treatment program." (Italics mine.)

Women who chance to become victim-wives or the mothers of victim-children find themselves, pre-diagnosed, suspect in the eyes of a system which renders them powerless and then mocks their powerlessness. Low self-esteem, indeed.

This book, then, also explores the impact the therapeutic response has had on those women. It traces the outlines of their disenfranchisement, their further victimization by the new "understanding" of their role in another's crime.

For some social scientists, as well as some treatment pioneers, family violences appeared a new Klondike. Here, also, experts appeared. Conferences abounded. Stakes were claimed. Victim populations were carved out. Skirmishes erupted. Turf was divvied up. A causality sweepstakes was set in motion. In place of low self-esteem, we got our violent culture, social isolation, the breakdown of the extended family, poor conflict management, and—when all else failed—the industrial revolution (for moving the workplace out of the home; devaluing and "privatizing" women's household contributions, etc.).

If family violences were brutal, and the subject volatile, the family violence industry seemed ferocious.

Wife-assault, the more active political issue for women, generated the greater amount of solid analysis of the problem as a social one—embedded in our social fabric, or, if one chose to be more optimistic, a problem vestigial to an older social order. Some searched out the motive behind the phenomenon we were witnessing: the victim being punished by the new understanding for *her* deviance. They explored—as I continue to do here—the interest continued violence permissions serve for those in power, to help secure their continuance in power (permissions which the new therapeutic understanding does not seriously threaten).

This, however, was quickly labeled naive. In the causality sweepstakes, complexity was a virtue and thoughts were meant—not to synthesize—but to subdivide. Studies were intended to be parthenogenetic. To breed littler studies. More research is needed.

From a starting point of zero in the 1960's, forests fell to raise a bald mountain of research papers. By 1980, if family violence studies had been currency, we would have been loading them into wheelbarrows. The Battered Wife Syndrome. The Battered Child Syndrome. The Sexually Abused Child Syndrome. The Battered Elderly Syndrome. It was highly inflationary—a case, it sometimes seemed, of too many researchers chasing too few relatives.

Briefly, a candidate for a new star appeared: The Battered Husband Syndrome. And flickered—a bit of schmutz, perhaps a tiny meteor. Out of its brief life emerged two bits of wit, rare on this grim front. One was a paper's title: "The Battered Data Syndrome." This picked out the flaws in the research on The Battered Husband Syndrome, a syndrome said first to afflict 250,000 husbands, then 20% of all husbands, and finally 12 million men—before it disappeared like Kahoutek, leaving behind no evidence that this was, or ever had been, a galactic problem.

Another was a paper exploring what it delightfully termed "The Woozle Effect." This one showed that—as with Pooh and Piglet tracking pawprints round and round a tree, creating their own evidence of the number of Woozles—even a false footprint in one study was almost bound to become a serious footnote the next study round, and that in the next.

If this was diverting, it was also diversionary.

The therapeutic response begged the question of whether we now found household mayhem—once traditional—offensive. It set up a halfway house to indifference. If we are not seriously offended (because we understand), there is no offense.

We were already well down the road to blaming the victims, to rehabilitating them back into the abusive home, before the new politics of family made these goals explicit.

Another chance will arise. Another time, to choose.

We may choose to be serious. Or not.

Either way, on the evidence, it is unwise to be unaware.

2
The Abuse of
the Psychological

It was with Freud that we left "The Age of Permitted Abuse," and entered "The Age of Denied Abuse."

Since a great deal of the therapeutic understanding attached to intervention, as presently marketed, stems from a discipline begun by Freud, it's instructive to look at Freud's understanding: at his response to crimes in the home.

As is only now being discussed by psychiatrists, Freud consistently refused to see them as such. He consistently identified the effects of the crime as located, in cause, in the unconscious wishes of the victims. Sometimes, as with actual paternal child molestation, this constituted a direct and deliberate reversal of his original perceptions.

That he first believed the women who told him of their childhood sexual abuse at the hands of fathers or close male relatives, that he then simply changed his mind and declared the "disease" in his female patients to be caused—not by the real molestation they testified to—but by their infantile sexual *wishes* for their fathers' sexual attentions, has by now been well-documented.

As psychiatrist Roland Summit recounts, "On February 11, 1897 [Freud] wrote to Fliess that he had been alarmed by the number of fathers named by his patients as molesters, and that he had come to fear through the presence of hysterical symptoms in his sisters that even his own father had been incriminated. . . ."

However, "Through *self*-analysis Freud moved from the belief that female children are damaged by adult seduction and that large numbers of fathers must be inherently incestuous to the recognition that all children (male and female) have sexual desires for a parent . . . ; all children are subject to maladjustments arising from their inability to cope with the psychic consequences of their own perverse sexual needs and vengeful fantasies." (italics mine) (cites omitted)

Author Florence Rush writes about Freud's conversion from the reality principle (the seduction theory) to the "phantasy" principle (the Oedipal complex):

> The seduction theory maintained that hysteria was a neurosis caused by sexual assault, and it incriminated incestuous fathers, while the Oedipal theory insisted the seduction was a fantasy, an invention, not a fact—and it incriminated daughters. . . . However, one must remember that when Freud arrived at the seduction theory, he did so by listening carefully and intently to his female patients; when he arrived at his Oedipal theory, he did so by listening carefully and intently to himself.

But this has not been made clear: That in some cases Freud did not identify the parent-abuse as causative of later illness because the parental behaviors involved *were no more than the norm of the time.* It was a social norm abusive of children by our standards, but a norm of which Freud was very much a part. Indeed, on March 10, 1910, Freud spoke, emphasizing that the increase in masochism which he saw in what he referred to as "our civilized society" was attributable to the fact that some children had "not been beaten enough or not at all." In one of his major cases, not only was the brutal behavior (as we would now see it) which the father directed toward his child normal—it was widely and enthusiastically applauded.

The case was that of Daniel Paul Schreber, a man whom Freud analyzed, although he had never met him.

Born in Germany in 1842, Daniel Paul Schreber became an eminent judge before going mad at the age of forty-two.

He got better for a bit and spent eight "quite happy" years at home with his wife before going mad again.

His was a quite colorful madness, and he left a published *Memoir* chronicling it. It was from this *Memoir* that Freud conducted his famous analysis of Schreber's case, and was able to trumpet evidence to support his pre-existing theory that it was the male child's homosexual wish for his father that caused paranoia.

This was the system of Daniel Paul's paranoid world: He was the victim of God's "miracling-up rays," and of "fleetingly made little men." That is, he felt himself afflicted with tormenting "miracles" and under siege of torturing "rays" directed toward his body.

There was, for instance, the "coccyx" miracle. This caused such agonizing pain as to make sitting or lying down excruciating. Daniel Paul wrote, with exasperation, that the "rays seemed to lack any understanding of the fact that a human being, since he really exists, *must be somewhere . . .*"

There was a "compression of the chest" miracle; a "being-tied-to-celestial-bodies" miracle; a "bellowing" miracle; a "multiple-headedness" miracle; a "putrefaction of the abdomen" miracle; an "eyes and eye lids" miracle; a "head-being-tied-to-machine" miracle; and a "writing-down" miracle.

He was also victimized by "voluptuous rays." "For well over six years," he wrote, "my body has been filled with these nerves of voluptuousness as a result of the ceaseless influx of rays of God's nerves. It is therefore understandable that my body is replete with nerves of voluptuousness to a degree unsurpassed by any female. . . ."

He wrote, "I, Daniel Paul Schreber, am appointed to redeem the world and to restore it to its lost state of bliss. This, however, can be brought about only if I am first transferred into a woman."

He speaks of himself often as "unmanned," and says of the rays, they "have the power of producing the miracle of unmanning. . . ."

While giving credence to the idea that the God referred

to was a displaced version of Daniel Paul's father, Freud's conclusion was that the symptoms reflected an early homosexual
wish for his father. We find ourselves once more, Freud says,
"upon the familiar ground of the father-complex." His construction is that:

> In infantile experiences such as this the father appears
> as an interferer with the gratification which the child is
> trying to obtain; this is usually of an auto-erotic character,
> though at a later date it is often replaced in phantasy
> by some other gratification of a less inglorious kind. In
> the final state of Shreber's delusion a glorious victory was
> scored by the infantile sexual tendencies; for voluptuous-
> ness became God-fearing, and God himself (*the father*)
> never tired of demanding it from him. . . . [italics mine].

(In Freud's constructions, children's alleged wishes were
consistently more powerful than adults' actual behavior. So
powerful, indeed, that the spectral image of those wishes, invoked, served to indemnify actual parental behavior.)

Indeed, Daniel Paul writes, "God demands constant enjoyment. . . . It is my duty to provide Him with it in the form
of highly developed soul-voluptuousness."

Undoubtedly, Daniel Paul's world-script would be seen now,
as then, as "deviant"; though it's likely he'd now be put on
thorazine, rather than camphor; and it's to be hoped that Daniel Paul would not now ring down the same diagnostic overkill:
"paranoid, schizophrenic, hallucinated, deluded, dissociated,
autistic, and ambivalent."

What is of interest is that Daniel Paul's father, a renowned
orthopedic physician, was seen then as not only utterly normal,
but an excellent father. Doctor Schreber wrote eighteen books
and booklets, many on proper child-rearing practices, including
one with the pithy title, *Education Toward Beauty by Natural
and Balanced Furtherance of Normal Body Growth, of Life-
Supporting Health, and of Mental Ennoblement, Especially
by the Use, if Possible, of Special Educational Means: for Parents, Educators, and Teachers.* This was dedicated to "the salva-

tion of future generations." The practices he advocated were
ones he himself used. The books were widely touted, went
through many editions and were translated into many lan-
guages. It is likely that Freud had read them, since he eulogized
the father in glowing terms. "His activities in favor of promoting the harmonious upbringing of the young, of securing coordi-
nation between educators in the home and in the school, of
introducing physical culture and manual work with a view to
raising the standards of health—all this exerted a lasting influence upon his contemporaries."

And Doctor Schreber was ranked by other physicians of
the time as a "giant . . . among those rare individuals who
through sheer force of personality are capable of effecting
change in the attitudes of their contemporaries."

He was virtually deified, described as a great leader, a pio-
neer, with the courage, strength, enthusiasm of a "religiously
inspired fighter for all the 'higher things' of life."

A professional colleague contributes that he had a "heart
full of *most devoted love,* prepared to live and die for his task."
Another speaks of Doctor Schreber's being "moved by the *philanthropic* ethic of a great human being." And speaks of his
"love of the people."

Yet every one of the practices which Doctor Schreber prescribed for child-rearing in his books, and cooked up as practice
in his own home, would lead us—as it is now leading some
psychiatrists, re-evaluating Freud—to call him a medically licensed sadist.

This is a retrospective diagnosis that avoids the facts of history. What Doctor Schreber recommended—though we might
in the present see it as child-torture—was in his time *laudable,*
and not just in Europe. His goals were, historically, the norm
here, as well; goals of destroying the child's autonomy, of breaking the child's will at all costs.

In the 1700's, in America, when life was seen as a state of
probation, a pass-fail test for eternity, the goal for the eventual
adult was "obedience to laws and authority, self-denial and
industry." Children were raised to "invariable obedience and

submission to government." Children's desires, as it was then seen, must be curbed, their appetites restrained, their inclinations thwarted. They had to learn to be denied and crossed. "Nay, you should even deny and cross them however innocent a thing it is they desire; whenever they discover an impetuous strong and impatient inclination toward it; for though the thing itself be ever so small and inconsiderable, yet custom, the custom of being indulged on all occasions, is a great thing and draws after it a pernicious train of evil consequences."

The fiery Calvinist minister, Jonathan Edwards, referred to "bad" children whose wills must be broken. "As innocent as children seem to us . . . they are young vipers, and are infinitely more hateful than vipers, and are in a most miserable condition. . . . They are naturally very senseless and stupid and need much to awaken them. Why should we conceal the truth from them?"

Disobedience was seen to be the original sin. "Disobedience to the father and his authority and the consequent disruption of the family sense of order seemed to threaten the very structure of modern society" during the eighteenth century.

And about the nineteenth century, Robert Sunley writes, "It was considered fatal to let the child win out. One mother, writing in the *Mother's Magazine* in 1834, described how her sixteen-month-old girl refused to say 'dear mama' upon the father's order. She was led into a room alone, where she screamed wildly for ten minutes; then she was commanded again, and again refused. She was then whipped, and asked again. This was kept up for four hours until the child finally obeyed."

The theory behind all of this, that of "infant depravity," was not contradicted, but was really carved in scientific, rather than religious, stone, by Freud's formulations. And Doctor Schreber was no more than the articulator of the idea of the mainstream.

All-powerful in his own home, Doctor Schreber advocated that all men be so. He wrote, "If one wants a planned upbringing based on principles to flourish, the father above anyone else must hold the reins of upbringing in his hands. . . . The main responsibility for the whole result of upbringing always belongs to the father."*

It was Doctor Schreber's admonishment to other fathers who would be good that they must strike early and act relentlessly to break a child's will and teach the child to regard this as self-determination. It was his apparent belief that children are criminal or ill at birth. About infants under one year, he wrote:

"Our entire effect on the direction of the child's will at this time will consist in accustoming it to absolute obedience, which has been in great part prepared for already by the applications of the principle laid down previously. . . . The thought should never even occur to the child that his will could be in control, rather should the habit of subordinating his will to the will of his parents or teachers be immutably planted in him. . . ."

Equally, for infants:

> One must look at the moods of the little ones that are announced by screaming without reason and crying. . . . If one has convinced oneself that no real need, no disturbing or painful condition [and Doctor Schreber insisted no infant be fed more than three times a day at prescribed hours], no sickness is present, one can be assured that the screaming is only and simply the expression of a mood, a whim, the first appearance of self-will. . . . One has to step forward in a positive manner: by quick distractions of the attention, stern words, threatening gestures, rapping against the bed . . . or, when all of this is to no avail: by moderate, intermittent, bodily admonishments consistently repeated until the child calms down or falls asleep.

Or, one might add, passes out.

The infant who was screaming for "no reason" is now screaming because you are administering bodily admonishments; if nothing else, it seems asking rather a lot of the infant

---

* It is ironic that this declaration of *paternal* accountability seems refreshing in the late twentieth century.

to intuit that you would stop those admonishments if he would stop using them as a reason to scream.

Doctor Schreber was, indeed, dedicated to the fine points of his task.

"If one asks a child to hand something to oneself with one specific hand but the child will use only the other hand, the intelligent upbringer will not rest until the act is done as demanded and the impure motive is removed."

Compliance was not enough. The child must obey for pure motives. Not because he's afraid you will sock him. And not while harboring a secret wish to do otherwise.

The doctor believed in surveillance. Present-day psychiatrists note the connection between Daniel Paul's "writing-down" miracles and his father's punishment board, which listed the children's names and every charge against them, including acts of omission and acts of commission; faults and weaknesses. Then, on the 30th of every month, came the totting-up—the hour of reckoning.

Psychiatrists also note the connection between other of Daniel Paul's "miracles" and actual barbarisms practiced on him by his father. One of Doctor Schreber's books, *The Harmful Positions and Habits of Children, Including a Statement of Counteracting Measures* (1853), recommended a contraption called a Geradhalter, an "iron crossbar fastened to the table at which a child sat . . . pressed against the collarbone and the front of the shoulders." With the added goody of a vertical bar to prevent any smarmy crossing of the legs.

Then there was the belt with ringshaped shoulder straps which fastened to the bed to keep the child from moving in his sleep.

And Doctor Schreber's design, later embodied in the "head-compressing" miracles—a head-compressing machine: a strap clamped at one end to the child's hair and at the other end to his underwear. If the child turned a fraction in the night, his hair was pulled.

There was also a helmet with a chinband to keep the kid's mouth held shut.

The combination of inventiveness and dictatorial passion

made Doctor Schreber a real special dad. Tortures for daytime, and torture all night. Apart from the constant psychological oppression, what the good doctor did with Daniel Paul from infancy was to effectively place him in one or another painful kind of traction for the better part of the day and all of the night. Naturally, and as always, for the child's own good. "Moral will power is the sword of victory in the coming battle of life. Be not afraid, loving parents, at these words. The true and high goal of human life can and should be achieved only through noble battling. . . ."

In other words, Doctor Schreber tormented Daniel Paul not in spite of the fact it was wrong—but *because he believed it was right.*

As was common in the 1800's, Doctor Schreber also developed his own version of comic-book sadism to prevent "pollutions." Other masturbation-prevention methods endorsed by physicians at the time included castration, circumcision, locked chastity belts, corporal punishment, electricity applied to the spine and genitals, and, before going to sleep, tying the hands or confining them in bags of pebbles to the back. For boys, the treatment included: "Enclosing the penis in bandages, infibulation (the placement of metal wires or rings through the prepuce in order to forestall its retraction behind the glands), section of the dorsal nerves of the penis, blistering of the prepuce, and wearing spiked or toothed metal rings on the penis at night, which would bite into the penis if it became erect."

Girls received: "ovarotomy (i.e. cutting into an ovary), clitoradectomy . . . infibulation of the preputial head from the clitoris, blistering of the prepuce, vulva and inside of the thighs, and, before going to sleep, putting the legs in splints, or tying them one to either side of the crib [sic] or bed."

Between 1850 and 1879, the most commonly recommended method for dealing with the dread dangers of masturbation was surgical treatment.

Doctor Schreber's method was, by comparison, fairly mellow. He recommended sixteen exercises, done between four and one hundred times daily. These were: "arm-circling, arm-raising sideways, elbows backwards, arm-striking forwards, arm-striking outwards, arm-striking upwards, sawing movements, striking the arms together, throwing the arms apart . . ." and on to mowing movements and arm-waving sideways.

Then, after the evening meal, you'd want to give the child a hip-bath at a temperature between 54° and 60° F. And a simple water enema at the same temperature. And in the morning you'd want to wash the sexual organs and the butt in cold water. Truly. A father's work was never done.

Since Doctor Schreber's books were so widely read and so widely praised, it must be assumed his creative techniques were not only applauded but widely practiced. Although it can be doubted that many or most fathers had either the time or the incredible energy for twenty-four-hour implementation of the doctor's regimen, it is certain that the practices in some or all measure would have represented conforming to a prescribed norm, not closet "deviance."

It is plausible, as well, that, apart from physical abuse (by our standards), Doctor Schreber sexually abused Daniel Paul. Not only would it be inconsistent to account for all the other of Daniel Paul's later "miraclings-up" as actual sense memory, hallucinated, yet make the sexual "miracles" an exception, but Doctor Schreber himself refers repeatedly to 'penetrating a child'; "in a seventy-five-page stretch of one book, he explicitly recommends penetrating (*dringen* or *eindringen*) a child ten times." As one psychiatrist notes, "The father in his language behavior implies that he may have wished to penetrate children."

During Daniel Paul's illness, when he saw God and heard Him speak, God called him *Luder*—a word applied to a lewd female, a hussy, or even a whore. Schreber thought that "rays of God" mocked him by calling him *Miss* Schreber. He believed that the goal of his doctor, Professor Flechsig, was to gain control over his soul and body and subject him to sexual abuse. He feared that his body would be thrown to the hospital attendants for sexual misuse.

While Doctor Schreber spoke of making ready the ground for the "seed of Godliness" in his son's body, Daniel Paul speaks of feeling that "God's nerves corresponding to male seed had been thrown into my body." Daniel Paul originally believed his emasculation—his transformation to a woman—was for the purpose of sexual abuse.

He spoke of "foul masses" being unloaded into his body. Among the questions that came into his mind were, "Imagine a presiding judge who lets himself be fucked."

Could this in part account for the fact that Chapter III of the *Memoirs* is missing?

> The contents of Chapter I and II were necessary in preparation for what follows. What could thus far be described only in part as axiom, will now be clarified, if at all possible, in view of the circumstances.
>
> I shall first deal with some occurrences involving other members of my family which might conceivably be related to the presupposed "soul murder," and which in any case are all of a more or less enigmatic nature, scarcely explainable in the light of common human experience.

There, the text stops cold, with the following decidedly enigmatic statement: "The further content of this Chapter is omitted from publication as unfit for print."

But all of the *other* things his father did to him were a matter of public record and public approbation. That paternal child molestation, most particularly of boys, was publicly unspoken of, would account for Daniel Paul's feeling that such was "scarcely explainable" in "common human experience."

Additionally, one of Daniel Paul's doctors, Doctor Weber, wrote in his report,

> When we survey the contents of this document and consider the mass of indiscretions in regard to himself and other persons which it contains, when we observe the unblushing manner in which he describes situations and events which are of the most delicate nature and indeed, in an aesthetic sense, utterly impossible, when

we reflect upon his use of strong language of the most offensive kind, and so forth, we shall find it quite impossible to understand how a man, distinguished apart from this by his tact and refinement, could contemplate taking a step so compromising to himself in the public eye. . . .

Nor are Daniel Paul's later sense-memory "hallucinations" unfamiliar in cases where there has been paternal child-rape and oral assault. Psychiatrist Roland Summit reports on Stephanie, who also wound up in a mental institution, a victim of childhood sexual assault. He says,

> Throughout the years of psychotic adjustment, Stephanie's delusional system was dominated by the belief that she was filled with malodorous slime which oozed from her mouth and from beneath her skin. It had become obvious through her association during psychotherapy that this was a childhood concept of semen, contaminated also by a traumatic exposure to the decomposing body of a beloved pet her father had unfairly blamed her for killing. With the reacquisition of oral rape memories, the actual source of the seminal incorporation became clear. . . .

And Doctor Schreber himself writes, "Experience proves that by far the largest number of those who have succumbed to *lust* in one way or another have sunk to this state by dint of their original ignorance of the dangers. . . . Such explanatory advice needs to be both more detailed and more weighty when it concerns boys than where girls are involved."

This giving of "detailed" and "weighty" explanatory advice rings mighty close to present-day fathers' explanations that they were not molesting: but were "teaching" and "initiating."

So it was not Doctor Schreber's actual assaults on the child-person of Daniel Paul, according to Freud, but Daniel Paul's homosexual wish for his father, that was at the root of his paranoia. And, the unthinkable sexual abuse aside, it certainly seems reasonable that part of Freud's myopia about parent-as-offender was likely due to the fact that some parent-offenses (as we now see them) were then perceived as normal.

Little Hans, for example, was a five-year-old boy who was afraid to go outside because a horse might bite him. This, Freud identified as "masked castration fear." Like the Schreber case, that of Little Hans also was, as Freud wrote, "not strictly speaking, derived from my observation." His interest in the case, reported to him by the child's father, was in furthering his collection of "observations on the sexual life of children." His goal—expressed to the father, who agreed—was to "let the child grow up and express himself without being intimidated."

Now Freud knew that, "It is by no means a rare thing, for instance, for a little boy, who is beginning to play with his penis in a naughty way and is not yet aware that one must conceal such activities, to be threatened by a parent or a nurse with having his penis or his sinful hand cut off. Parents will often admit this when they are asked. . . ."

Nor was he at all unaware of Little Hans's parents' system of "non-intimidation:"

"When he was three-and-a-half his mother found him with his hand to his penis. She threatened him in these words: 'If you do that, I shall send for Dr. A. to cut off your widdler. And then what'll you widdle with?' "

She threatened to abandon him before he was four for being "naughty."

And the same concept of will-breaking and mind-control so advocated by Doctor Shreber was practiced by Hans's father as well:

HANS: But I don't put my hand to my widdler anymore.
I: (the father) But you still want to.
HANS: Yes I do. But wanting's not doing, and doing's not wanting.
I: Well, but to prevent your wanting to, this evening you're going to have a bag to sleep in.

DIAGNOSIS: Castration complex.

And so Freud, by locating illness in the victim, derived deviance from norms, as we continue to do today where crimes in the home are concerned. The ones with the problem are the source of the problem. William Ryan writes: "We cannot comfortably believe that we are the cause of that which is problematic to us; therefore we are almost compelled to believe that *they*—the problematic ones—are the cause and this immediately prompts us to search for deviance. Identification of that deviance as the cause of the problem is a simple step that ordinarily does not even require evidence."

Apart from the dislike, the social and legal stigma this places on victims of household crimes, ignoring the norms involved permits us to neglect the fact that these norms support a particular order. The desired family system is highly suggestive of the desired social system.

Doctor Schreber's patriarchal and brutally repressive construct was entirely within the bounds of the appropriate where the social system that required support was an authoritarian state.

> The father's authoritarian position reflects his political role and discloses the relationship of family and authoritarian state. The same position which the boss holds in the production process, the father maintains in the family. He in turn produces submission to authority in his children, especially in his sons. This is the basis of the passive, submissive attitude of middle-class individuals toward Führer figures.

In terms of all Freud's major cases, some psychiatrists are now re-examining and re-evaluating the cause-reversal of Freud's case analyses—thereby questioning his very formulations: the castration complex, the Oedipal complex, the etiology of paranoia. Curiously, Doctor Schreber—in retrospective diagnosis—is now said to have been sadistic or disturbed. Once more, it is so much simpler to say "that's sick" than to examine that which we now think of as abuse in terms of social ideation. (The Huns may seem, in our eyes, to have been barbaric. But to diagnose them, individually, as psychotic, would be a distinctly dangerous avoidance of the potential for approved

social barbarism; for collective, political, human destructiveness.)

While it is reassuring that the re-evaluation of Freud take
place, Florence Rush says, "It is possible that we closed the
barn door too late." She says, "We are now told that Freud
was right the first time" about the reality of paternal child
molestation. "But his second theory, the Oedipal complex, now
firmly implanted in the public mind, remains dominant." Male
psychiatrists who speak out in contradiction of Freud are still
apt to face a professional firing squad. Summit writes: "Freud's
. . . early speculation led him and many of his followers to
arm themselves with a dogma of disbelief. The messenger of
incest risks provoking not only ordinary, common-sense denial
but also inviting charges of heresy among the most highly
trained and sophisticated professionals." And analyst-scholar,
Jeffrey Masson, who had been assigned to edit new and unpublished letters from Freud to Wilhelm Fliess, was declared heret-
ical when he cited from this material to prove that Freud recognized the reality of childhood seductions even after renouncing
the theory, and was fired as projects director of the Sigmund
Freud Archives. In parting, Masson said that, if *real* seduction
was the cause of neurosis, analysts "would have to recall every
patient since 1901. It would be like the Pinto." As for "the
public mind," males, even professionals disputing Freud in
print, risk being accused of trying to kill their father in some
Oedipal drama.

So it is entirely possible that acknowledgment of actual sexual aggression by adult caretaking males toward girl and boy
children will not necessarily eradicate—or even be seen to
seriously contradict—the essential mother-causative, victim-
blaming message in the Oedipal construction. Because this formulation has been so widely accepted as primal, and because
so many factors evidence a vested interest in maintaining it,
it may well continue to be considered to have more and deeper
weight than actual molestation (or actual castration threats)—
and an intrinsic truth, beyond them.

The seemingly ineradicable Oedipal thesis is that "the infant's sexual feelings and fantasies center first around the intake of nourishment, then around the retention and elimination of his feces, and only later around genital sensations. The child enters the genital or phallic state of his development only when he has been forced to give up oral and anal gratification—to feed and evacuate according to his parents' pleasure instead of his own." Yet that "force" has differed tremendously, not only in degree but in kind, between Doctor Schreber's (and Freud's) time and our own. Surely Doctor Schreber's virtual coopting of the infant's bodily processes—by food deprivation, indeed food *teasing;* by constant surveillance and challenge, by enema—would produce an altogether different effect than demand feeding, than toilet training encouragement beginning at two.

But it is the next leap that requires faith: "At this point, he [the child] becomes aware of his father as a rival for the sexual favors of his mother and dreams of taking his place." We've gotten quite used to the formulation, but the words "sexual favors" imply a reasonably amazing sophistication for a small child; suggesting he was born with a pocket sex manual, and, of course, the ability to read it. And, without arguing childhood sensuality, or the capacity for pleasure sensations, there is a demand that we accept a child's awareness of adult sexual activity in its specifics for the syllogism to work.

> Sometimes, however, the fear and guilt aroused by these fantasies overwhelm the child, and he represses his genital wishes with particular severity. Still enthralled by the earliest associations aroused by his mother, those of nursing at the breast, he fears that his genital desires will themselves be governed by oral-sadistic impulses. The aggressive impulses inevitably directed against the mother, which originate in her frustration of the child's oral and anal pleasures, become so intense that they threaten to dominate every other activity.

Now we reach the place where it becomes not just necessary but crucial that the child know the mechanics of adult sexuality:

> Under these conditions, the penis presents itself to the child's mind as a dangerous weapon, the presence of which in the mother's vagina makes the vagina itself a dangerous place by association. In the child's fantasies, she becomes a vampire, a devouring bird with an open beak. "This dread of the mother is so overwhelming," writes Melanie Klein, "because there is combined with it an intense dread of castration by the father."

Whether or not one can make the leaps of faith involved, and assuming one can do that *and* integrate the information that both sexual molestation of children and castration threats are often *real*, this is where we come out on this construct:

"The essence of the Oedipus complex and its resolution is that the son transforms the wish to get rid of the father into the wish to succeed him. Without by any means overcoming his original longing for the mother and hatred of the father, he transfers the maternal longing to another woman, while redirecting many of his aggressive impulses against himself. . . ."

Many, perhaps, but, alas, not enough. Because, if we follow this formulation through, what is being transferred is not just "longing" but mother-dread and oral-sadistic impulses. And we are left with the idea that men, by natural process, displace (or put in the bank, with interest collecting) a rare and inevitable amount of mixed rage and longing which they then "transfer" to another woman. We are then left with a lurking primordial menace, only partially tamable by what psychiatrists call a "successful resolution." What we have here can only be described as "normal pathology" and it is *one* way of accounting for, or justifying, the tremendous eagerness to blame women for failing to be what they are supposed to be—men's mothers.

Florence Rush says, "To blame Freud is pointless. Many counter theories have been promulgated, but it is his concept of the primacy of the unconscious, which relegates prevalent social problems to individual maladjustment and relieves society of responsibility, that has been embraced." It is important to add that it is the concept of the primacy of the *victim's* unconscious—where undeniably real wrong-doings have occurred; the denial of the significance of the offense.

Freud's reluctance to believe the reality he was presented with was, to some degree, based on sheer prevalence. He knew parents threatened their children with castration. But he could not believe, he said, that so many did. Or, perhaps more likely, what he could not believe was that that which was so normal could produce so much "deviance." To have given credence to what he was hearing would have been to question the *social order.**

Certainly, "Freud's theory about women not only reflected the patriarchal and authoritarian society of his era in Europe but also tended to preserve that type of society." And paternal child molestation of girls did work to preserve a type of society in which women were meant to be socialized to subjection.

To have challenged the social order would have been far more dangerous for Freud than what he actually did, which was to recast the existing specter of children as born vicious, with wills which needed to be broken, in a new mode: the unconscious.

That what he identified as illness in the adult was caused by the *usual* childhoods of the time might partially account for his oversight, then, However, in reversing his seduction theory, some authorities suggest that the motive was his need to avoid acknowledging excesses on the part of his own father. As we witness, in evolution, the therapeutic response today to crimes in the home where they are committed by an adult male, it is impossible not to conclude that the profound need to avoid seriously condemning those crimes, to avoid accepting the male head of household as offender, *is the most significant universal to be found in all of Freud.*

The father in Freud's case of Rat Man, for instance, was "tyrannical, brutal . . . murderous."

Yet "(a)s Freud continued his case history of the Rat Man,

* Had he done so, would Freud have been, not the father of psychiatry, but—of sociology? Of political science? (Would Freud have been—as it were—Marx?)

he was forced to play down what he was reluctant, but nonetheless obliged to admit—the undeniable brute force of the father."

But it was an oblique admission. Freud wrote:

"That he [the father] could be hasty and violent was certainly not inconsistent with his other qualities, but was rather a necessary complement to them: but it occasionally brought down the most severe castigations upon the children while they were young and naughty." But this was no more than a minor shortcoming because, "When they grew up . . . he differed from other fathers in not attempting to exalt himself into a sacrosanct authority, but in sharing with them a knowledge of the little failures and misfortunes of his life with good-natured candour."

As with Doctor Schreber, this father, hasty and violent toward his children, was an "excellent one." And the child, Freud alleged, only became a "coward—*out of fear of the violence of his own rage*" (my italics).

Today's understanding of crimes in the home, then, is most particularly consistent with Freud's in its failure to identify the offender when the offender is the adult male. And there is reason to worry, based on recent analyses, with their heavy dosage of mother-blame, that a re-thinking of Freudianism may get us no further than Rheingoldism.

Dr. Joseph C. Rheingold, a much-respected psychiatrist with claim to 2,500 cases, controverted Freud in the 1960's by decisively attributing the cause of neurosis in the patient to the real behavior of a parent. That of the mother. It was she whom he identified as the child-destroyer. He says that Freud's failure to identify actual parental destructiveness of children was due to his "defense against recognizing *his own mother's destructiveness.*" (Italics mine.)

In the section of his book, *The Fear of Being a Woman,* on "nonviolent parental abuse" he elaborates with great emphasis on the "nonviolent abuses" the mother heaped on her daughter by making her clean, cook, etc.

Those were her offenses.

Here is what the non-offending parent did:

He pounded and kicked his daughter. He dragged her by the hair. He struck her in the face. He shot at her, missed, then "pulled her into the parlor by the hair, said he would 'fix it right now' and shot her, the bullet clipping the patient's hair."

It would seem difficult in the face of the evidence, but he held his point. The real abuser was Mom.

In another book, *The Mother, Anxiety, and Death*, written in 1967, he says:

> It is acknowledged as more or less relevant to certain neurotic trends and personality problems and to certain clinical syndromes, but its pertinency to the whole sweep of psychiatric and psychosomatic disorders is not conceptualized. We may not say that maternal destructiveness is the prime factor in all pathological states, but the total evidence at hand seems to permit one to say that it enters causatively into a greater range of disorders than any other factor, and that it is the prepotent determinant in more individual cases.

Even the nurturant mother "is not without destructive effect."

It is her mutilative impulse "in its castrative form" which

> cannot be separated from the mother's sexual seduction of the child. Here, as in the case of cruelty, one deals with behavior that is more frequent and more obtrusive than we have allowed ourselves to believe. The father is seductive too (of the daughter, very rarely the son), but the clinical evidence indicates that seduction of the girl is without significant pathogenic effect, even where it involves actual incest and in the presence of the father's reactive guilt and punitiveness [sic]. It is the father's indifference to her femininity or his surreptitious interest that is detrimental to the girl's self-concept and the reason for strong protest against him later in life. But even a nonsensual relationship between father and daughter may become pathogenic if the mother is jealous and intervenes threateningly.

The reader will, please, note the—not only permission—
but *prescription* for paternal child molestation, so as to ward
off any "strong protest against him later in life." The scientific
imprimatur was given by a psychiatrist at Harvard Medical
School.

("Sick," I can hear my young friend muttering. "That's
sick.")

Notice, also, the medicalized mother-blame, the no-win for
even the "nurturant" mother. (Acording to his line of reason-
ing, it would be the mother reporting her child's abuse by
her husband to the authorities who would be, intervening
threateningly, creating pathology.) This blame is inherent in
virtually every "non-judgmental" understanding currently applied to crimes in the home, where committed by an adult
male.

But even if that blame were not there: even if "non-judgmental" meant what it promised—what would we have?

"The Age of No-Fault Abuse." That's what we'd have.

3
The War on the Ground

"Once married, the risk of abuse falls significantly only for the widowed."

Stark, Flitcraft, Frazier, Medicine and Patriarchal Violence: The Social Construction of a "Private" Event.

An English law professor writes, reasonably, "Once within the Family Court setting and a social welfare counseling orientation we may lose track of the fact that wife-beating may be a brutal criminal assault and not just the symptom of a troubled marriage."

Suppose.

You have been married three years. You are pregnant. One night, you have gone to bed early. He has a late meeting at the office. On returning home, he comes into the bedroom, turns on the light, and starts slugging you. (Remember—most of the bashing starts without even an argument.)

Your reality now is that the *result*—your shock, your pain, your rage, your fear—will be taken as one with the cause, should you be forced by your injuries to go public with your battering the first time it occurs. (And if you do not, it will later be examined why you did not.) Every characteristic of yours will now be searched by the mental health customs officials for its relevance as a defect as you cross the border into your new identity: that of battered wife.

"The symptoms are not read to illuminate a person's history, but the reverse. The social dimensions of the patient's experience, her history as she has lived it in the presence of the medical system, disappear behind a developing catalogue of prior symptoms. . . ." Her symptoms seen as psychopathologies, it is the woman herself, not the offender, who appears defective, and the fitting object for personality dissection, and rehabilitation.

The luggage of your past and present will be combed, your personality strip-searched, for what has suddenly been proclaimed to be, if not an outright defect, then an anachronism in *you:* "Victims of spouse assault may have unrealistic or stereotypic expectations of themselves and their marriages. . . . Most of these women believe the man should be the head of the house and the major breadwinner."

While he gets off with "low self-esteem" and "poor impulse control," these insights will be reserved for you:

First, as a battered wife, you play a "crucial role" in your own battering. (It is, again, like the Zero Mostel routine "in which he impersonated a Dixiecrat Senator conducting an investigation of the origins of World War II. At the climax of the sketch, the Senator boomed out, in an excruciating mixture of triumph and suspicion, 'What was Pearl Harbor *doing* in the Pacific?' ") You may, indeed, be the kind of woman who fears "kind husbands and good men, lest such individuals go away" or otherwise hurt you. You may be aggressive. You may be castrating.

> Along with their high hopes, the women brought to the marriage very traditional ideas about marital behavior. Although almost all claimed that marriage is a fifty-fifty partnership, a large proportion also believed that the man should be the head of the house and that a woman's greatest job is to be a wife and mother. In addition, a third of the sample clung to the notion that it is the wife's duty to obey her husband in family matters and to submit to him sexually whenever he wishes.

This ought not to pass without comment—most particularly now, amidst calls for a return to "traditional" ideas about marital behavior: as a battered wife, you are being diagnosed as a nerd for having been what until five minutes ago (in historical time, not real time) was thought to be what a wife should be

(and in five minutes may be so thought again). "The solution
to the problem the patient *has* suddenly appears to lie in the
problem the patient *is.*"

All this is reminiscent of Trial by Ordeal in the 1300's—of
the water-test for witches. Tie them up, toss them in the drink.
See if they sink and drown like a normal person. Or, if they
escape, call them witch; burn them.

The battered wife, diagnosed for her symptoms, is now labeled mentally ill. One battered woman in eight is eventually
committed to a mental hospital.

This, also—for both women- and child-victims—is *historical.*
In the 1700's, "in the United States it was easy to get rid of
a troublesome wife by having her committed to an insane asylum. . . ." And the legal doctrine giving parents immunity
from suit by their offspring was first expressed in 1891, in a
suit brought by a Mississippi child against her parents for false
imprisonment in an insane asylum.

For the battered wife, the peril only begins with her diagnosis. Once labeled mentally ill, the battered wife "must depend
on the good will of the 'helper' in such future attempts at
independence as working outside the home or *gaining custody
of the children.*" (Italics mine.)

The dangers facing her, then, are legal as well as physical.
Apart from the precious, and few, shelters existing, our average
battered wife—on a waiting list for a shelter, perhaps, but still
under siege—is left with this advice, virtually a Combat Training Manual:

> If you have the space in your home, select a room
> that can be locked from the inside in order to get away
> from an attack. Or, if you sense an attack coming, move
> closer to the door to avoid getting cornered and to help
> you get out of the house. Consider the things you could
> arrange to hide in order to help you during a crisis: money
> and/or a spare set of car keys to get you to safety. If
> you will need to get out of the house in a hurry, you
> may want quickly to get such things as food, extra clothing,
> diapers, extra glasses, medication, identification cards,

medical insurance or welfare cards, important legal papers and so on. . . .

During an attack, there is probably nothing you can
say or do to make him stop. Because he is not in a rational
state of mind, it is unlikely you can reason with him. However, there are things to keep in mind that may aid you.
First, try not to panic or lose your temper. . . . Getting
angry and insulting may make him angrier which will
be worse for you.. . . Some people feel that it is important
to stand up for yourself and show that you won't be pushed
around. Others claim that this may subject you to greater
violence. Knowing your own strength and your husband's
personality will tell you whether fighting back will benefit
or harm you. . . .

DEFEND AND PROTECT YOURSELF, especially
your head and stomach.

CALL FOR HELP. Scream, or if you can get away,
run to the nearest person or home, say you are being
hurt and that you need help. . . .

CALL THE POLICE. . . .

GET AWAY. . . .

This—in my opinion—is a less than reasonable risk.

What chance will "the family" have if women realize that,
in marrying, they place themselves effectively outside the protection of the law, and men outside its censure? No wonder,
the fear, the unwillingness to believe our ears, our eyes. Yet
it really is too dangerous not to.

Although "(c)ontrary to popular myth most mothers are
not aware of ongoing sexual abuse," the literature of the major
interveners in cases of child molestation continues to be replete
with allegations of the mother's invariable collusion. Underlying the language of pathology, the clear statement is that it
was her job to have stopped the man, that he would not have
committed the offense against her daughter had she engaged
in sufficient "preventive flattery," or offered sufficient preventive sexual activity.

If Freud's "Age of Denied Abuse" reinforced in women the

sense that they'd best shut up, "The Age of No-Fault Abuse" now beckons them to come forward. Only to find themselves in a legal dark alley—a set-up for being therapeutically mugged. Where, before the "discovery" of prevalent wife-battering and paternal child molestation in homes "across all socioeconomic lines," women knew enough to know they would face censure or disbelief; knew they'd be told "you made your bed, you lie in it"; knew they would be stigmatized for their own inadequacy as demonstrated by their man's violence toward them; knew their daughters would be stigmatized (if believed) by exposure of paternal molestation—now they are widely admonished to speak up; are widely told they should not accept this behavior; are widely told they must not permit this behavior. And they now find themselves entirely unsupported, unprotected, and implicated when they do what they are told.

During the 1970's, platoons of experts, battalions of professionals swept over the horizon. Although there was no article on family violence in the prestigious *Journal of Marriage and Family* during the 1960's, by 1971 the better part of an issue was devoted to family violence; and by 1980 there was a review of the research. We now had, not only the psychological model, but the social-psychological model, and the socio-cultural model. We had the "resource theory," the "general systems theory," the "ecological perspective," the "evolutionary perspective."

Rarely was the question addressed, which Doctor Summit poses, as to why "normal men slip rather easily into exploiting whatever potential sexual object is most available and most easily subordinated." Nor why normal men batter their wives. Nor, more importantly, why, as a society which claims to have moved beyond at least primitive patriarchy, we continue to be so entirely loath to accept husband/father crimes as such, that virtually any theory or understanding will be embraced which permits us to sidestep that. This question becomes even more dramatic when laid alongside the fact that—although a statistically significant number of normal men do commit such crimes—*most* men do not.

Yet Freud's true legacy—the revulsion at confronting the fact of husband/father culpability in household crimes—carries forward today, under the banner of a new "scientific" rationale, flying benign and enlightened motives, beaming with self-described neutrality, aiming to "preserve the family," by curing "the family," which—as an entity—has a "disease."

(What are you saying? [I can hear some reader say.] Are you saying lock them all up? Throw away the key?

Well—let's wait on that one. Let's go on with our evidence-gathering, keeping in mind that the criminal justice system, with its procedures and protections, is separate from the correctional system.)

Let's work, for the moment, toward reason.

A lonely voice, that of lawyer Michael Rosenthal, speaks to the reasons *for* criminalizing child abuse, and sums up with this absurdity:

> JUDGE (to the defendant): You are charged with killing (or seriously assaulting) your two-year-old son. How do you plead?
>
> DEFENDANT: Your honor, I admit I killed (or seriously assaulted) my son, but I have a defense.
>
> JUDGE: What is your defense?
>
> DEFENDANT: Your honor, my defense is that it was child abuse.*

There is a highly controversial category of offense within the juvenile justice system: the Status Offense—that is, an offense which would not be seen as such if it were committed by an adult—truancy, running away; . . . an offense which can only be seen as such because of the status of the individual

---

* This can be taken further with sexual abuse. Were it *literally* de-criminalized, it would be fairly bizarre. Presumably, where you had *"Lewdness with a child* under 14: Any lewd or lascivious act other than sexual assault with a child under 14"—you would have to amend it to read *"except when the child is the offender's daughter or stepdaughter."* (For statutes see Leigh H. Bienen, "The Incest Statutes" in J. L. Herman, *Father-Daughter Incest,* Nevada at p. 240).

as dependent youth. What we seem to have with crimes in the home are Status Non-Offenses. Crimes which would be crimes if the victim were a stranger, but are not because the only victim is "only" a part of the family.

Why do we, as individuals, not only buy this, but *embrace* it?

In women, I sense fear.

A friend says, "The problem I have with what you're saying is it's so negative. You don't talk about the families that work, where people do respect each other. And you say, 'Men do this, men do that. . . .' And my husband doesn't do those things. But listening to you, what you're saying implicates him. And that makes me feel disloyal."

Author Florence Rush says, "You're questioning things that are frightening. Women who are strong, successful, and self-supporting, live in an aura of fear."

Why?

"Because they're alone. Our society has no room for the strong, independent woman. Our world provides no structure for human association other than the family. The woman who turns from marriage and family faces isolation. To be alone is frightening. So for all its hazards, women chose marriage. Without ever thinking it through, they sense the terrible consequences of independence."

Certainly, women have been well-warned, well-primed to fear before.

In the 1920's, a minister wrote that,

> Marriage is, after a fashion, a trades union of women for their own protection. The prostitute and the vamp are the scabs who underbid the union wage. When men begin to believe, with Samuel Butler, that it is cheaper to buy milk than to keep a cow, their discovery is a sad one for those among the dairy maids who have begun to discover now and then a gray hair in the comb. . . . Married women will do well to reserve their union cards, and keep their dues well paid, and also keep up the high quality of their goods. They have competition.

And in a 1974 book, which is a massively well-informed re-thinking of mysogyny, we find this, historically debatable,* but nonetheless instructive wag of the finger in our direction:

> . . . As early as 1919, Soviet authorities decreed that "the family has ceased to be a necessity both to its members and for the state" . . .
>
> In a few short years the great experiment began to fall apart. Men, stripped of their former paternal power and responsibilities, became neglectful toward their families and left the burden of the upbringing of the younger generation to the women. . . . The collapse of family solidarity resulted in the mushrooming of juvenile delinquency on a staggering scale, and far from raising the status of women, the revolution proved to be utterly demoralizing. Rather than freeing woman, it had freed *man* from sexual restraints and domestic responsibility, the two great gifts of stable marriage to women. . . . In fact, the new Soviet female was sexually oppressed as she never had been before.

The warnings continue today. Shared job opportunities, shared child-rearing, will lead to the man's simply vanishing. He will not be there. "The woman will open her marriage only to a stiffening and probing technocracy of the child-care

---

* Margaret Mead, *Childhood in Contemporary Culture*, (p. 181) tells us that the bourgeois family was indeed to be abolished in Russia at that time— with women free to choose mates, divorce made easy, and women working as men did, the state taking care of the children. She says that the Russian state did attempt direct control—abolishing property and the idea of people as property; that there was a "nationalization of women."

However, Jesse Bernard says: "One of the first fronts in the Russian Revolution was in this battle: 'Among the Soviet Communists it was a foregone conclusion that parenthood was a declining occupation that was to be replaced by social rearing.' [Cites omitted.] In the words of one woman, 'We must rescue these children from the nefarious influences of family life. In other words, we must nationalize them. They will be taught the ABC's of communism and later become true communists. Our task now is to oblige the mother to give her children to us—to the Soviet State.' "

So there is at least a substantial likelihood that it was the *children* who were being "nationalized" and not the women—whatever the language of female liberation.

state." Without his role of provider and protector—and by implication the *rights* attending those roles—he will simply vamoose.

So it is not surprising to find fear: "Tell me that's sick." "Tell me that's not normal." "Tell me (in effect) that can't happen to me, to my daughter."

But it can. Any woman can find herself in a battering relationship by accident. Surely legal protections and safeguards in that event are a better security blanket than imprecations to the therapeutic gods?

Apparently not.

A friend calls to tell me she's read about a new treatment program for batterers.

Another treatment program for batterers?

There follows a most uncharitable pause.

"Look. This is not fruitful for me. You have your own way of looking at all this, your own reasons for thinking about it the way you do. But that way is not fruitful for me. I read that there's a program for battering husbands, and I think, 'Oh good. Someone is doing something about it.' More than that, I simply don't want to know. Knowing more than that is not fruitful for me."

No, not fruitful—if she is lucky. If her life does not undergo one simple change of context. If she does not find herself married to a batterer or a child molester by accident. Then, she would be blamed for that which she did not find it fruitful to know. Scenario:

You are the best and most family-loving woman on your block. You worked for ten years before your girls (now seven and nine) were born. Now you are a happy homemaker (though perhaps you plan to go back to work part-time when the children do not need you home so much—whether you plan to work as a dental technician or distribute leaflets for the Moral Majority is of no moment). You have a set pattern of doing your grocery shopping on Thursday nights when the market is open late (and you often ask your oldest girl to unload the dishwasher for you while you're out). This leaves your days free for cleaning and mending and cooking and helping the kids with their homework. It also gives your husband a little time alone with the children.

The pattern of your life is—the pattern of your life. To the best of your knowlege, it is ordinary, routine.

One Thursday evening, you get done shopping more quickly than usual (no one in line has brought coupons). You come home to interrupt your husband sexually molesting your older girl. (Or you come home, and your younger daughter reports this has happened, has been happening.)

You are shattered. You are furious. You feel betrayed. For an instant, you hate your daughter. Then you hate your husband. You don't want to believe your eyes or your ears. You wish yourself back in time.

You confront him. He threatens to kill you (or else says that everyone is lying; or is making a fuss over just affection). But now—untrained as you are for this situation (it was not part of the drill in your family-of-origin's boot camp)—you are a soldier. You are fierce and brave.

You call the police.

Since "criminal justice" is widely deemed to be an "inappropriate response" to such matters, the policeman does his duty and reports your complaint to the central registry of child protective services. You are now a known casualty, although your case has not yet been "substantiated." (Within 24–72 hours, an investigation should begin. Within 60 days, your husband should get either a visit, a phone call, or a form letter.) This is how, in theory, you can expect your situation to be appraised.

Your husband is probably middle-aged, maybe in his late thirties or forties. He's beginning to realize he's growing older without, perhaps, having accomplished everything he wanted to. He is, most likely, of normal or above-average intelligence. He tends to be a good worker. He has probably never been involved with other criminal activities.

He's a scout. Then what led to this (a) heinous deed, (b) inappropriate behavior?

Your marital relationship is poor. Your sexual relationship tends to be non-existent or very unsatisfying. Your husband,

however, is not having an extra-marital affair. (Indeed, not only
is the sexually abusive father not a sexual pig, or sexually rapa-
cious, he tends to be positively conservative.)

All these years, he has been frustrated—the idea seems to
be—but he's been a terrific sport about it.

You, on the other hand, are the key to the problem. All
evidence indicates that you have colluded in the sexual abuse
of your child, and—though you may deny knowledge of it—
you are most likely aware of the relationship between your
husband and your daughter. What you have done is you've
ignored the situation. You have failed to fulfill your role in
the family of protecting the children.

It is entirely possible that this will come as a surprise to
you: that your primary role in the family is—and has been
all along—to protect your children from their father. But while
ignorance of the law for the paternal child molester is acceptable as an "excuse" (since the criminal laws are seldom invoked),
ignorance of this expectation—which has nowhere been made
clear in any marriage or family literature—is, for you, no excuse.
It is a symptom of your denial, your avoidance, your pathology.

You may be charged with neglect for having "allowed" your
child to be sexually abused.

What is certain is you will be newly understood. Now the
fact of your having asked your daughter to unload the dishwasher on Thursday nights will take on a new and sinister
significance. It will be taken as evidence of your having maneu-
vered an exchange of roles with her.

That which yesterday may have been seen as "teaching
responsibility"—today will be seen as your having avoided it.

A letter arrives.

> To begin: A timetable of events as they progressed.
> NOV. 2—My son made a comment at dinner which I
> clarified with him later. He had apparently seen my hus-
> band sexually abusing my daughter or some part of an
> episode. It was not pursued out of fear of bodily harm
> to all of us at this time.
> NOV. 3—I received confirmation of the abuse from

my daughter when we were alone. I took her to school and went to our Department of Social Services . . . and asked for help. . . .

I talked to the supervisor of Social Services. He was polite and comforting, soliciting basic information such as names and ages of children, place of employment, etc. He asked if I could get my husband to contact him personally and I said I would try. I requested he make arrangements for a temporary foster home for my daughter as I was not prepared to help her deal with this trauma. I felt she would receive some counseling and direction from "professional" parents while I had time to sort things out as well . . . After talking to my husband, we returned to Social Services about 2:00 that afternoon. The supervisor was present as well as a deputy sheriff. The policeman read my husband his rights and asked him if he wanted to contact a lawyer. He was shown to another room and given total privacy and telephone access for three hours.

During this period, I was asked a number of questions. A first, they were innocuous, informational. The questions took a nasty turn and consisted of "How frequently do you have sex with your husband?" "Have you ever had an orgasm?" "Did your daughter enjoy having sex?" "Did she ever have an orgasm?" "Did she have oral sex?" "Did she enjoy it?" etc. Of course I objected to these questions and refused to answer most of them when I realized what was being asked (the whole atmosphere was low key and hushed, like "You can trust me—your husband and kid are really rotten, aren't they?") I asked to speak to an attorney, but was refused access to a phone. They said I didn't need an attorney as our District Attorney would be representing me. They said I had to answer their questions so they would know what kind of help to give me. They said I was in violation of both federal and state laws if I didn't answer their questions and I would be arrested. I told them to arrest me.

This display of feistiness, plus her other active efforts to sort out the situation led to the diagnosis that this woman had usurped her husband's authority in the family. It was the written summation about the situation, then, that "the problems in the family and perhaps even the alleged abuse were not entirely emotional or psychological problems of the alleged abuser alone but the result of less than satisfactory personal relationships within the family."

In other words, as the supervisor at the Department of Social Services said, looking her straight in the eyes, "Lady, this is all your fault. If you had been sleeping with your husband, this wouldn't have happened."

She writes: "Neither my daughter nor I were allowed to file charges, and in fact were threatened with exposure and publicity if we tried. We were not asked if there had been prior abuse, if we were afraid of physical harm for reporting the abuse, or even if we wanted to stay a family." The counselor she had gone to had *refused* to counsel her in the absence of her husband because "we only treat families."

> No one ever asked my daughter if she wanted to move away from her father. . . .
>
> I discovered I cannot protect my children from anything. After suffering with them through cancer, brain surgery, auto accidents, poor education, I realize I cannot protect them from outside forces. And I do not have the energy or the resources to protect them from within the family. . . . As matters stand now, my husband can beat his children, rape them, kill them, and I could not stop him. Nor would I make any attempt to report it. The abuse of the law in our case has given my husband full power to abuse all of us and there is nothing I can do to prevent it from happening. In fact, by divorcing my husband now, I still run the risk of him obtaining full custody, or, at the very least, shared custody of them and then there is no semblance of protection from his abuse at all.

Given that her diagnosis by the social services is now a matter of record, that last part is probably true.

We are now being asked to support equal rights for men. How can anyone be against *equal* rights for men?

But the dangers of building civilized visions—equal caretaking, equal nurturance—on a fractured foundation, where bottom-line issues have been avoided, is nowhere clearer than on the issue of custody.

With the rise of the "father's rights" movement, the issue of custody after divorce has become a mined field for mothers. Calls for "equal rights" for men threatens to "progress" us back to the 1700's, and the presumption of men's natural guardianship rights.

In 63% of *contested* custody cases, the children are now awarded to the father. So if 90% of all child-custody awards are made to the mother, it is only because the fathers are not contesting in most cases. And the men may challenge the custody award at any later date. Since men re-marry often and quickly, and women do not, a later suit by the man for custody presents the court with these two pictures: the working mother, struggling to make ends meet and arrange for childcare; and a freshly formed nuclear family, with a working father, and a new wife ensconced in the home, full-time. The fathers, challenging, are judged on their "parenting potential." The mother is judged on her *actual* parenting, which—for all of us—is never as good as what *could* be.

Where a woman is battered and threatens to leave, the batterer may counter-threaten that he will sue for custody. "Go on, leave. You'll never get the kids." At the least, he can use the threat to trade her financial demands down. Where the battered wife or mother of the sexually abused child, just wanting out, seeks the seemingly simpler "no-fault" divorce, she foregoes establishing the battering or molestation. This makes any later claims seem no more than vindictive. With "no-fault," he will normally be awarded weekend custody, and therefore constant access to her and the children. A constant opportunity to continue the battering, to continue the child molestation.

Even where she alleges battering to begin with, the courts do not consider a husband's violence toward his wife as evidence of his custodial or visitation right unfitness.

Where the assault continues (as it most often does), where the molestation is ongoing, she may attempt to frustrate the visitation—and lose custody altogether.

If the woman then turns to the system, she will be gaslighted.

Once still higher levels of mental health professionals are called in to adjudicate a mother's report of her child's molestation at the hands of her ex-husband, we reach a level of fact-finding which could not thinkably be reached outside the wickedest satire.

As psychiatrist Roland Summit writes:

> If a woman allows [sic] sexual abuse to occur under her roof, she is accused of setting up the abuse. If she separates with her children, she is accused of inventing prejudicial stories to block her husband's legitimate access to his children. Clinical evaluation of the disputing parties and the children provides the major evidence in such suits, and the "objective" evaluation almost invariably faults the woman. The man is evaluated as normal if he is sufficiently self-assured and if he confides no more conflicted material than the average, unemotional, well-defended male. The woman is evaluated as within the normal limits, but with marked anxieties in the area of sexuality.

Indeed, her very concern about the ongoing molestation of her child by her husband (or ex-husband) is evaluated as a symptom of her sexual obsession and her own sexual over-stimulation of the child.

The husband's guilt or innocence is determined by diagnosis—by medical interpretations of him, and the (ex)wife and the child. These diagnoses are rebuttable only by other diagnosers. Thus, a goodly portion of the guilt-or-innocence debate rests on attacks by one diagnoser on the emotionality or credentials (or lack thereof) of another. The most relevant "fact" is whether the alleged perpetrator fits a stereotypic profile of a perpetrator. If the alleged, well-heeled offender is deemed normal, that is taken as assurance he would not have done something considered pathological.

What this amounts to is a fancily decked-out way of deciding that a felony was not committed because the man is simply Not the Type.

Literally.

Type is exactly the point: a tool for identifying psychological determinism not unlike the old methods for identifying physical determinism for criminality in the past; where the shape of a person's jaw, head, facial features, were themselves indicators of criminal characteristics.

Witness the Myers-Briggs Type Indicator. It's a psychiatric evaluation concoction which, when completed by the testee and scored by the testor, spits out something very like a highfallutin' version of the cards you once got from public, penny-cost weighing machines, or the cards you can still obtain from amusement park horoscope machines: ("You are sensitive to the feelings of others . . .").

For example, the "Introverted Sensing Type." This combination "makes the super-dependable. He has a complete, realistic, practical respect for the facts. . . ." Now how could a father with a character witness like that be suspected of lying about child molestation?

That is the type of the father in the case of a kid code-named Sheldon. Give him the last name of Samuels. Call his mother Jan. His father George. His baby sister Kim.

Jan writes:

> I was married for eight plus years and left my now ex-husband in late February 1980, and filed for divorce. I have two children, Sheldon (b. 1976) and Kim (b. 1979).
>
> (Before I left, I had the uneasy feeling that my son was being fondled during bath time given by George. I could not determine that this was the case and, of course, really did not want to think it was so. I shared this feeling with my attorney, who thought I was crazy; or vindictive, probably.)
>
> We stipulated to joint custody with the children resid-

ing with me. George had them alternate weekends, although Kim was brought home Saturday nights as she was still nursing in the AM and PM. By the end of March, Sheldon was reporting that he and Dad fondled each other during visitation.

I reported this to the Child Abuse Registry. I am myself a social worker, and I am mandated to report.

The irony here, in light of what was to happen, is so blatant as to make even pointing it out seem like rubbing it in.

Records of the Emergency Room where then three-year-old Sheldon was examined report that the child told the mother that he had been playing with his father, mutual masturbation, and the mother claimed the child told her that he took his father's penis in his mouth and they were playing and sticking fingers in each other's anus. The mother claimed the child told her that the father threatened to shoot him and cut his penis off if he told. The parents, the report said, were separated, and this molestation had occurred over a three-month period. Shortly before the examination, Sheldon was taken into custody and placed in a child-care center.

According to Jan Samuels, the medical exam—using a test which has a 2 percent error rate—showed that both children had pharyngeal gonorrhea. One psychiatrist, involved in evaluating the case, noted that Jan Samuels "called to announce that both children have gonorrhea of the mouth and I had not wanted them examined. I told her that I referred to invasive examination under anaesthetic, not a swab of the mouth. She was coldly furious."

The Outpatient Clinic Record says that while in the examining room, Sheldon was very reluctant to talk about the molestation, first only talking about getting big and strong and killing his father. As he became more comfortable playing with a doctor kit, he talked about bleeding from the penis, about his father putting a screwdriver in his penis and also his rectum, but he didn't know if he bled from the rectum.

He also said that his daddy hurt his "baby" (meaning Kim, his sister) in her vaginal area and made her cry. When questioned about scissors (Sheldon had told his mother that his father had threatened to cut off his penis with scissors), he refused to discuss the scissors.

Now comes Round I in the expert joust.

Our first court-ordered evaluation of Mr. Samuels asserts that:

> Defendant/subject is not mentally disordered, and there is no evidence from his history or clinical examination that he is sexually perverse or tends to pedophilia.
>
> He has a somewhat aggressive and rigid manner, with relatively little emphathy [sic] expressed in this procedure—but much of his defensiveness and criticism of his wife are appropriate to the circumstances in which the wife's charges have placed him and to other behavior on her part which he described.
>
> His religiosity, character, history, record, concern for children's welfare, and the tender age of alleged victim make the charges against him most unlikely to be based on facts of his behavior.
>
> If committed, offense acts were precipitated by loneliness, anger at wife, and intimate circumstances—very unlikely to be repeated. He is not a danger, not in need of hospital treatment, and not a "mentally disordered sex offender."
>
> Save for the charges, there appears no reason subject is unfit for child custody; and to the degree his description of his wife's behavior is accurate her emotional stability is questionable. . . .

Now a second expert, a clinical psychologist, is called in. And he administers—besides a Diagnostic Interview—a Minnesota Multiphasic Personality Inventory (MMPI), Projective Drawings (HTP), Revised Bender Gestalt, Myers-Briggs Type Indicator, Rorschach and Thematic Apperception Test (TAT).

Results? The man is normal.

> On the MMPI, the validation scores fall well within normal limits so I would accept the results as valid. Ego strength is fair indicating that he may have some difficulty

coping with personal problems. Suicide potential is moderate. All of the clinical scales fall well within normal limits indicating no psychopathology. The profile is not at all consonant with those of persons in my sex offenders group.

On the Projective Drawings, "there is a normal male identification. He would like to be younger than his forty-four years. There is evidence of a fair degree of anxiety which would be normal for his circumstances. He tends to be a rather closed person who has the potential for warmth which is currently not being experienced or expressed."

On the Revised Bender Gestalt, "the gestalten are intact indicating good contact with reality. The sequence is methodical indicating good judgment or planning ability. Ego functioning appears to be intact. Again there is evidence of some anxiety. There appears to be passive, dependent needs. There is some simplification which suggests passive-aggressive tendencies. No organicity is indicated."

On the Myers-Briggs Type Indicator, he scores as that "Introverted Sensing Type"—(that's the one who has

a complete, realistic, practical, respect for the facts. He absorbs, remembers and uses an immense number of them. He likes everything put on a factual basis, clearly stated and not too unfamiliar or complex. Only when you know him very well do you discover that behind his outer calm he is looking at the facts from an intensely individual angle, often a very droll one. His private reaction, the way a thing will strike him, is quite unpredictable, but what he actually does about it will be sound and sensible.

He is conservative, consistent, responsible, stable, painstaking, systematic, hard-working, and patient with detail and routine . . .).

The Rorschach shows "high intellectual control. . . ."

In all, George Samuels is "neither neurotic nor psychotic . . . nor does he have a character disorder."

Now another clinical psychologist interviews Sheldon and finds him quite open and approachable. When asked why he'd been temporarily removed to a foster care home, the child said, "because my daddy's gonna do something to me." When asked what, he said he didn't remember.

The psychologist, finding he couldn't get any confirmation out of Sheldon in that interview, recommended giving the father back visitation rights.

Now another battery of tests, this time for Jan Samuels. She is found to be "open and cooperative," volunteering that she had, as a child, been sexually molested by her stepfather. She also brought handwritten documents with her, and reported she did not feel good about coming in for the tests.

She, too, is found to be normal—but with somewhat less benign language. She is described as "narcissistic, egocentric."

How did she do on the Myers-Briggs Type Indicator? She scores as an "Extroverted Feeling Type."

> The feeling extravert [sic] is concerned chiefly with people. He [sic] radiates a fellowship, valuing harmonious human contacts above all things. He is friendly, tactful, sympathetic, always able to express the correct feeling. He is particularly warmed by approval and bothered by indifference. . . . If his perception is underdeveloped or not allowed to influence his judgment, he will jump to conclusions; for lack of a first-hand knowledge of a person or situation, he will act upon assumptions, and while he means well, his actions may go wide of the mark. . . . Again, he may be unable to admit the truth of a disagreeable fact or a criticism that hurts, and may seek somehow to escape the issue.

Obviously, such a Type has nowhere near the reliability of Mr. Samuels' Type.

Besides, her inner values are "so far outstripped by her instinctual drives as to result in appreciable impulsivity. . . . There is an unusual number of sexual responses indicating a marked sensitivity in this area. . . ."

One bites one's tongue. Her three-year-old is repeating stories of having been and being molested by his father. Surely an occasion for "marked sensitivity?"

No such connection is made.

On the TAT, "the themas center around feeling sad because a child was being hurt, family fighting with uncommunicative husband, taking responsibility to end relationship."

Although Jan, too, is adjudged to be non-neurotic, not psychotic, or suffering from a character disorder, "She appears to be preoccupied with sex, to have been sexually frustrated, throughout her marriage and sexually molested by her stepfather when she was a child."

Opinion: Re-instate George Samuels' visitation rights.

Round two.

Another psychiatrist, writing on behalf of Jan Samuels, counters the previous psychiatrist's evaluation (that George Samuels did not engage in such behavior), introducing casually a remark of glistening good sense: "one cannot disprove such an allegation, merely by performing a clinical examination of the accused."

He also writes to the probation officer, asking that the matter be further observed and investigated, and recounting a conversation he had with Jan Samuels' mother.

> During that phone conversation [she] told me that Sheldon reported his father said, "I have a fever—let's go to bed." And that when his father takes him to bed when he has a fever "he nices my pudo." She states Sheldon reported to her that he is not supposed to talk about matters because his father would therefore get in trouble and go to jail, and Sheldon mentioned something about a gun.

Third round.

Yet another psychiatric evaluation. It is now some five months later. This one "involved a few hours of reviewing multiple records" ($400), "two hours of consultation with the Samuels couple together for an hour and separately for a half hour each" ($160)—two hours with the entire family ($160), and a supplemental review of records and reports ($200).

What we learn for our $920, is that other reports reviewed show intense emotional bias which "obfuscate the truth." According to this expert's sorting of fact from opinion, "We see a mother and father, neither of whom is severely mentally ill, who each have emotional problems but not out of the range of normal, who both love their children within their limited capacities, who are unable to make a marriage and in their warring with one another both profoundly misunderstood their son Sheldon and this misunderstanding is further compounded by well-meaning mental health professionals who became overly emotional and prematurely committed themselves before adequately weighing their observations." The "tragic result" of this was that Sheldon had not seen his father for six months.

He sympathizes with the doctor who said "how difficult it is for a psychiatrist to evaluate whether someone is a sex offender from a clinical interview"—but does think that doctor became "rather extreme in his criticism."

He reiterates what a normal man the tests show George Samuels to be, and notes that Jan Samuels' tests showed her as subject to "jump to conclusions" and to "act upon assumptions."

But he saves his big guns for a report submitted by a person whom he is not even sure is a *professional* person, a report of her interview with Sheldon.

This woman's report described how Sheldon "played with stamps in a drawer as Mommy and Daddy stamps and how at one point he put Daddy's stamp in the drawer, because 'he was bad.' " Sheldon then arranged the stamps in a "variety of ways seeming to express family tensions. Then he took a piece of scotch tape to cover the staples on the inside of the stapler" . . . and the reporter says that she "felt that this was very strange and said, 'You are covering the staples with scotch

tape?' " And she then asked, "What happens under the covers?"
And Sheldon then said, "Daddy feels my nice" . . . And she
asked him, "What did he do to be bad?" And Sheldon replied
that he "stuck his thumb up my bottom." And added, "In my
mouth too." And he showed her.
Here our evaluating psychiatrist becomes impatient.

> I must comment that what is so remarkable and psychi-
> atrically naive is that what Sheldon was telling [her] was
> undoubtedly a fantasy. Not only is it common psychiatric
> knowledge that children of all ages, and especially chil-
> dren from the ages of 3 to 5, engage in quite intensive
> sexual fantasies about their own and their parents' bodies
> but also fantasize any manner of sexuality that would be
> considered "perverse" by adults. I am not saying that I
> can claim with certainty that Sheldon is not reporting
> real events, but the distinction between reality and fan-
> tasy is not clear in children which is one reason that chil-
> dren of this age can become so intensely involved in a
> symbolic play. However, I am saying that "perverse" sex-
> ual fantasies are to be expected at this age and if a child
> did not have some of them, that would be considered
> an abnormality. I am also not saying that one should not
> consider the possibility that such statements by children
> could represent real events, even in this age group. Of
> course they could. What is amazing to me in this instance
> is that the possibility that these could be sexual fantasies,
> which is also the overwhelming probability in a child this
> age, was never considered. Dr.——— is more astute in this
> regard and seems to imply that they could be fantasies,
> but if so, they are not the fantasies of a "normal" child.
> . . . In a certain sense I would agree that these are not
> strictly "normal" fantasies. This is not to say that fantasies
> with this content are abnormal at this age. They clearly
> are normal, however, I think the frequency, repetitivity
> and intensity with which these fantasies are expressed
> by Sheldon is indicative of an anxious child. They are
> the fantasies of a child who is anxious about the affectional
> bonds with both his parents and is perhaps sexually over-
> stimulated unconciously by both of them, although most

certainly by the mother, who is quite sexually preoccupied. . . .
 There is also abundant other data that these are fantasies that we are involved with, e.g. the theme of castration
by his father. This particular anxiety is part of the growing
Oedipal attachment to the mother, and the fantasy that
the father is going to cut off his penis is as predictable
as the rising of the sun.

Before our eyes, Little Sheldon turns into Little Hans; and
the mother reporting her child's molestation turns into the
destructive, seductive villain.

In sum? "I found nothing to support the contention that
Mr. Samuels sexually molested or in any other way physically
abused his children, but again one can never prove with cer-
tainty on psychiatric grounds that a molestation did not take
place." He thinks it is, however, highly improbable. He thinks
Sheldon said what he is said to have said, but made it up in
keeping with his fantasies, due to his mother's "over-zealous
preoccupation with his sexuality"—and he recommends that
the father be granted full visitation rights at once.

As with the old Anglo-Saxon ministration of justice, the Trial
by Ordeal, this is surely "less trial than tribulation." Ordeal,
too, was reliant on divination; and it, too, confused health with
truth. Then, the accused would have to (for example) carry a
hot iron in his bare hands, or dip his arm in boiling water. If
he was in good health, and the wound healed, voilà, he was
innocent. . . .

Jan Samuels writes, "The police told me I should go to Washington because I'd never get justice here. I thought that was
ridiculous. *I protect kids all the time!*"

Further pressure on her part to protect Sheldon against
what increasingly seemed the inevitable loss of at least partial
custody and the inevitable continuation of the abuse, produced
a further psychiatric report: one for her team. This one is im-
pressed that Sheldon is the "victim of both sexual assault and
of threats of severe bodily harm" and "should be protected
from his father."

This re-excites the ire of the psychiatrist so committed to Sheldon's fantasies. He instantly labels it evidence of Jan Samuels' continued effort to traumatize Sheldon; evidence of a continued invasion of the child's fantasy life; further proof that Jan Samuels "is again projecting her unresolved problems onto Sheldon."

He is impatient. But he is clear in the proof of his case: A man who would do such a thing to a three-year-old boy would also predictably have a severe mental disorder, and George Samuels does not.

He is more than impatient. He is growing dangerously impatient:

> . . . due to the growing evidence of Mrs. Samuels' continued lack of empathy, sexual over-stimulating and traumatization of Sheldon and her evident lack of insight and resultant inability to change this behavior, I would recommend that custody of Sheldon be granted to the court and foster care placement be arranged for him with visitation by both parents. It might even eventually be found suitable to grant custody of Sheldon to his father.

As Doctor Summit, commenting, puts it:

> A normal child's complaint may be taken as valid if he happened to be molested by a disturbed adult.
>
> A normal child complaining against a "normal" adult has no basis for complaint.
>
> A normal child seeking intervention from a normal mother against a father jeopardizes his mother. If the father is disturbed (capable of being seen as guilty by examining professionals) and the mother leaves him, she may be condemned for failing to stick by her emotionally needy husband. If she does not take action (report him or leave him) she *will* be condemned as responsible for allowing the abuse. If the father is not 'disturbed' and she leaves him, she is condemned for deserting a good husband. If she persists in the belief that the child's complaints are valid and that her husband is a menace, she

is condemned for setting up the child's complaints and of overstimulating, confusing and traumatizing the child out of *her* need to deny the child his natural right to a loving father.

This, then, is part of the "something" that the (oh good) "somebody" is "doing about it."

4

Storming the Castle

We were speaking, friends and I. The conversation, begun with a recounting of a next-door battering incident overheard by one of us the previous night (cries of no, don't, stop, please, don't, thud—horrid to hear), had segued through talk of the attraction of a type labeled psychopath: charming one moment, a menace the next. And we'd reached—not too illogically in life, though a bit more so in print—speculation over the phenomenon of women who court involvement with notorious men doing jail time.

"I don't see what's in it for the woman. All she can do is visit him once in a while."

"It's a total romance—all in the mind."

"And in the mail."

"She doesn't have him around at all."

"Imagine being involved with someone you just get to visit briefly—and seldom—through a double-plate window with a microphone, or through a screen. . . ."

There was a short silence for thought.

"You know? . . ."

"Maybe that's not such a bad idea?"

"They can't get at you."

"Why *not* marry a guy who's already in jail?"

Man-haters? But know (she said, whipping out credentials): each of the three of us talking remain in a long-standing marriage; each has children. (Such credentials.)

Each is non-battered.

And nonplussed.

Why, in a society so proud of its niceties of feeling that relationships must be fulfilling and mutual or end—why is such effort put into maintaining those units which are behaviorally barbaric (when the effort is not being put into denying the barbarism)?

Why did it seem more useful to choose a medical-bureaucratic response, one which has led to appalling language abuse—whether deliberately obfuscatory, or just professionalese—which threatens to murder thought?

Shelters are imprecated to "operationalize their goals."

About child or adolescent abuse, we are told, " 'Fact-finding' can be a quagmire if the 'facts' are concerned only with who did what." (Presumably, the quagmire would only shake more violently underfoot, were we also concerned with when, and where, and to whom.)

All intervention "services" should focus on injury and family dynamics in order to prevent "crisis intervention efforts from becoming mired in inconclusive cross-examinations and from *scapegoating one family member.*" (Italics mine.)

Is it alarmist to think that it's but a hop and a skip from de-criminalizing crimes against women and children in the home, to de-criminalizing crimes against them in the street? To not wanting to "scapegoat" any man for a crime against any woman? No.

The logic of medicalization-theory perhaps reaches a less cloud-covered peak with the attempt to de-criminalize stranger-rape. Here also the incredible power of women is at the root of all matter. Here, also, that woman is mother; the mother who makes a rapist. (I'm reminded of a nice bit of graffiti: "My mother made me a homosexual." Followed by, "If I get her some wool, will she make me one too?")

"The attitudes of these men [rapists] toward women, including their relationships with their mothers and other women, were explored. Results indicated that 90% of the aggressive males and 61% of the nonaggressive males reported either not loving their mothers or having had painful experiences (rejection) with females they had dated." Having rejection with one female, then, obviously leads to having rape with another.

Also, "These men often have a history of pre-pubertal or post-pubertal sexual trauma with women, frequently the mother." Aside from the fact that pre-pubertal or post-pubertal allows for all the ages of man, what sort of trauma? Well, one man, whose father died when he was seven, had a mother who gave him everything he wanted but at the same time was quite controlling of "what he did, when he did it, and with whom he did it." Since she was a black single parent, had she not been so controlling of her eight-year-old, of what he did, when he did, it, and with whom he did it, she would have been a sitting target for a presumption of neglect.

In any case, however controlling this woman was (of what he did, when he did it, and with whom he did it), her control over him was, eventually, this: whenever she argued with him, he went out and raped.

"The mother [of the rapist] is usually a warm, compassionate, overly permissive individual." When she is not controlling.

So the path of medicalizing crimes in the family is not a cul-de-sac. We embark on a course of enlightened problem management—where the problem is a female or child victim— and the farther we go, the further we diminish male accountability, until it becomes impossible not to wonder that men are willing to trade the respect due adult autonomy for the impunity accorded the naturally feeble.

"The therapist's goal is to develop successes for the rapist in his heterosexual skills, components that can be mastered by the rapist." (In the context, the toilet-training-manual-for-new-mothers-style is surreal.) "Rapists with poor heterosexual skills are frequently overcritical of their own heterosocial skills, feeling that nothing they do is right. In actuality, many of their conversations, if they would initiate them, fall very close to normal conversations."

Hey, baby.

The authors feel that, "The tragedy of many treatment programs for rapists is that they do not attend to issues such as how to relate to women socially. *Furthermore, many of the environments in which rapists are placed (such as prisons) remove them from contact with women. . . ."* (Italics mine.)

This is no more than a somewhat screwy extension of the contention that incest should be de-criminalized because, as one law paper puts it, "At the minimum, imprisonment of the parent simply delays the difficult task of treatment until his release."

We are now implored to gird up for a tough decision regarding rape: "The issue that society must face squarely is whether the current, primarily punitive method of dealing with rapists is conducive to their rehabilitation."

Let's set aside for the moment that these therapists' idea of rehabilitation seems not to be getting little Johnny to stop molesting the other kids, but teaching him to practice his interpersonal skills while he does it. Let's even set aside the complete absence of any evidence that we *are* dealing with rapists in any widespread punitive way by placing them in skill-depriving environments. (In 1978, in the United States, there were an estimated 171,145 rapes. 83,665 were reported to the police. 29,660 were cleared by arrest. That is, 17.3% of all victimizations resulted in an arrest. Of those arrested, some 36.1% were eventually charged. That is, 12.7% of all rapes *reported,* and 6.25% of all victimization. Of those charged, 35% were found guilty. That is 11.9% of all those arrested, and 4.2% of all rapes reported—and *2.06% of all rape victimizations.*) In light of the statistics, there seems little reason, God knows, for any uproar about enforcing rapists' social isolation.

But what is one to make of this letter, dated August 28, 1981?

Dear Colleague,

The Sexual Behavior Clinic has recently received funding from the National Institute of Mental Health to provide evaluation and *treatment* to *incest offenders* and

> *child molesters.* Patients are seen on an outpatient basis, and there is no charge for any of the services provided.
> There are several requirements for participation. First the patient/client must be 18 years of age or older and nonpsychotic. Second, he must have involved himself sexually with a female child, either related or unrelated to him. Thirdly, he must want to do something to stop that behavior. Finally, he must not be under legal coercion to participate in this treatment program. Treatment can only be given to those men voluntarily seeking treatment for their sexual behavior. *Likewise, if the patient/client is dissatisfied with the treatment at any time, he can simply stop the treatment without further consequence.* . . . [Italics mine.]

Surely this is the therapeutic response run riot?

Let's look briefly into the history of this idea of rehabilitation—of, ideally, prevention, and, failing that, treatment, which is the promise, the appeal to our better natures, made by the therapeutic state.

For all practical purposes, rational (as opposed to theistic) principles for justice came along with Cesare di Beccaria in 1764.

He said the rules should be clearly stated: What constituted a crime? What constituted the punishment for that crime?

He said the punishment and the crime should stand in proportionate relationship. And the punishments should be standard, regardless of the individual's class or wealth.

He advocated protection of individual's rights and liberties, including a presumption of innocence. Better that a guilty man should go free than an innocent one do time.

Along came science, and scientific criminology. We got social determinism—that is, crime as a result of social conditions in which criminals are bred. And we got positivism—the idea that criminals are born that way; that there are anatomical types predisposed to crime—a long lower jaw, flat nose, sparse beard, and low sensitivity to pain.

Psychiatric determinism began as a reflection of the state

of the art of psychiatry, which early on dealt only with containing crazies. Crime was explained as moral insanity; and criminals were adjudged to be of inferior mental type.

Then in the late 1800's, Italian Criminal Law Professor Enrico Ferri pulled a bit from all parts, and the search was on to explain the causes of individuals' criminal behavior. The law should no longer "be concerned with questions of guilt and its degree nor with measuring a fit punishment, but should humanely apply whatever measures are necessary to protect society from further transgressions by the same individual." Punishment should be tailored to the offender, not the offense.

This idea of custom-fitted justice made room for a natural partnership between law and psychiatry. Where once, illness had been thought to be due to sin, now sin (or evil- or wrongdoing) was seen as due to illness. The concept of punishment, then, naturally gave way to the concept of "treatment."

Author-philosopher, Michel Foucault, writing of "the constitution of a medico-legal apparatus, through which on the one hand psychiatry is utilised in the penal system while, conversely, penal types of control and interventions are developed and multiplied to deal with the actions or behavior of abnormal subjects," wonders why doctors should have wanted to "intervene in the penal domain just when they had barely and then only with difficulty, succeeded in detaching psychiatry from the sort of magma constituted by the practices of internment which occupied precisely the heart of the 'medico-legal' domain except for the fact that they were neither medical nor legal. . . ." He concludes that although psychiatry had achieved an autonomous stronghold, it yet needed to gain a recognized piece of the planet, "to secure a basis for its intervention by gaining recognition as a component of public hygiene."

In other words, psychiatrists had to secure a broader base for their "professionalizing." Professionalizing requires an identifiable specialization. It engages a considerable number of people in full time paid employment. It requires skills and expertise. And a conviction on the part of the public that the

professionals serve an essential function. It requires that there
be a something necessary to do, which is best done by them.
Following that, of course, it wants membership organizations,
associations, exclusive channels of entrance—and the apparatus
of boundary defenses: the ownership of a problem; turf.

Psychiatry could "establish this basis only through the fact
that there was a disease (mental alienation) for it to mop up.
There had also to be a danger for it to combat, comparable
with that of an epidemic, a lack of hygiene, or suchlike. . . ."
Since they had identified themselves as experts on those whom
society found to be outside the norm (and therefore by going
to psychiatrists declared themselves outside the norm, since
psychiatrists deal with people outside the norm: sick), an obvious place to expand was to those who might act outside the
norm, or whose situation was seen to threaten the norm.

Jacques Donzelot writes:

> In the last third of the nineteenth century, psychiatrists
> began to refuse the terms according to which they were
> asked to offer their opinions regarding a particular defen-
> dant, even when adults were involved. To declare
> whether a criminal had acted in a state of insanity ap-
> peared pointless and metaphysical to them. To be called
> upon in cases involving major crime, "monstrous" affairs
> that baffled the judicial apparatus, seemed to them a vexa-
> tious limitation of their practice, as did the restriction
> of their field of action to adults . . . for them it was not
> so much a question of giving up an old function as of
> extending the existing one. They wanted to be able to
> concern themselves more with minors than with adults,
> more with petty offenses than with major crimes, more
> with the detection of anomalies, with orienting those sen-
> tenced to a particular mechanism of correction, than with
> grading the responsibility of those accused.
>
> Again, then, the number of actual gross offenses—
> whether outside the home, or within—are *finite*. Secur-
> ing the broadest possible population for your service re-
> quires the broadest possible definition of those requiring
> it. The psychiatrists then proposed to go beyond their

minor function in the judiciary and achieve an autonomous position as prime movers in the prevention and
treatment of delinquency, which in their eyes had become
a mere symptom of mental aberration, on a par with all
the other "antisocial reactions" such as running away, lying, sexual perversions, suicide, and so on. For them, delinquency . . . was the manifestation of a deficiency that
was present at the start, a constitutive—hence detectable,
foreseeable—anomaly.

It was hardly a passing thought, then, to treatment instead
of punishment, to treatment as a form of punishment; or to
treatment before any overt act had even been committed, in
the name of *prevention.* Hardly a blink to the Senate Sub-
committee Hearing held in October of 1981, where we find
experts imploring us to ransack the cribs and playgrounds of
America in search of the newly coined "proto-delinquent build-
up."

Nor, because it was *medical,* was psychiatry ever discomfit-
ted by the need to make distinctions between voluntary and
involuntary assistance. Based on the medical idea that prevention is preferable to cure, and that it is better to intervene
unnecessarily, preventively, than to miss intervening where
it is necessary (or may become necessary), it was able to justify
coercive intervention where the law would not otherwise permit it.

Thus, for example, commitment to a mental institution without legal review, could be posited as being no more than preserving the "dignity" of the patient, and ensuring his comfort
by raising no unnecessary "*obstacles* to his admission." (Italics
mine.) And where, in both juvenile proceedings and those "on
behalf of" the allegedly mentally ill, the state's powers were
posed as benign—as *parens patriae*—psychiatry supplied the
scientific rationale for the purported benevolence.

When the issue arose of due process protections for those
facing mental commitment, psychiatrists argued that hearings,
with relatives and friends testifying that the patient should
be committed, would be counter-therapeutic to the mentally

ill patient. Legal scholars as well said that rules and regulations set by law would get in the way of the needs of the mentally ill. Those same arguments arose over therapeutic interventions into the family to combat pre-delinquency. And they arise, once more, with crimes in the home—where criminal justice interventions are widely said to be "counter-therapeutic," stigmatizing the offender, and destructive of the potential for "family harmony."

That there is a fundamental confusion inherent in the two intervention-powers of the state, that—where the family is concerned—there is overlap which allows the state to choose its weapon, based on interest, is evident from this explanation in the *Harvard Law Review:* "The state's power to regulate the family derives from two distinct sources, the police power and the *parens patriae* power. The police power is the state's inherent plenary power both to prevent its citizens from harming one another and to promote all aspects of the public welfare." So, in theory at least, citizens harming one another do justify police power intervention, leaving only the question of public welfare. "A large number of state ends have been considered legitimate objectives of the police power, including the promotion not only of the 'public health, safety, morals or general welfare,' but also of more abstract goals like aesthetic and family values. Individual conduct that fails to implicate any of these legitimate collective interests, however, lies outside the scope of police power." Well, okay. So police power would be justified if the state saw crimes in the home as threatening, let's say, "family values?"

"The *parens patriae* power, by contrast, is the state's limited paternalistic power to protect or promote the welfare of certain individuals like young children and mental incompetents, who lack the capacity to act in their own best interests. Acting under its *parens patriae* power, the state may pursue ends that would be impermissible under the police power because they are unrelated to any harm to third parties . . ." Oops. Presumably, in stranger-rape, the three parties are the state, the rapist, and the stranger-victim. Then, in paternal child molestation, it must be that the child-victim is seen as part of the party molesting her? Onward: ". . . unrelated to any harm to third parties or to the public welfare. At the same time, however, when the state acts as *parens patriae,* it should advance only the best interests of the incompetent individual and not attempt to further other objectives, deriving from its police power, that may conflict with the individual's welfare."[11]

Police power interest is "in preventing or punishing those acts that directly threaten the existence or stability of the state itself or the personal security of its citizens."

Then are we to deduce that once one is a member of a family, one is less than, or at least other than, a citizen?

It is argued that "in the case of interpersonal assaults in the privacy of the home the 'public's interest is not at stake.' " Is it not?

> Criminal law . . . deals with the regulation of those aspects of personal conduct deemed essential for the maintenance of the community. Infractions of criminal statutes harm not only the persons directly offended, but the whole community. *A bank robbery, for example, is considered to injure not only the depositors of the particular bank, but the whole business community as well, by undermining the confidence necessary to maintain normal banking operations.* [Italics mine.]

Well, but preserving the family is an often-stated state goal. Surely it can be posed that crimes in the home, revealed, alongside the "non-punitive" response to the offender and the concomitant implication of the victim, can threaten the confidence necessary to maintain continuing family operations?

Do crimes in the home pose a threat to the state end of preserving "the family"?

Yes and no.

Yes, for the credibility reason just suggested.

No, if the question is read differently.

Ask this: Does embezzlement pose a threat to "the corporation"? Yes, but no. When all is well, the corporation is perceived as a "fictitious person" including all those who are parties to it. However, the embezzler of funds is promptly identified as an individual isolated from his corporate identity by the act of embezzlement. He is prosecuted as an individual; the fact that his status as a member of the board gave him access to the funds does not come into issue. The corporation is not implicated in its own embezzlement.* No questions are asked of it as to why it allowed him access to those funds or why it didn't stop him, or whether it knew all along he was doing it. It is not identified as a "dysfunctional corporation." It is not imprecated to keep the offender on the job. Yet, where the family is concerned, the greater the evidence of gross misbehaviors, the greater the insistence on subsuming the individual under the family unit.

Again, one asks why? Why are individuals so happy, why are the powers that be so happy, with this effectively man-absolving, woman-blaming solution to the "discovery" of widespread crimes in the home?

Perhaps there is something in this:

> The displacement of blame onto women for things perceived as individual failures rather than as social injuries—inadequate income, accidental pregnancies, unsatisfying work and leisure—makes it all the more difficult to move beyond guilt into resistance. As long as families

* Interestingly, this was a question early on about the corporation: "In the year 1429, an action was brought against the Mayor, Bailiff, and Commonality of Ipswich and one J. Jabe (presumably a member of what we should call the 'corporation') for trespass in respect to the seizure of the plaintiff's beasts for non-payment of toll. Apparently, the facts could not be disputed, for the defendant's counsel resorted to plea which was of the most technical kind, but not less interesting on that account. He pleaded that, inasmuch as the defendant Jabe was a member of the 'commonality' of Ipswich, he had been named twice over in the writ commencing the action, which was, therefore, bad. Presumably, if Jabe, instead of being sued with the corporation, had been prosecuted by it for stealing the 'corporation plate,' he would have set up the plea that, being a member of the corporation, he could not be convicted of stealing 'his own plate.'" Which would have been, of course, identical to the logic behind old permissions for paternal and spousal violence and sexual assault.

remain microcosms of male domination and class conflict, they will absorb energies into personal and painful battles between women and men, thinly concealed behind veneers of domestic harmony and romantic love.

But suppose that absorption of energies is the very idea? Suppose that household violence is perceived as *domesticated* violence, with the violence potential of less powerful males perceived as a fixed quantitative phenomenon which has to go *somewhere*. Then, surely, it would not hurt as a hedge against mobilized energies to leave each individual male an "appropriate" victim or two. This is kind of the woman and child as lightning rod theory.

"A man's home is his castle" is often enlisted as an idea relevant to male misbehaviors in the home. It is traced in Bartlett to Sir Edward Coke (1549–1634): "for a man's house is his castle, *et domus sua cuique tutissimum refugium.*" "The house of everyone is to him as his castle and fortress, as well for his defense against injury and violence as for his repose." (cites omitted)

In its time, that was kind of a declaration of olly-olly-in-free, a safety-zone declaration, a right to freedom from marauders or state intrusion—but it can also be seen as a truly inspired political platform; one with all the features of slogan appeal: a Basic Selling Premise. It confirmed the individual male's dominance over his terrain: even the lowliest among you can have your personal property—including the cow, the wife, the kid. Even the poorest among you is sovereign in your domain. You, too, have an earthly "kingdom." A realm in which you, also, are above the law. Don't bother your head about My goings-on.

Most men now, as then, are in fact powerless in the larger matters; and often in the smaller ones pertaining to the outside world. Powerlessness has been suspected of causing rage for a lot longer than there've been mental health professionals to shake. What is now thought to lead to stress and low self-esteem, has always been suspected of leading to peasant revolts or riots in the streets.

Ending poverty is among many solutions looked to by sociologists studing family violences—even though the violences are over and over shown to take place in all social spheres. But poverty is only one aspect of powerlessness (as physical oppression is only one aspect of oppression); and aggregate anger, collectively acted on, is a danger to people in power—a danger, therefore, to existing society.

It seems possible that the state (which in modern times includes all major institutions of power, including corporations) might be considerably reluctant to seriously remove the more "natural" or "harmless" or at least "discreet" forms of ventilation for that rage.

And what of the thought put forth by a court in 1840 that the "father-child nexus" was—far more than a formalistic legal relationship. It was the "generational glue of society." Why? Because the child provided "for the father's thrift and industry." And *"any disruption of that tie might remove a valuable incentive for labor."* (Italics mine.)

Are women and children perceived by the state as grounding devices for individual male aggression? Are they, as "the family," a way of keeping men in thrall to the state? It does sound fancy. But here it is:

Were it not that he is one of the "intellectuals" connected with the current administration, author of "Wealth and Poverty," turning to George Gilder's constructions might seem whimsical. Were he "fringe," it would be no more than making points off an odd phenomenon. But he is presently being taken seriously. And, as I was to discover, what he is saying is neither odd nor even particularly new.

He is seriously warning us, as we have been warned before (and at the same time as we have never been warned before) of what the "breakdown of the family," due to women's failure to do their duty to society, would mean.

Men would run amok.

The marketplace would disintegrate.

Civilization would collapse.

It is Gilder's thesis that men are naturally inferior. That, without women as wives, socializing them, they would rampage, loot, pillage, rape, and so on. That their natural fragility and insecurity must be bolstered with cultural leg-ups and with female subordination—because women are superior. A society, he says, which permits that superiority to become evident will drive men to commit sexual suicide. He cites the Iks.

When the Ugandan government banished the Iks from their lands, the mode of life went agricultural; the men had no role in life. Family ties collapsed, along with compassion and cooperation. Predation, opportunism, and hate and contempt for human life ensued. All this, not because of poverty and scarcity but because the men had lost their *crucial roles.*

It is Gilder's thesis that men have no sexual authenticity as women do; that "males are the sexual outsiders and inferiors"; that "the man must be made equal by society."

And men can only be made equal by women's taking it upon themselves to socialize them, and giving up the idea of threatening men in the job market.

> The crucial process of civilization is the subordination of male sexual impulses and psychology to long-term horizons of female biology. If one compares female overall sexual behavior now with women's life in primitive societies, the difference is relatively small. It is male behavior that must be changed to create a civilized order. Modern society relies increasingly on predictable, regular, long-term human activities, corresponding to the female sexual patterns. It has little latitude for the pattern of impulsiveness, aggressiveness, and immediacy, arising from male insecurity without women—and further enhanced by hormonal activity. This is the ultimate and growing source of female power in the modern world. Women domesticate and civilize male nature. They can destroy civilized male identity merely by giving up the role.

Sexual "suicide," then, seems euphemistic: what he *really* seems to mean is sexual slaughter.

Nor is this view of the power of uppity-women to create societal disaster unique to Gilder.

It is also said that we brought down Rome.

"Roman women unwittingly wrecked with their own hands their feminine strongholds within a patriarchal society; from the proud, dignified and influential mothers they had been in early republican times, they became despisers of their prime biological function in imperial times and began competing on men's terms."

Roman women's assertiveness "led to the crippling of Rome's family structure and largely destroyed family loyalty and solidarity. Roman legislation and social evolution steadily eroded what was left of male privileges and responsibilities, and, under Domitius Ulpanius's inspiration, proclaimed that women were entitled to the same rights as men . . ." Infanticide, lewdness . . . "The Romans actually committed ethnic suicide."

As then, so now, is the urgency of Gilder's theme.

Man is naturally outlaw.

Deprived of his role as provider and protector, the man, like males all over the world throughout human history, will leave. As a general rule of anthropology the likelihood of his presence in the home decreases in direct proportion to the aggressiveness of the woman. Instead, he will conduct male rituals, drink, commit crimes, hunt, seek power, take drugs, pursue women on male terms. Unless he is performing a masculine service for the marriage commensurate in some way with the bearing of a child, the marriage will cramp his manhood. He will feel unworthy of the woman and thus unable to love her. The relationship will fail. . . .

Turning away from the family, he "frequents all-male bars and behaves loudly and abusively . . . watches televised football and other male sports for hours on end and argues about them incessantly; or he bombards himself with the music of male sexuality. . . . Otherwise he is obsessed with women. He tries as much as possible to reduce them to their sexual parts and to reduce their sexuality to his own limited terms—to meaningless but insistent copulation."

That's pretty portentous stuff.

It manages to ignore the fact that male barbarity toward women never seems to have much diminished during periods of total patriarchy; periods when the male "role" was secure. Perhaps that is because there was not, then, televised sports, or continuous access to the music of male sexuality. Perhaps. But the very absence of reason makes the fear more palpable, and the imperative more menacing.

"Such single males—and married ones whose socialization fails—constitute our major social problem. They are the murderers, the rapists, the burglars, the suicides, the assailants, the psychopaths." Men, he has told us, commit 100% of the rapes, 95% of the burglaries, represent 94% of the drunken drivers, 70% of the suicides, *and "91% of the offenders against family and children."* (Italics mine) Peculiarly, he adds after this last that, "More specifically, the chief perpetrators are single men." It is difficult to know how they arrange this.

Society needs women to need men as providers so that men will work—not because they're better at working, but so they won't go hogwild.

"Male dominance in the marketplace . . . is a social artifice maintained not for the dubious benefits it confers on men but for the indispensable benefits it offers the society. . . ." Surely the permission for domesticated violence and domesticated child sexual assault could be seen as a social artifice serving as a benefit to society as well.

"Conventional male power, in fact, might be considered more the ideological myth. It is designed to induce the majority of men to accept a bondage to the machine and the marketplace, to a large extent in the service of women and in the interests of civilization."

It is women's job, then, to harness men, to corral them and pen them in family units. By ensnaring him into the role of provider, the woman (and her brood) becomes his ever-demanding incentive. Men, only then, become responsible creatures. Otherwise, women (and society) will be victimized, possibly terminated, by the "disruptive energies of unsocialized males."

So the essential function of women is to tie men to the marketplace, thereby keeping the social machine running, and, yes, domesticating their violence. And the point of the family is not—as it has been so often said—to socialize children (Gilder barely mentions them): it is to socialize adult men.

So crimes in the home can be seen to pit two police power interests against one another: the security of the state vs. the security of citizens. If men are perceived (by men) to be naturally "outlaws," the choice presented becomes predation on the streets, or predation in the home. Since the state must first defend itself against male outlawry, women, in conjugal service to the nation though they be, are on their own. Shouldn't there, then, be due compensation, due honor, for service? If women's enlistment is essential, as Gilder says, to the very survival of civilization? Yes, but. To let on that women, marrying, were at high risk of volunteering for hazardous duty might seriously affect the rate of enlistment. It is more frightening, far less fair, but probably seems more attractive, to eliminate insofar as possible, any other alternatives. At the far end of that spectrum lies this: if civilization itself depends on female subordination, then insubordination is seditious.

It is not a pretty picture. If individual male violence is a form of social control of women, the permission for that violence is a form of social control of men. It smacks unpleasantly of puppeteering. Nor does it raise a lot of hope to feel one could argue he is wrong. As long as women are *perceived* by those in power as agents of social control, it matters little whether the reason is men's inferiority, or the state's need to offer men a "harmless" diversion—to offer them women as scapegoats.

Men presently in power endorse Gilder's beliefs. His premise is tied to all of the (anti)social issues we presently confront.

Neither welfare, nor abortion, busing, gun control, or marijuana are primarily subject to either logic or the U.S. Constitution. They also are subject to the primacy of the Sexual Constitution.

Guns may be nasty, but, Gilder says, they affirm the "validity of the family itself and the man's part in it"—in protecting his wife and children. Since the crime this man is protecting his family against is itself a signal of male incapacitation by females unwilling to socialize the intruders, "controls may exacerbate the syndrome of male insecurity, violence, and frustration that they are designed to restrict." In other words, I gather, those men might run amok as well.

Abortion threatens the male sexual organ itself. In the good old days, "Male potency was not simply a matter of erectile reliability; it was a fell weapon of procreation. Women viewed male potency with some awe, and males were affirmed by this response." One should think so. But that is all gone, now; the penis is no more than "an optimal accessory of the woman's will and body," "an empty plaything." Abortion, he says threatens to interfere with "our deepest human experiences."

Busing. Here, again, it encroaches on "the sexual constitution"—reflecting "a breakdown and incapacitation of the family, particularly in its role of socializing ghetto males." Gilder says, "As with guns and abortion, people are being treated not principally as members of families and subject to familial disciplines but as individuals primarily subject to the state and its social and legal priorities." Now that sounds nice—about family integrity and domestic privacy; about people not being primarily subject to the state and its priorities. Except for this: he has told us that the subsumption of women under "family" *is* the state's priority. That the only possible solution to civilization is to keep men under the force of the "civilizing constraints of female sexuality."

The idea of more nurturant men, he finds ridiculous: it fails to affirm male roles.

Women's new sexual compliancy only threatens men, who, unsocialized—as if unstrung—by this, are pushed toward their natural patterns of barbarism.

In the old "1-2" of the Sexual Constitution, "1" is flattery; "2" is threat.

That we are being threatened with a chestnut makes it more, not less, alarming. The same-olds simply do not seem to go away: "Men can find partners too easily. Women become so available on male terms that men are not induced to submit to the futurity of feminine love. Wives fail to teach their husbands the cycles of femininity. Thus, even though the marriage may be happy, the man is not durably bound to the woman through her womb and the hope or presence of progeny." Once again, the old cow and milk routine. As in Rome where, "The chief sufferers were the virtuous women themselves, often superseded in their husband's affections by the bolder exotic courtesans of those cosmopolitan times. . . ."

The suggestion that women, working, remove pressure on the man, he finds "similarly upsetting." It destroys the importance of man's role as provider without replacing it with anything else. All of these things may *seem* to grant new powers to a man, but "what he requires are signs and assurances that women really need his submission to them, that they are as dependent on his masculinity as he is on their femininity."

Just how this who is submitting to whom really works has what James Thurber has called "a muzziness of thought so great as to almost defy analysis."

> If masculinity is reaffirmed, many of the resentments that women now bear toward it will be dissipated. Women now associate maleness with their own oppression. In fact, it is the restriction of masculine fulfillment in modern society that leads men to seek sexual validation by oppressing women. If men grow sexually stronger, women will become more powerful as well, because men will be able to submit to them more happily.

I tried it this way: "If masterhood is reaffirmed, many of the resentments that puppies now bear toward it will be dissipated. Puppies now associate masterhood with their own oppression. In fact, it is the restriction of masterhood fulfillment in modern society that leads masters to seek validation by oppressing puppies. If masters grow stronger, puppies will become more powerful as well, because masters will be able to submit to them more happily."

I don't know. If you can make head or tail out of it, send in your solution with any boxtop.

I grow peevish. Irritable.

I do not like knowing about this. Not only that—no one else is going to either.

A friend, reading this over, confirms that.

"This is really hard to take. It's slit-your-throat time. Reading it, I go, what's the use? Who wants to get married if that's what they think it's for?"

"They" don't all, of course. But the political concept of using women to restrain individual men—who might otherwise turn collectively aggressive—must be pretty appealing when you're trying to run things.

As I try *not* to think about it—to block the idea that if women and children are justifiable trade-offs in keeping men in tow, there can be no bottom-line in permitted behaviors— it pops up elsewhere (it *seems* like everywhere):

"Marriage, like Hobbes' *Leviathan,* was instituted in order to preserve the social order and prevent males from mutual destruction."

"(I)t is the woman who also acts as the protector of the man in the home by providing a social life for him and acting as the nourishing mother who feeds and clothes him. . . ."

As women moved into the low-paid job market in the late 1800's, "the men if they were not actually displaced from their jobs by women, were at least under greatest risk of unemployment, and in any case were the victims of a process of disqualification of labor that caused them to lose both their rights over women and children, and by the same token, their responsibilities." Then, it was by promoting professional motherhood— in the home, and as a social career—that men regained "the impression if not the reality of their former patriarchal power by guaranteeing them the primary responsibility in providing for the home, and placed women in the position of constant watchfulness over the men, since wives would have an interest in the regularity of their husbands' professional and hence social life, as their own chances of betterment depended on it."

It ought not to go unremarked that if a woman had formulated this denigrating analysis of men, and for certain if any woman had had the power to implement the manipulative policy implicit in it, she would have been stoned for man-hating. Should one be open-minded—prepared to entertain Gilder's thesis that men are, naturally, biologically, even criminally, inferior? (Men have, after all, from time to time, entertained that thought about women.)

"(T)he woman's place *is* the home, and she does her best when she can get the man there too." What does that mean, please? How? By pulling on the leash? But she's not holding the leash—she *is* the leash.

Ah, here: this getting the man in the home "she cannot easily do alone. The society has to provide a role for him, usually as provider, that connects him to the family in a masculine way. But if social conditions are right, the woman can induce the man to submit most human activity to the domestic values of civilization."

Never mind that "if social conditions are right" he will have a job, and the elation of being sole provider in an economy where the two-paycheck family is often a matter of basic survival *need*. Implicit in this domestication of male aggression is that household violences on the part of men are part of the integral value of domesticity. They are the natural cost of purchasing social tranquility.

It is ironic that the "liberal" efforts to de-criminalize crimes in the home, to "treat" the victims, with the aim of keeping the abusive families intact, should mesh so nicely with reactionary goals.

In the face of this, one reaches for a serious and convincingly authoritative expression to wear.

Because if women's role is critical, the fulcrum of the Sexual Constitution which keeps the jungle from society's door—surely there should be a Bill of Rights under that Constitution?

As a soldier, as things stand, you are not even a citizen. Like an anti-hero in an Eric Ambler novel, you can be disowned in time of crisis by those unknowns whose power and purpose you serve.

Battered by your husband, or discovering him to be molesting your child, you will be identified as one with him. "It is objectively sound, therefore," Gilder says,

> to define the society as chiefly an assemblage of families, family aspirants, and unmarried units within the familial order. Unless we take this reality into account, our politics will fail to achieve its goals—will fail to foster the happiness and fulfillment of our citizens. A sound social policy will devote itself to promoting the creation and maintenance of family connections.

Getting married, having children within that marriage, is a little like having your passport revoked. The passport which, identifying you as a citizen, affords you the police power protections of the state.

"It has long been recognized," writes John Kenneth Galbraith, "that women are kept on political leash by urging their higher commitment to the family."

His analysis, in the essay, "The Higher Economic Purpose of Women", seems to me to shed some light on the higher political purpose of women, as well. Far from the hortatory tone of Gilder's books, Galbraith's incisiveness is considerably more reassuring. But not his point.

Information about women's economic value, Galbraith says, has been selectively withheld. Information about their victim-value, as put forward by Gilder, would seem to have been withheld as well.

Galbraith points out that the avowed focus of economics is on the individual. Yet, as he says, the act of marriage, the formation of the family unit, creates an assumption that the interests of individuals are presto–change-o identical.

In the area of crimes in the home, the insistence on this unit's value loudens markedly in direct relation to the evidence of the horrors at hand. That is, the more overwhelming the case of systematic brutality, the keener the insistence on "the family" being maintained.

It is, Galbraith points out, precisely at the point where to include the individual woman's household economic function in the Gross National Product would create an inconvenient re-estimation of her value, that the individual becomes the "household." And it is at precisely that point where the question of serious and chronic victimization arises that our concern for the citizen (for the *individual*) is suddenly subsumed under a reverent solicitude for the family.

"The concept of the household is an outrageous assault on personality," Galbraith writes. Particularly, one might add, where that assault is superimposed on a real and grievous assault. "People are not people; they are parts of a composite or collective . . ." which overpowers, I add, in social value those severely brutalized within it.

Writing of the economist's concern with the individual, Galbraith says, "Were this preoccupation with the individual pursued to the limit, namely to the individual, there would be a grave danger that the role of women would attract attention." Were this same preoccupation with the individual, the citizen, pursued to its limit in law—to the individual maimed on the family battlefield—there would be some similar danger that the risk women run in marrying and having children, in joining the family unit, would attract attention as well. Because, examined, it's pretty clear that where the individuals who make up this (theoretically voluntary) unit do not by their own individual, fortuitously civilized makeups, embrace a docile behavioral accord, the "head of household" continues to be empowered to structure for himself as barbarian a landscape as he chooses. And his victim, by relationship, will be said to have *acquiesced* in her victimization.

Both Galbraith and Gilder are showing us the *pragmatics* behind the insistent depersonalization involved in the politics of "the family." It's a kind of puppeteering in which sexism seems to comprise the strings. Gilder celebrates sexism as essential, "based on the exaltation of women, acknowledgment of the supremacy of domestic values, and the necessity of inducing men to support them [women] in civilized society."

We ignore the state's commitment to this principle at considerable risk. So long as it exists, truly civilized suggestions for improving family life—for rendering it more civil than martial—continue to be naive.

Charlotte Perkins Gilman noted in the 1800's that men could do what they want as work, for less wages, and not what they had to, if they weren't burdened with total home support. Logical. But ingenuous so long as the definition of civilization itself is written on the premise that women's dependence is fundamental to society's control of men.

More recently, the same suggestion:

> First, we hear a great deal about men "caught" in unsatisfying jobs, but because of their provider duties they are unable and/or unwilling to take risks—either go back to school or to try some whole new field of occupational endeavor. A self-interest appeal could be made to these kinds of men. If they would be willing to change their norms and behaviors regarding the status of provider so that that status could be occupied equally and interchangeably with wives, men would be free to exercise a variety of occupational options not now open to them.

Exactly. But the "self-interest appeal" would be in conflict with state interest.

From the perspective of bottom-line protections against crimes in the home, the only wedge may lie here.

Galbraith writes:

> In modern society power rests extensively on persuasion. Such reverse incentives as flogging, though there are law-and-order circles that seek their revival, are in limbo. So, with increasing affluence, is the threat of starvation. And even affirmative pecuniary reward is impaired. For some, at least, enough is enough—the hope for more ceases to drive. In consequence, those who have need for a particular behavior in others resort to persuasion—

to instilling the belief that the action they need is reputable, moral, virtuous, socially beneficent or otherwise good. It follows that what women are persuaded to believe about their social role and, more important what they are taught to overlook, are of prime importance in winning the requisite behavior.

Were we to penetrate beyond the language addressed to heart and hearth, could we still be persuaded by the chilling analysis of our social role as leeches and leashes? As, individually, *expendable* ones in the bargain?

Were we to see past that which insistently tried to teach us that the fallen, the wounded, are "sick"—which promises us that they are *different* by the evidence of their having been in a marital accident—would we still volunteer for the "requisite behavior"?

Any call for basic civilian protections for those in the home will require a willingness to re-examine and re-negotiate the trade-off. This, in turn, will require that we have the nerve to operate from the due process principle, demanding basic protections as individuals under the law—rather than the fear principle: "Oh good, someone is doing something about it."

Two battered women who killed their husbands, Francine Hughes and Cynthia Hutto, appeared on the Phil Donahue Show. Donahue was a bit nervous, or at the least a bit ameliorating, in the face of the support the audience was showing the women. They had both, after all, gone free.

DONAHUE (returning after a break): Francine Hughes, who's on the right, was with us, oh my, this is a year and a half, two years ago, in Philadelphia. I'll never forget it. You told the story of the death of your husband. And we had about 3,000 to 4,000 people in the audience at that time, and when you finished telling that story everybody applauded. And I was very struck by that, and I guess, now, as I review it, I understand it, but it was a real surprise to me to see—And it's a little unnerving, you know. I know that you're not asking for that, but it was like, you know, it was almost like cheerleading, you know. "Get the bum. Get the bum."

A sobering thought. And the audience, now, was somewhat subdued, listening as Cynthia Hutto described how she hadn't picked her husband up in the car because she'd thought he had a ride, and she met him on the road and picked him up and . . .

> he just started beatin' me around. And we live right down the road, so I just wanted to get home so nobody would see him hittin' me. So when we got home and he started beatin' me more and tellin' me that I had 45 minutes to get everything out of the house except for the kids, and I talked to him, you know, 'cause usually, when he'd get like that, I could talk to him and he'd calm down. And I figured, you know, it'd be like that again, but he didn't. He got worse. I said, "Bubba, I'm not leavin' . . . I'm not leavin' the kids; you know. Just let's work it out or somethin'." Then he went and got the shotgun from down off the wall, and I was sittin' on the couch, where he'd slung me there. And he pointed it at me, and it was loaded. And he said either he was gonna kill me or I was gonna kill him. And that's the only way he was gonna stop beatin' me. Then he handed it to me, turned around and walked away and went and laid down on the bed. And he was still yellin' at me, and I just sat there, you know. "When's this gonna stop?" 'Cause I was wantin' it to stop so we could be happy. So, I walked into the bedroom, and I seen him layin' there. And I don't know why, I just pointed it at him, and I pulled the trigger. And he moved, and I thought he was gonna get up and hit me some more. So I shot him again.

During this, the audience seemed attentive, somber. Donahue then reminded those who may have tuned in late, that Cynthia Hutto had been acquitted; that this was a painful thing to review; and the only reason for doing so was to "turn other wheels."

MS. HUTTO: That's the only reason.

MR. DONAHUE: That's why you're here, because you want others who may be similarly entrapped to get out before—

MS. HUTTO:—They don't do this. They don't know what it's like to go through it.

And then:

AUDIENCE: Would either of you be wanting to get married again?

And—from Francine Hughes:

MS. HUGHES: I have remarried. I remarried in February.

AUDIENCE: (Applause.)

Applause? As I remember, they went wild. After all, all was well.

5
A Little War History

"Experience should teach us to be most on our guard to protect liberty when the government's purposes are beneficent. Men born to freedom are naturally alert to repel invasion of their liberty by evil-minded rulers. The greatest dangers to liberty lurk in insidious encroachment by men of zeal, well-meaning but without understanding."

Brandeis, J., dissenting in Olmstead
v. United States, 277 U.S. 438, 479 (1928)

". . . the decision to treat deviance as a social problem is itself a political decision."

Anthony Platt, The Child Savers, *p. 100*

A book comes in, an annual report on the Child Protective Services of New York State. It is titled, somewhat chillingly, *The Children of the State*. Here, we learn that:

• child protective workers in New York are inadequately trained.

• the Commission evaluating them is "appalled" that child protective workers are regularly promoted out of protective services, and "income maintenance" workers promoted into it.

• that the workers do not necessarily know what should be reported.

• that they rely "heavily on their own backgrounds and experience" in making judgments.

• that there is no standardized pattern of action—so that "investigation of a report might variously count as a letter, a phone call, a visit."

• that, in one county, they are told to simply close down validated cases in order to reduce their workload.

• that paperwork has top priority, with some workers saying "the only feedback they receive from the state on their work is when a child abuse reporting form is filled out incorrectly."

• that the state hotline is often impossible to reach.

• that with a 50% turnover, "experienced staff" are those who've been around for six months or more.

• that the carbon paper is so lousy that carbon copies of the (Series DSS-222) forms which are used to make out reports are often so faint as to be unreadable.

All of which would be poignant, except for this: its inefficiency is the only safeguard in the system.

Peremptory? Perhaps. How can anyone be negative about a "service" to "protect" children? But at the very least a cautious negativity is called for. Unlike financial services (welfare, AFDC, etc.), Child Protective Services are a service only in the most misleading sense. Arguably, they are a service to children. Unquestionably, they are a service to the state. And they are not voluntary.

Nor in most states are they concerned as often with cases of abuse as they are with cases of neglect.

Many states now have computerized central registers to count, keep record of, and monitor cases. Yet the Commission investigating the New York child protective services says it was unable to learn: annual statistics on the number of days it takes to investigate a case; the average number of contacts in each investigation; the types of allegation which most often result in protective removal. With all that the system is said to be crushingly overloaded, workers are admonished to extend their "outreach"—beyond abuse, beyond sexual abuse, beyond "neglect"—to emotional neglect. In some places, to moral and religious neglect.

It's no wonder at all that arguments continue in law journals over the Family Court/Juvenile Court/child welfare system.

The voices of dissent were there from the beginning. To review the development of juvenile "justice" and child welfare is to watch the law struggle and squirm to get around itself.

The dangers of the system have often been pointed out. "The powers of the Star Chamber were a trifle in comparison with those of juvenile court." Each negative charge was met with yet more positive language: the lack of protections in the system were "informalities"—for the child's own good, in the child's best interests. Who could be against the good of children? Or against their best interests?

Interestingly, the history of child welfare/juvenile justice parallels the rise to a crashing cymbal of mother-blame, and the dramatic escalation of women's culpability in their personae as wives and mothers. Women, unhappily, played a significant role in both developments. (But then neither of the genders is perfect.)

Dissolving back to the eighteenth-century definition of good womanhood, we find that, if fairly discouraging to the contemporary mind, it certainly contained no hint that any woman was powerful enough to affect what a big strong man did. In "perfecting" themselves, then, women sought to develop virtues which would be seen as clinically neuraesthenic today. They were to be excessively modest, entirely delicate. They were thought to be vain and fickle creatures, filled with womanish fears. They referred to themselves as "weak and imperfect" creatures. In less-than-perfect circumstances (spinsterhood, widowhood), they were referred to as helpless, and referred to themselves that way (as in, "being a Poor helpless Widow . . . "). Said to possess trifling minds, they were thought to be a fund of small talk. Drearily, they wrote of "my own Imbecility and Weakness"; "my brain is so vacant that it seems to be void of Ideas." Their Virtue lay in discharging their "every duty" to husbands, households, and children. This, however, was no more than pursuit of their "humble duties," in their "Narrow sphere," concerned with their "little Domestick affairs."

By and large, they had no choice. Not only was divorce extremely rare, it was mainly incomplete. It was the granting of separation only, empty of the option of remarriage, and it was dependent on mutual agreement.

Custody of the children went fairly automatically to the head of household. Prior to 1800, the courts' presumption of the father's common law prerogative of guardianship was virtually complete.

The good news was this: that women "clearly perceived their dependent status, their lack of options, and the insufficient protection afforded them by law." They knew about marriage-as-lottery; knew that "if it is our fate to be conected with a Tyrant; it is then a temporary Hell." They were stuck. Without a separation *agreement,* without that the husband agreed—women were not able to conduct business or to earn money that could not later be claimed by their husbands. Were he to take the children, or to place them with his relatives or friends, she had little in the way of recourse—except what she could muster in ingenuity.

And there was some considerable spunk and ingenuity under the itty-bitty-me-woman personified in the public ideal.

A New Hampshire farm wife, Abigail Bailey, had been married to Asa Bailey for twenty-two years before she discovered he had sexually forced himself on one of her daughters. We don't know how old the girl was—only that Abigail had "mostly young children."

Abigail confronted Asa (not much has changed . . .). She told him to cut out his "abominable wickedness" (. . . except the idiom). And Asa replied smartly that "she was under his legal control: and he could overrule all (her) plans as he pleased."

What was she to do? She needed him to agree to a separation. She kicked him out. He kept coming back to the house to "play on her Fears" that she was incapable of "taking the whole charge of so great a family, and mostly young children, and all of (its) numberous affairs, without head or helper."

Obviously, she kept going somehow, to his greater pique.

Because one day old Asa came around and told her he'd agreed
to a settlement. She thought there was a "but." And of course
there was: but, he said, in order to make the settlement, they
needed to sell the farm, a transaction which, he claimed, would
have to take place in New York. Abigail smelled a trick, but
she felt she had no choice. So Asa traveled her up to the "rough
New York frontier town" of Unadilla, and just left her there.
Then he hot-footed it back to settle things up in New Hampshire, putting the kids in the care of a friend of his.

Abigail struggled back over the 270 miles and was able to
have Asa arrested. *Incest was then a capital crime.*

Aha! The good old days!

No. Not really aha.

The crime of incest most significantly referred to intermar-
riage within a proscribed familial degree. It carried an implication of complicity. Where a girl charged sexual assault (within
a proscribed familial degree), there was a strong tendency on
the part of judges to find it incredible that such an act by a
father could have occurred without the daughter's consent.
Which consent would then make her an "accomplice-witness."
Robert Frassetto, a law student at California's University of
Santa Clara, commenting on incest laws in the 1800's and early
1900's, writes:

> The ironic twist lies, of course, not only in the fact
> that, under the . . . rules, prosecutrix/victims were almost
> invariably found to be accomplices, but also in the fact
> that the victim witness could be found to be an accomplice
> to a crime which the courts would not acknowledge had
> been committed. Further irony appears in the fact that,
> even in some cases where incestuous copulation was vio-
> lence-induced, failure of the victim to make an outcry
> or subsequently to report the act has been considered
> submission, sufficiently qualifying her as a consenting ac-
> complice.

As long as the accomplice-witness component was present—
alongside a belief that such a thing could not occur otherwise—
far more likely than that the offender would be convicted,

was that the child-victim would be adjudged a "wayward girl"
trying " 'to hang' her father for her own delinquencies." Where
she might complain, for example, of the *threat* of force? Of
whipping? ". . . the court pointed out that there was not one
word of testimony that she declined to engage in the alleged
act of incestuous intercourse or that she resisted or protested,
and since there was no protest or resistance to overcome, a
resort to means calculated to overcome it was unnecessary."

Which seems to mean that although he threatened to beat
her, and she succumbed to the threat, that succumbing rendered the carrying-out of the threat unnecessary, and therefore
rendered the threat itself invalid.

However. Old Asa did get arrested. And the nice thing
about a law which looks serious is that the offender can't be
sure how it will come out.

But—even with Asa in jail—how was Abigail going to get
the kids back? A lawyer, assuring her that it was indeed the
father's absolute right to "move them where he should think
best"—also suggested that there would be no harm in having
a go at the ignorance of the law of the man who was holding
the children.

So Abigail threatened to have that man arrested as well.
Which worked.

She then dropped all charges against Asa in exchange for
a property settlement.

Happy ending. And notice—no suggestion in any of this
that Abigail either *made* him molest the girl, or *let* him do
it. No suggestion that she had any power except that of fina-
gling.

Another Abigail, Abigail Adams, had another problem. Her
daughter, Nabby, had married an "irresponsible scoundrel
given to business failures and frequent unexplained absences."
Yet, "I make no reflection but in my own Breast," Abigail was
able to write to her sister in 1797. "It is some comfort, to
know that she has not been the cause, and that she could not
prevent the misfortune to which she is brought."

Fifty years later, she could not have been so sure.

The Cult of Motherhood had no one birthday, but July 4, 1790, is as good as any to assign it. Then, in a July Fourth oration, James Tilton, president of the Delaware Society of the Cincinnati (an organization of former Revolutionary War officers), declared: "The men possess more ostensible powers of making and executing the laws." But . . . "the women, in every free country, have an absolute control of manners; and it is confessed, that in a republic, manners are of equal importance with laws." And he went on, "From the most savage to the most enlightened people, the female parent is considered of greatest importance to their descendants, by stamping their manners and sentiments in the early periods of childhood and youth."

From there, the Cult of True Womanhood grew, as a gift horse, to magnificent dimensions. "By the mother's forming hand," one manual asserted in 1848, the child "receives its shape to a great extent for all its future existence. And, perhaps there is no proposition that is so hackneyed and at the same time so little understood as that women are the prime cause of all the good and evil in human actions. . . . Yes, mothers, in a certain sense, the destiny of a redeemed world is put into your hands."

It is truly amazing how, for women, the elevator never seems to stop at equality (or, if it does, the doors don't open), but just zips up and down, from the pit to the pedestal.

Circumstances allowed for this new exaltation of woman/ mother's role: reduced home industry, increasingly urban life, a greater number of women married to men who were increasingly well off. In the mid-1800's, Americans seemed engaged in an endless homage to Mom. Mother was a creature, not of politics or power, but of *influence*. If every boy could grow up to be George Washington, every girl could grow up to be his mother.

If "circumstances" permitted the elevation of women, it was the clergy which decidedly encouraged it.

Women far outnumbered men as church supporters. Even in the 1650's, more women than men attended church. And revivals—among Baptists, among evangelical sects—usually won more women converts than men. At the end of the eighteenth century, in four Connecticut towns only one-third of the converts were male. Throughout the nineteenth century, women predominated as the major consumers of religious services. Church was someplace "proper" to go. It provided women with a safe and sanctified place around which to organize social activities. Women were said to be more susceptible to religion because of their "superior delicacy"—which is, as a compliment, a little like stronger fragility. It was only natural that they should be moved to do good works for the church.

One of the good works they did was to raise money.

They formed prayer groups, charitable institutions, missionary and education societies (to raise funds to educate the ministers).

In turn (in exchange), the ministers declared women of equal rank with men in "all the felicities of the soul." They rescued men from their baser passions; they domesticated them. As a visitor of the time observed:

> It is from the clergy only that the women of America receive that sort of attention which is so dearly valued by every female heart throughout the world. With the priests of America the women hold that degree of influential importance which in the countries of Europe is allowed them throughout all orders and ranks of society . . . and in return for this they seem to give their hearts and souls into their keeping. I never saw or read of any country where religion had so strong a hold upon the women or a slighter hold upon the men.

Women's exalted status was, however, something *conferred* by the ministers of the Christian churches, and the ministers used that as a control button. They "threatened that women would suffer more than men if the Christian social order dissolved." And their view of the Christian social order was that, superior or not, it was women's duty to submit to men. "Should 'the wife who possesses a mind of superior cultivation and

power to her husband's . . . be in subjection to his authority'?
asked Richardson, and answered, 'yes, because this is conforma-
ble to the general order God has established.' " Change that,
challenge the "order of the social state and women must become the most abject and helpless of all slaves."

Since the ministers saw fit to remind women of the bargain
rather frequently, the women could not help but understand
it. "It is that, which prevents our being treated like the beasts
of burden—which secures us the honourable privilege of human companionship in social life, and raises us in the domestic
relations to the elevated stations of wives and mothers." They
said, "To the Christian religion we owe the rank we hold in
society, and we should feel our obligations."

Science, also, was enjoying a sacred boom. And doctors increasingly appealed to the power of motherhood for reasons
of hygiene. And for reasons of their own expanding expertise.
They played to the mothers' movement with huge success.
One mother wrote:

> Scientific motherhood means more than a casual
> thought can grasp. It means a grander, nobler race, and
> altruistic humanity which shall fit the earth for the Savi-
> our's advent. It means the reformation of the drunkard,
> the redemption of the criminal, the repentance of the
> murderer, the abolition of asylums for the blind, dumb
> and insane . . . the elimination of selfishness, the death
> of oppression, the birth of brotherly love, the uplifting
> of mankind through true spiritual Christianity.

Giddiness aside, the promotion was more or less from cleaning personnel to administrative assistant. It was only a promotion enabling women to exercise their "superior sensibility"
within the female sphere. It did encourage women to move
outside the home, but only to suitable activities: activities at
which they might be naturally better equipped because of their
greater womanly gifts. It was a promotion—not to power—
but to pious *influence*.

"The doctrine of woman's sphere opened to women (reserved for them) the avenues of domestic influence, religious

morality, and child nurture. It articulated a social power based
on their special female power rather than on human rights.
For women who previously held no particular avenue of power
of their own—no unique defense of their integrity and dignity—this represented an advance."

The image was everywhere presented of Mother, ensconced
on her hearthside throne, the moral guardian of her children—
and of her husband as well. Men's behavior was to be molded
by women. Without her influence of grace, man would revert
to his natural barbarousness (notice how repetitious this all
gets?). He was, in other words, reasonably childish, hers to
control.

In fact, the two objects of her ministrations were becoming
increasingly indistinguishable. Substitute mother for wife, and
child for man, in this hymn to Her:

> A good wife [mother] is heaven's last, best gift to man
> [child]—his angel and minister of graces innumerable—
> his gem of many virtues—his casket of jewels; her voice
> is sweet music—her smiles, his brightest day—her kiss,
> the guardian of [his] innocence—her arms the pale of his
> safety, the balm of his health, the balsam of his life—her
> industry, his surest wealth—her economy, his safest stew-
> ard—her lips, his faithful counselors—and her prayers,
> the ablest advocate of heaven's blessedness on his head.

Whereas in the sixteenth and seventeenth centuries, it had
been father who'd been primary in the rearing of children,
him to whom the manuals directed advice—by the early nineteenth century, the literature spoke almost entirely to mothers.
It was a far cry from the time when a stern fatherly eye on
both wife and children was the rule. When it was the father's
job to maintain surveillance, discipline, subjection. What remained now was male authority—and female responsibility.
If women, after all, were imbued with a naturally superior
moral sense, and with a virtually limitless molding power over
their husbands, then his behaviors, his failures, were not a matter of his control, but a failure of hers.

Someone should have had the gift horse checked out by a
(female) vet.

"This has been called the *woman's age,*" begins *Maternity, A Book for every Wife and Mother,* "and perhaps with justice, for *never* has she held such a prominent position before in the world, as at present.

"Her labors and successes, in the various fields and affairs of life, are calling for more and more attention. . . ." Yes, but:

> . . . we must not lose sight of the fundamental principle of her organism, her most divine and sublime mission in life—*womanhood* and *motherhood.* The hand that rocks the cradle, *the mother of the coming man,* is too important a factor to be disregarded ever so slightly; and while all the world is alive to *women's* progress, accomplishments, and attainments; while artists and thinkers in the various fields are assisting her with stepping stones to attain her goal, we should be doubly anxious to keep up a corresponding development in the physical and moral elements of her being.

Because only she can *sustain* a "perfect evolution" and remain "perfectly secure on her lofty plane."

"Men may *rule* the *race,* but *women govern its destiny."*
Yes.

"Great men of all times have traced their lofty ideals and talents, and indeed the whole of their success, to their mothers. A mother's influence, both on the body and on the mind, and her powers of transmission of habits, good or bad, are always stonger than are those of the father. . . ." They are not kidding. *"Her* life, *her* morals, and *her* teachings, both pre-natally and subsequently, affect the child to control its actions to a great extent and for its entire existence."

They are not kidding about *pre-natally.*

We are here presented with a "very reasonable law of embryonic molding" whereby a mother can *electrotype* her unborn fetus. Evidence? Please.

> A lady, who, during the period of gestation was chiefly employed in reading the poets and in giving form to her daydreams of the ideal world, at the same time gave to

her child (in phrenological parlance) large *ideality,* and a highly imaginative turn of mind.

Some time since we met with a youth who had finely molded limbs and a symmetrical form throughout. His mother has a large, lean, attenuated frame, that does not offer so much as a single suggestion of the beautiful. The boy is doubtless indebted for his fine form to the presence of a beautiful French lithograph in his mother's sleeping apartment, and which presented for her contemplation the faultless form of a naked child.

This electrotyping process—literally a process of causing, through electricity, "the deposit of fine particles of metal . . . dissolved in a powerful acid, upon the surface of any article which it is desired should receive a coating of such metal"— is, by the author, reasonably supposed to have a parallel pre-natal molding process. One which is effected by the vital forces of the mother, and to some extent controllable by her mental operations and emotions which imprints on "the human embryo in all its various parts."

This was remarkable not so much because it was a new idea, but because it was such an old one. The Hottentots, too, believed that the conduct of the mother before birth affected the child's personality. They thought that if a pregnant woman ate lion's or leopard's flesh, the child would have the characteristics of those animals. And in European folklore, if a pregnant woman walked over a grave, it was said that the child would die. And in Transylvania, if anyone threw a flower in the mother's face, the child would have a mole on that part of the face.

The difference is that, here, in the American *Maternity,* the power was suffusive. The author offers another case by way of illustration.

A teacher in a western state was working with five children from one family. The two oldest were dull and slow to learn. The third, however, was quick and poetic and appreciative of the beauties of nature. She could also "write a theme in prose or verse with ease and facility." This would be puzzling, unless one unearthed the following facts:

Some months prior to the birth of the favored child, the mother (who, though reared in an Eastern State, in the enjoyment of fair advantages, had become the wife of a farmer in a new county, deprived of literary and social privileges, and overworked in the struggle to acquire a competence) had her attention attracted to a volume of Walter Scott's poems, brought to the house by a canvasser; and she was so seized with a desire to possess and read the book, that, not having at hand the money to purchase it, she had walked four miles at night to borrow of a friend a sufficient sum for the purpose.

Whereupon, she read it so often she learned it by rote. "Here, no doubt, was the source of the superior intelligence, refinement and poetic tendencies in the child."

And, no doubt, the source of the dull-wittedness in the others: pre-natal cultural neglect.

And so our *woman* facing *maternity* has the power to *consciously* and *purposely* at every moment of her *pregnancy* shape the "mental, moral and spiritual features of her child to an extent to which no limit could be assigned." Not only that but this *culture before birth* must begin even before the "mere nine or twelve months" preceding birth. "To this end does it not behoove every one who aspires to the god-like honor of begetting a being in his or her own likeness, to first enter in thorough earnest upon the work of self-improvement, self-discipline, and moral and spiritual purgation?" These are "not the work of a day, or even a year. In fact, the whole previous life is none too long a period in which to prepare for so serious an undertaking as the reproduction of one's self." If the author keeps working backward, she will, of course, reach the incipient mother's mother and *her* prenatal culture and whole life's preparation, and back to . . .

However. Just as the pip begins to rise, we discover in *Maternity* a very crafty under-message which our female physician/author slips into this phrenological blitz. It is *the sacred right of mothers to be free of marital rape.*

Couched in the language of "the sacred right of mothers

to choose, in accordance with her own highest monitions, the
time and circumstances under which she would assume the
maternal function," this doctor tells us that "so often" a woman
is "compelled, or made to believe it her religious duty to accept
this function at the husband's imperious desire, even against
the vehement protest of both soul and body on her part, causing
an aversion, if not a loathing." From her "so often" one can
only infer how often.

In fact, the issue of marital rape first arose alongside the
movement to make abortion illegal for the first time in this
country. "The true and *greatest* cause of abortion," wrote one
woman anonymously in 1866, "is one hidden from the world,
viz: unhappiness and want of consideration towards wives in
the marriage relation, the more refined education of girls, and
their subsequent revolting from the degradation of being a
mere thing—an appendage." Abortion was an alternative, she
said, for women who "are victims of selfish and gross husbands,
who are allowed no choice of time or convenience, whose
hearts ache with disappointment and degradation. . . ."

However, as we know, it was abortion which was criminal-
ized. Not marital rape.

And women like our physician/author were left with
"please." With appeals to the very better nature men were
thought not to possess to refrain from such "outrages of the
most flagrant character, the same in essence as positive physical
violence, and the same within as without the legal marriage
relation . . ."

Her marital rape effort is almost enough to make one want
to overlook the more disastrous effect of the mother-power
message of her book.

She is excellent, too, on admonishments to basic health and
hygiene, excoriating "indigestible hot bread, pastry, greasy
food . . . and the many abominations of modern un-hygienic
cookery." Good on the powers of fresh air. Excellent on rational
dress, abhorring those methods of "compressing the body about
the waist, chest, or abdomen. . . ."

But, inescapably, she returns to the gestating mother's purity of *thought* and *feeling* and the direct causal connection between what a woman is, does, thinks, feels, looks at, reads, with the implanting in the child not only of desirable traits but its *future occupation*. During the "ten or twelve" months before birth, the parents should think, talk, read, or study about the department of human interest to which they wish to destine the child. It is the mother's cherishing of strong aspirations which will give the child its aptitude for that career.

This is her *power*. It is her *duty*.

What a setup.

So there was this pool of piety, this new natural liquid asset of zest and newfound power, an engine in search of an engineer. There was the clergy defining appropriate boundaries. And there was a new band of medicals, professionalizing. All were ripe and ready to merge interests in a zeal of righteous social reform, to combat what they perceived as a moral disease in (woman's sphere) children. Poor children. And the state, encouraging them in its own interests, perceived the same problem as one meriting social control.

Increasing immigration, growing urbanization, made for a vastly increased, and increasingly visible, number of those afflicted with the plague of pauperism. The practice of indenture, suitable to earlier, smaller social situations—whereby towns could find relief from providing for poor children by selling them to masters for their entire minority, to learn a trade— was impracticable with larger populations, and with more centralized working conditions. Almshouses, workhouses, and poorhouses were built and filled up rapidly with a mélange of children, adult vagrants, criminals, and just plain poor people.

Women, with their newly starched attire of moral superiority and their new mandate to engage in a "larger housekeeping" set out to rescue children from the contagiousness of their degraded parents. Their concern was not with abused or severely neglected children, since in their minds that was a redundancy. In their minds, abuse and neglect *defined* children whose parents were in the morally degraded circumstance of poverty.

Physicians of the body, physicians of the soul, and soon physicians of the mind, saw poverty as a disease—one widely associated with criminality—with, at the least, wantonness, mendicancy, lewdness. And criminality was widely thought to be hereditary. Therefore, these were children who must be rescued, must be cured. They were *pre-delinquent.* This did not mean they had not done anything wrong. It meant they had not done anything wrong *yet.* That they would was regarded as inevitable. Because criminals were conditioned by biological heritage and brutish living conditions, the children must be rescued and "reconstituted."

Idleness and lack of ambition, too, were crimes/diseases. But concern was not limited to children in idleness. It was not spared children who worked, in mills and factories—where children under twelve sometimes made up one-fourth of the labor force. There, as well, the children were said to be in grave moral danger, from exposure to the influences of the adult poor working people. They might pick up foul habits, foul language. More important, if they worked, they did not learn to read. And if they did not learn to read, they could not read the Bible. And this would lead to moral illiteracy. The concerns of the rich for the poor working child far and away exceeded the concern of the poor working child's parent(s). For them, the alternative was often the almshouse or the poorhouse for the whole family, children included.

Upper-middle-class women joined philanthropic institutions. They joined charity organizations. They became "friendly visitors" to the poor, with each well-to-do woman maintaining a patronage of three families, intending to negotiate the uplifting idea that the rich were the buddies of the industrious poor.

Meanwhile, what the women saw as a social hygiene problem, and the state saw as a public order problem, a number of men saw as an exciting entrepreneurial challenge—not unnatural in an industrializing age. Since the government had sponsored almshouses and poorhouses, it seemed natural to assume that it would continue to share the costs of building and maintaining more suitably specialized institutions for destitute, pre-delinquent children whom (everyone agreed) it was cruel and disease-enhancing to shut up in institutions with derelict and criminal adults. So orphan asylums were built under private sponsorship—with funds raised largely by women—in which the government shared the costs.

But then—what of children who were not orphans, yet were exposed to conditions that would, inevitably, result in their hopeless corruption (and who were, then *pre-corrupt;* already infected)?

The first step toward colonizing those children was to separate out the ones already part of a captive poor population. To "liberate" them from the workhouses and almshouses they were in, and from their parents. To build a system which would de-contaminate them.

The first House of Refuge, built in New York in 1825, and organized by a private corporation, was billed as a reformatory. It was called a "haven" for children who otherwise would go hopelessly wrong. Although it began by taking children from almshouses and poorhouses, it quickly was authorized to take children whose parents "volunteered" them to it. Kids who were dumped into the system. Kids who—as beyond control, or in need of supervision—continue to make up one-third of the juvenile court cases today.

From there, it was but a short step to the idea that the state should assume control of all children under fourteen who lacked "proper care or guardianship." And it was certainly an attractive feature that the institutions these children were placed in would be state subsidized, under the supervision of private citizens and charity organizations, with a bounty of so much per month per head.

Given the goal of child-salvation, the vista of children receiving moral training, religion, and the habits of industriousness—given the need to "remedy the neglect and vice of parents," to rescue every child who was "cradled in infamy, imbibing with its earliest natural nourishment the germs of a depraved appetite and reared in the midst of people whose lives are an atrocious crime against natural and divine law and the rights of society"—it was no wonder that some reformers were peevish about the hamstringing presented by the technicalities of the Constitution and the Bill of Rights: about the dreary questions raised from the beginning over legal technicalities that might be at issue in snatching children and incarcerating them through their minority, based on no proven, or often even claimed, wrongdoing. Based on what they were, not what they had done.

It was no wonder at all that Frederick Wines, Secretary of the Illinois Board of Public Charities, said testily:

> The object of reformatory institutions is well stated; it is not punishment for past offenses, but training for future usefulness. . . . (T)he operation of the Illinois law is positively injurious. It proceeds from a *morbid sensibility on the subject of personal liberty,* and from a false idea of the relation of the juvenile offender to society, as well as of the object sought in sending him to a reformatory. It destroys the potency of the agencies employed for his reformation, by encouraging in his mind the hope that obstinate resistance to their influence, for a comparatively short period, will enable him to triumph over authority and to enter upon a life of vicious indulgence. . . . The statutes of Illinois fail to recognize the fact that confinement and control have a humane as well as a severe aspect nor do they distinguish between confinement for the protection of society and for the protection of the individual himself. . . . (Italics mine.)

If there was one thing the child savers were able to do from the start, it was to look on the bright side of indefinite incarceration.

The laws, the primacy of due process protections for individuals against unwarranted time spent under lock and key, the right to fair warning, to trial, to specific sentence on conviction for a crime, protections of all citizens' rights against having their children summarily "saved," were indeed a nuisance, one which had to be faced—somehow.

When the first court challenge came, in 1838, it was met head-on—with what was to become the major artillery weapon: Language. The case was *Ex Parte Crouse.* Mary Ann Crouse's mother complained that she was incorrigible. Since the Pennsylvania law agreeably provided that children determined to be vagrants, criminal offenders, or incorrigible to the extent that they were beyond parental control could be placed in the Philadelphia House of Refuge, Mary Ann was so remanded.

Mary Ann's father then challenged the child's incarceration, calling for due process procedures for her—for a trial by jury.

The Pennsylvania Supreme Court countered that the House was not a prison but a school intended to reform children "by training its inmates to industry; by imbuing their minds with the means to earn a living; and, above all, by separating them from the corrupting influences of improper associates." It was as simple as this: when parents failed to "properly instruct a child," it was the state's right and duty to take over. To snatch the kid.

"The infant has been snatched from a course which must have ended in confirmed depravity and, not only is the restraint lawful, but it would be an act of extreme cruelty to release her from it."

And so it was decided, "The House of Refuge is not a prison but a school. . . . Where reformation and not punishment is the end it may indeed be used as a prison for juvenile convicts who would else be committed to a common gaol. . . ." What a public relations performance. You get common agreement that children who have committed misdeeds should not be incarcerated with adults. Then you incarcerate children separately—where they have not yet committed misdeeds—saying that the only other alternative is their incarceration with adults, which, agreement has it, would be a bad thing. "To this end may not the natural parents, when unequal to the task of education or unworthy of it, be superseded by the *parens patriae*, or common guardian of the community."

This was the first invocation in this country of the doctrine of *parens patriae*. Since it forms the legal (or quasi-legal, or socio-legal) base on which rests an entire present subsystem with a massive family intervention capability, it is worth looking backward to its parentage.

It had a royal birth, traced back as far as the eleventh century—to Anglo-Saxon King Aethelred II, old Aethelred the Unready. Under him, it was decreed: "If an attempt is made to deprive any wise man in orders or a stranger of either his goods or his life, the king shall act as his kinsman and protector . . . unless he has some other." Later, in the fourteenth century, it showed up in Edward II's assertion of the "sovereign's responsibility toward the property and later the person of the insane."

Notice: *property*, and later the person.

It was extended to children of *property*, to protect feudal succession—as well as to "idiots and lunatics."

> The guardianship of the person and control of the property of the legally disabled in medieval England was originally a role performed by the feudal lord of the manor on which the lunatic resided. This function, however, was assumed by the king after the Crown's consolidation in England in the thirteenth century. As *parens patriae* the sovereign functioned as the protector of the proprietary and personal interests of his subjects. "The King," says an early legal commentator, "as the political father and guardian of his kingdom, has the protection of all his subjects, and of their land and goods; and he is bound, in a more peculiar manner, to take care of those who, by reason of their imbecility and want of understanding, are incapable of taking care of themselves."

It is useful to remember, here, that during this period, the king was the Universal Landlord. He parceled property out to counts and dukes in return for services; and they, in turn, parceled out to smaller subtenants, and so on down to the peasant.

Propertied children, whose fathers died, were a commodity of some interest. There was a tidy bit to be gained from estate administration. And you could always marry your ward off to one of your heirs. Or you could sell the right of marriage and pocket the profit.

Even *honest* guardians did well. One case shows that a ward, left with £300, found himself after thirteen years' minority, possessed of £580 1s. 4d., even after all expenses of food and maintenance had been paid, "through the good management of his guardian, who had traded with the money at an interest of 4s, in the pound, half of which he had kept himself."

Not everybody was as lucky as that boy.

The guardian could deal with the child's inheritance in such a way as to blackmail the child into the marriage of the guardian's choice. "In Britain, the sons of noblemen come into the power of guardians if their father dies; this right is bought or obtained from the King. Whenever such a guardianship falls out of the family then the ward's possessions are sometimes so dealt with that he can hope for little fruit from his lands unless he marries the wife purchased by his guardian. . . ."

The requirements for the guardianship job were simple: like a Ming vase at Sotheby's, it was awarded to the highest bidder. A girl named Grace, an heiress of considerable proportions, was the daughter of Thomas of Saleby. On his death, the king gave her in ward to Adam Neville, the chief forester's brother. When she was four years old, Adam proposed to marry her himself. The bishop said no, but then left town, and while he was away, Adam got a priest to officiate the marriage. It's unclear what happened to Adam, but next we hear, the king (John) sold Grace to his chamberlain Norman for 200 marks. When Norman died, the king sold her again for 300 marks to the "third and worst" of all her husbands, Brian de Lisle. We are told she died childless. But, having started wedlock at four, she may have died pre-pubescent.

To administrate all this, as government regulator, there was first a Master of Wards, then a Court of Wards, and then (possibly spotting the missed profit), the Court of Wards was abolished in favor of direct control by the king. Lord Somers states that "with the dissolution of the Court of Wards, *parens patriae* responsibility fell to the king for the care of charities, infants, idiots and lunatics. . . ." There still had to be guardians, however. They were still the highest bidders. But now the courts could intervene in protecting wards from the exploitation of guardians. Eventually, they were empowered to protect them from exploitation by third parties.

The extent of the power principle potential involved in court intervention as *parens patriae* was not stated until 1827. Then, it was stated pretty baldly.

In *Wellesley v. Beaufort,* Lord Eldon ruled "this Court has not the means of acting except where it has property to act upon. It is not, however, from any want of jurisdiction that it does not act, but from means to exercise that jurisdiction: because the court cannot take on itself the maintenance of all the children in the kingdom."

In other words, it could if it would—and it would if it could. This, at least, has the beauty of the clearcut, a rather lucid expression of power and state self-interest, aligned with a respectable touch of the pragmatic—compared to the fanciful justifying language that was to come later.

Not unnaturally, this bald statement of principle led to the court deciding later that it could intervene to protect a child from his parent or guardian, even when property was absent. Lord Chancellor Cottenham:

> I have no doubt about the jurisdiction. The cases in which the Court interferes on behalf of infants, are not confined to those in which there is property. Courts of law interfere by *habeus* for the protection of the person of any body who is suggested to be improperly detained. This Court interferes for the protection of infants, *qua* infants, by virtue of the prerogative which belongs to the Crown as *parens patriae,* and the exercise of which is delegated to the Great Seal.

(I like the Great Seal, which I envision as a marvelous creature of coastal waters. But what is truly impressive is the language: the word *interfere*. Not intervene.)

This decision gave the state a straight-out course for increasingly *interfering* between parent and child among the poor
"in order to effectuate a number of public policies ranging
from the provision of relief at minimum cost to the prevention
of future crime."

Unquestionably, if not from its inception, then quickly
thereafter, the doctrine of *parens patriae* was a doctrine designed to effectuate the state's social control of the poor. And
at the beginning, in England, there were no bones made about
it.

Blackstone said: "The rich, indeed, are left at their own
option, whether they will breed up their children to be orna-
ments or disgraces to their family."

The first statutes in the Colonies, in the 1700's, focused
entirely on parental poverty. In the late 1700's, the court began
to expand its authority in child custody disputes. Without that
the father was an outrageous drunk or wastrel, the paternal
custody presumption was virtually unchallenged. Even where
the father had been particularly brutal, the court's decision
to deny him custody could be so loaded as to border on its
own subliminal reversal.

For instance. In 1833, in South Carolina, Mr. Kottman had
severely beaten his son, Frederick. He then simply left the
child with Mrs. Mary Thompson, who "gratuitously" fed and
housed little Frederick. Mr. Kottman later decided he wanted
Frederick back. He sued for custody. The court said no. Knott-
man appealed the decision, his lawyer claiming the father's
"supreme and inalienable right to custody and government"
of his child.

Frederick, by this time fifteen years old, insisted on remain-
ing with Mrs. Thompson. The court did fail to actually reverse
the original decision, the "no." What it did was to turn the
"no" into a "not exactly." The judge, Justice Harper, was "certain that Mrs. Thompson was not legally entitled to custody."

The father alone possessed that right. Therefore, he reasoned, the court ought to permit Kottman to "take" his son "where he can find him." It admonished him only not to commit a trespass in doing so. "It must be at his own risk." In other words, he was advised to kidnap his child—and further advised not to get caught at it.

In another case, Eliza Barry and her husband, John, agreed on a "voluntary" separation.

He did "covenant and agree" to allow his daughter, Mercein, to remain with her mother for the next year. Whereupon John turned up wanting them all to get back together.

Eliza said no.

So John got a habeus corpus demanding Mercein be delivered to his custody.

Eliza countered with a description of John as of "irascible temper, of domineering and vindictive spirit and of intemperate habits." She called his conduct toward her "harsh, tyrannical, cruel."

Since Mercein was a sickly child, the first court decision was that Eliza could keep Mercein with her. But John kept trying, until one judge, Justice Bronson, ruled, "In these unhappy controversies between husband and wife, the former, if he chooses to assert his right, has a better title to the custody of their minor children. His claim cannot be set aside upon light grounds, or upon mere conjecture that the interests of the child require it." The father would have to be proven guilty of grossly immoral conduct. The judge said further that the husband and wife could not be witnesses against one another. And, while Eliza might have some cause for complaint, it was nothing like divorce-type cause. He refused to recognize the separation agreement, saying, "It is simply a covenant between husband and wife, who are not competent to covenant with each other."

Eliza's choice, then, was either to return to John in order to keep control of Mercein, or to return to him because she had no other alternative.

The ideological foundation presented in the opinion was

that under natural law, wife and children were equal to the father, but inferior and subject to the sovereign. "As husband and father, male authority was perfectly balanced by wife and child's, but in his capacity as sovereign family head he was supreme. With the rise of civil society the father's sovereign power passed to the 'chief or government of the nation.' " However, since obviously the sovereign couldn't provide for all the children of the state, the duty of education and maintenance reverted to the father, and a "right" of guardianship.

Here we have the early parameters of *parens patriae* intervention, the beginnings of the state as Superpop. And as, during the 1800's, the "rescuing societies" expanded their outreach; as custodians became criminologists; and phrenologists gave way to psychologists; and volunteers gave way to social workers—all beginning to professionalize and institutionalize child-saving—the seeds were being planted for the eventual use of the caseworker as Supermom. For social work as an arm of the law. All that was needed was some way to make all this legal.

The doing-good business was doing well.

Reformatories were expanded. Industrial *schools* were built—to provide education and moral training, religion and labor. And descriptions of children's innate character swung from pole to pole, depending on whether the desired string would pull sympathy ("helpless infants,") or fear (depraved pre-delinquents). Where the latter was desired, it was said that "the placing of vicious children should take place without the intervention of the courts."

Society was being saved from the children in the name of the children's being saved, through such benign practices as military drill, physical exercise, and constant supervision. There were dress parades. Proud language proclaimed the likeness between the children's situation and that of the military; and likened their treatment to that of convicts under martial law. They were said to be under constant watch, with any sign of impending disobedience subject to instant suppression.

Under the subsidy system, vested interests flourished. And

the women, elated by the discovery of the effectiveness of their influence, continued in their crusade—unsuspecting, volunteering, fund-raising, and coming up with new good ideas, fresh populations of children to "serve" and to save. In 1876, Mrs. Louise R. Wardner, member of the Women's Centennial Association, which group had strangely found itself with $500 left in the kitty "at the end of their tasks," piped up with the difficulty she and her colleagues were experiencing in "placing out" girls released from the local orphanage. These girls, over twelve, were obviously likely to become delinquent if left unsupervised, yet shockingly, there was no institution in which to warehouse them.

What a good idea.

Land was donated. An industrial school was built. And in just one year they had corralled forty-one girls who were now being supervised, under "purifying, refining influences"—in "the atmosphere of a Christian home."

However, the "untiring exertions" needed to keep this school funded pointed up a distressing problem: *the association had no legal authority to retain dependent girls.* The solution? Appoint a well-appointed and well-connected investigative committee from among their friends: Judge and Mrs. Bradwell and ex-Governor Beveridge. . . . *Their* solution, smartly enough, was to *make* it legal, and—once legal—funded by the state.

Voilà, the "Industrial School for Girls Bill" whereby dependent girls could be committed by the county court to any industrial school established by seven or more persons, the majority of whom were women. "Dependent" meaning:

> Every female infant who begs or receives alms while actually selling, or pretending to sell any article in public; or who frequents any street, alley or other place, for the purpose of begging or receiving alms; or who having no permanent place of abode, proper parental care, or guardianship, or sufficient means of subsistence, or who for other causes is a wanderer through streets and alleys and in

other public places; or, who lives with, or frequents the company of, or consorts with reputed thieves, or other vicious persons; or who is found in a house of ill-fame, or in a poor house.

Any "responsible" person could petition the court under circumstances where, for instance, "the parent or guardian is not a fit person to have the custody of such an infant." The county would then pay $10 a month for the keeping of her body (and soul, of course) until she became eighteen.

It was an awfully good business. It saved the courts a lot of rigamarole. And it got the unpleasantness off the streets. And all in the name of greater social and moral beneficence. How could anybody be against cultivating in children "good manners, cleanliness of person, decency of language, habits of industry, and an appreciation of good morals and industry . . ."?

Women did, increasingly, observe and resent "having the door shut in their face when the work they . . . initiated and long maintained is taken over into the halls of the state." But they were able to keep their volunteer toes in the doors of the institutions by pleading that, without their presence, the schools would be "like a home without a mother—a place of desolation. In reformatory work woman is the good mother. The pulse of the school or home throbs in her breast. She is the one to whom all look for comfort and relief." With all this goodness going on, why fuss over "morbid sensibilities" about civil liberties?

But the morbid sensibilities just would not lie down and die.

In 1870, the Superior Court of Illinois declared unconstitutional a statute providing for the commitment to reform school of children "destitute of proper parental care, and growing up in mendicancy, ignorance, idleness, or vice."

(This was the decision that so piqued Frederick Wines.)

Mr. Justice Thornton held that committing fourteen-year-old Daniel O'Connell to the Chicago Reform School was unconstitutional because it was without the benefit of a trial that the child had been committed to an "infant penitentiary."

The judge asked:

> Can the state, as parens patriae, exceed the power of the natural parent, except in punishing crime? These laws provide for the "safe keeping" of the child; they direct his "commitment" and only a "ticket of leave" or the uncontrolled discretion of a board of guardians, will permit the imprisoned boy to breathe the pure air of heaven outside his prison walls, and to feel the instincts of manhood by contact with the busy world. . . . The confinement may be from one to fifteen years, according to the age of the child. Executive clemency cannot open the prison doors for no offense has been committed. The writ of habeus corpus, a writ for the security of liberty, can afford no relief, for the sovereign power of the State as parens patriae has determined the imprisonment beyond recall. Such a restraint upon natural liberty is tyranny and oppression. If, without crime, without the conviction of an offense, the children of the State are thus to be confined for the "good of Society," then Society had better be reduced to its original elements and free government acknowledged a failure. . . . The welfare and rights of the child are also to be considered. . . . Even criminals cannot be convicted and imprisoned without due process of law.

This, however, did little or nothing to turn the course of events either around or aside. In 1874, we got the disputable story of Mary Ellen. The romantic version is that Mary Ellen was eight and was being treated with shocking brutality by her stepparents. A church worker discovered that there were no laws to protect children as even the meanest of beasts were protected. And so a case was brought before the court based on the plea that Mary Ellen was a member of the animal kingdom and thus entitled to protection under the laws protecting animals.

Then, that version of the folkloric tale goes, she was removed from the cruel foster parents and placed with the church worker who had originally brought the case to the attention of the Society for the Prevention of Cruelty to Animals.

In another version, Mary Ellen was nine, and those who beat her brutally were her parents. Here, it was a nurse making her rounds through the streets of New York who discovered Mary Ellen and sought aid from the police and the district attorney. We are told, in this version that "there was no statute clearly giving these officials the right to intervene." And that "removal of children from the homes of parents who abused them was virtually without precedent." This is confusing, since we know that the state was empowered to take children into custody who were "without proper parental care." What it suggests is that, previously, children were removed *only* from the homes of "improper" parents, and not from those parents who actively abused them.

Anyway, in version two, the nurse contacted the Society for the Prevention of Cruelty to Animals and implored it to take the case on the "member of the animal kingdom" connection. And in April, Henry Bergh, founder and president of the SPCA, "Petitioned the court for the removal of the child, Mary Ellen Wilson, from her *guardian.*" Mysteriously, the parents are from here on in absent; and we are dealing with a guardian.

The New York Times on April 10th, quoted the child as saying:

> My mother and father are dead. I don't know how old I am. I have no recollection of a time when I did not live with the Connollys. I call Mrs. Connolly Mama. I have never had but one pair of shoes, but I cannot recollect when that was. I have had no shoes or stockings on this winter. I have never been allowed to go out of the room where the Connollys were, except at night into the yard. My bed at night has only been a piece of carpet stretched on the floor underneath a window. I am never allowed to play with any children or have any company whatsoever. Mama has been in the habit of whipping and beating me almost every day. She used to whip me with

> a twisted whip . . . a raw hide. The whip always left a
> black and blue mark on my body. I now have also a cut
> on the left side of my forehead which she made with a
> scissors. She struck me with the scissors and cut me. . . .
> Mama never said anything to me when she whipped me.

According to another version of the story, a lawyer's, the
Society's attorney, Elbridge Gerry, brought the case—not on
the "child as member of the animal kingdom" principle, but
under an old English writ of law which permitted the removal
of custody from one person by another. The girl was placed
for seven months, while they looked for relatives. Finding none,
she was committed to the "Sheltering Arms," an orphan asylum.

Now Gerry or Bergh, or both, looked up and around, and
noticed that, while there were a number of agencies serving
dependent and orphaned children, and institutions that provided for their placement—there were no agencies aggressively seeking out and removing neglected or abused children.
Thus, the Society for the Prevention of Cruelty to Children
was formed.

It acquired police power. It placed agents in magistrate's
courts to investigate cases. It gained the power of arrest—although I have seen no evidence in support of the usual charge
that the SPCC went in for the wholesale "punitive" arrest of
parents. (Indeed, it was no more than a misdemeanor to ob-
struct or interfere with agents.)

In fact, the record shows that poverty, not cruelty, was the
basis for most intervention. And a "surprisingly large number
of the cases involved organ grinders who were using children
to aid in their begging routines." (Perhaps the kids were reported by SPCA workers, who were gathering up the monkeys.)
The focus of the great bulk of all intervention and removal
continued to be destitute, neglected, and wayward children.
Not abused children. Attacking pauperism remained the better
business.

Besides, though the advocacy of child-whipping had abated
somewhat by the late 1800's, one cannot help suspecting that

the real crime against Mary Ellen was seen to be—not the whipping, but—that she "never had but one pair of shoes."

As a matter of curiosity and convenience—and perhaps co-incidence—Industrial Schools were proliferating at the very time reform forces were seeking an end to child labor. Since industrial schools were being used to provide child labor, this made for an interesting situation; one fortuitously enabling small businesses to sidestep the increasing demands placed on them by unionization, which was a major force in seeking the end of child labor. (Circuitous sentence for a circuitous situation.)

When, in 1871, the State Reform School was opened at Pontiac, in Illinois, "Dr. J. D. Scouller, who was formerly a physician was appointed Superintendent"

> immediately contracted with private industry for the cheap labor of inmates. Although the trustees of the reformatory were prevented by law from "leasing the labor" of inmates for more than six hours a day, a contract was made with a Chicago shoe firm for the labor of fifty boys who were to be employed seven hours a day. A similar contract was made with Clark and Hill and Company for the manufacture of brushes. After these contracts were dissolved due to legal difficulties, many of the inmates were employed in cane-seating chairs for the Bloomington Manufacturing Company under the direction of the officers of the school.

If "reformatory" was a linguistic reform of prison, "industrial school" was a similar reform of workhouse.

By the 1890's, the child-saving industry was in excellent health. It was a "field" with its own "experts." All that was needed was to legitimate the otherwise doubtful idea that the state, in collaboration with private organizations, was engaged in the wholesale removal and incarceration of poor children, in total abrogation of the rights of both parents and children.

The doctrine of *parens patriae* had been established.

What was needed was that it be institutionalized. Set into a system. Packaged. And some flexible language to not only justify it, but crown it once and for all as irrefutably benign—messianic.

The language poured fourth: medical language, of treatment, of cure, of prevention.

The system emerged. The Juvenile Court.

Because their focus continued to be on delinquency, and *pre-delinquency* (described also as waywardness and incorrigibility), the objectives were police power objectives, masquerading as *parens patriae.*

Yet it was denied emphatically that this was a system for social defense.

> The action is not for the trial of a child charged with a crime, but is mercifully to save it from such an ordeal, with the prison or the penitentiary in its wake, if the child's own good and the best interests of the state [sic] justify such salvation. Whether the child deserves to be saved by the state is no more a question for a jury than whether the father, if able to save it, ought to save it. No constitutional right is violated.

Compassion and salvation replaced rights and punishments. After all, the involuntary commitment of a child did not amount to a deprivation of liberty. No. The state was merely ensuring "that these children received the parental custody to which they were entitled." The absence of due process was the benefit of benign informality. The lock-up was to cure; it was not to punish. Where incarceration of "pre-offensive" children was concerned, they always saw only the silver lining.

The "best interest of the state" remained part of the language, however. It did not get dropped—leaving only the "best interests of the child"—until later. "The problem for determination . . . is not 'Has this boy or girl committed a specific wrong,' but 'What is he, how has he become what he is, and what had best be done in his interest and in the interest of the state to save him from a downward career?' "

The passage of the Juvenile Court Act in 1899 was an accomplishment claimed by women of influence. Julia Lathrop's father was a lawyer. Lucy Flower was married to one. "This is a legal matter," Julia Lathrop is supposed to have said in teacup fashion. "It must not go to the legislature of a woman's measure; we must get the Bar Association to handle it."

They did. Whereupon, after a number of Whereases, it was

> *Resolved,* That the president of this association appoint a committee of five of its members to investigate existing conditions relative to delinquent and dependent children, and to cooperate with committees of other organizations in formulating and securing such legislation as may be necessary to cure existing evils and bring the State of Illinois and the City of Chicago up to the standard of the leading states and cities of the Union.

First, they pled the *delinquency* aspects, avoiding the dependency/neglect aspects. They stressed the importance of removing children from jails, thereby appealing to the social concern about crime and its contagiousness. Then they punched an appeal to sentiment: "You cannot take a boy of tender years" (said Major R. W. McClaughty, Warden of Joliet State Penitentiary)—and knocked that home with a follow-up reiteration of threat: "and lock him up with thieves, drunkards, and half-crazy men of all classes and nationalities without teaching him lessons in crime."

Crime was the prime concern. Yet when the legislation was drafted and passed, the focus of the language was on benevolence toward the dependent and neglected:

> For the purposes of this Act the words dependent child and neglected child shall mean any child who for any reason is destitute or homeless or abandoned; or dependent upon the public for support; or has not proper parental care or guardianship; or who habitually begs or receives alms; or who is found living in any house of ill fame or with any vicious or disreputable person; or whose home, by reason of neglect, cruelty or depravity on the part of his parents, guardian or other person in whose care it may be, is an unfit place for such a child; and

any child under the age of 8 years who is found peddling or selling any article or singing or playing any musical instrument upon the street or giving any public entertainment.

Philanthropist Louise Bowen, taking credit for the Juvenile Court Act's passage, wrote:

> I happened to know at that time a noted Illinois politician; I asked him to my house and told him I wanted to get this law passed at once. The legislature was in session; he went to the telephone in my library, called up one of the bosses in the Senate, and one in the House and said to each one, "There is a bill, number so and so, which I want passed; see that it is done at once." One of the men whom he evidently called said, "What is there in it?" and the reply was, "There is nothing in it, but a woman I know wants it passed." And it was passed. I thought with horror at the time, supposing it had been a bad bill, it would have passed in exactly the same way.

Easy as pie, then.

Hailed as humane, non-punitive, the greatest step forward since the Magna Carta, the juvenile court gradually extended its medical metaphor, replacing the piety of religious doctrine with the piety of psychiatric doctrine, of benevolent understanding. And leaving a situation ripe for a kind of medicalized tyranny aimed at social control, which—evading the issue of what a person has done—could suit a variety of interests.

It has left us with a situation where crimes against children, crimes committed by parents against children, are a subconcern of a civil subsystem which views them either as a custody dispute between parent and state—or as a pre-delinquency concern. Whereas safeguards have been won for children accused of delinquent behavior, few if any have been secured for children who are victimized by their parents. Nor for the parents who find themselves under surveillance by agents of the state. That there is no punishment involved for a parent in the removal of a child is certainly specious. (Should we call it, at least, *disciplinary?*) That there is no punishment involved for a mother in the removal of a child, where it is the child's father who is abusive, is absurd.

Ironically, the court as Superpop suits a number of parents quite nicely. Those seeking to dump their children into the system—as beyond control, incorrigible, in need of supervision—are very often successful.

Whether any of this—unmonitored, unchecked, unreviewed—is in the "best interests of the child" is doubtful. However, where the male parent is the abuser, it is in the worst possible interests of mothers.

During a telephone call, a psychiatrist tells me of yet another man, accused of sexually molesting his child during weekend visitation. The ruling now is that his visitation must take place in the presence of his younger brother.

"What is this," I ask, "with the court-ordered babysitting of grown men?"

Anthony Platt writes, "[T]o abandon punishing means to abandon the very idea of crime. . . . Therefore as long as we choose to call some forms of conduct criminal, we already provide for the fitness of punitive sanctions and the search for further justification merely confuses the issue."

Just how confused the confusion can get is evident in this update from Jan Samuels.

Sheldon is now five.

Kim is now two.

As you know, we had our trial 8 months ago, before a woman judge in Family Court. One psychiatrist testified my ex-husband, George, was just fine—that if he molested the kids, which he didn't, he did so because he was angry with me and was lonely—but it's good to get molested anyway. A psychologist testified that Sheldon wasn't molested but did not give reasons why he thought so explicitly. Another psychiatrist said it was as if *I* were brain damaged and so persisted in this erroneous belief about the molestation—even though many professionals also persisted and he did not think them brain damaged—

and custody should be removed as I was interfering with my son's fantasy life—and that it was impossible to determine from a psychiatric evaluation if someone did or did not molest a child, but he was sure, despite this, that it did not—and could not have—happened. One psychiatrist testified that Sheldon was traumatized by molestation. Another (on the Court panel) testified that Sheldon was emotionally disturbed and that the source of that disturbance was the father. Another psychiatrist testified that children do not fantasize painful sexual experiences, details of sexual position, ejaculation, etc., and if a child of Sheldon's age lies it is by omission, not commission. I testified as to Sheldon's statements, positions, ejaculation descriptions and castration and other threats. A physician testified as to the gonorrhea. . . . A leading psychiatrist expert on sexual abuse in the United States testified as to the way you go about verifying incest, how mental health professionals theorize fantasies even in the presence of physical evidence and the more outrageous the acts against children, the less the Court and mental health professional is willing to protect the child or believe the child. One neighbor and one friend testified about Sheldon's statements to them about the abuse. Three of the psychiatrists testified that incest and molestation cut across all diagnostic categories of perpetrators, including normals.

The Judge ordered, pending her decision, that George's mother alternate weekend visitation and that she be present at all times.

The first weekend after the trial, Sheldon came back with an irritated anus, said his father put his finger up his rear end while Grandma was sleeping, and said that no one could stop him—not the Court, not the police, not the doctors, not even his mother's being a social worker. My neighbor came over shortly after the kids came home. She saw the red ring around the anus and heard from Sheldon what had happened. Sheldon also told her that he just didn't want his dad anymore. Later in the week, Sheldon panicked because he didn't see the neighbor's car. He indicated that his father said he would shoot the neighbor and her husband and my friend who testified, and the man she lives with, and my parents (my dad testified). Rather specific fantasies!

The next week I told George he could see the kids in front of me—he said he'd haul my ass into Court. The attorneys agreed to Saturday and Sunday visitation (but not overnight) in Grandma's presence, pending the decision (so a mistrial would not result).

The Judge in March gave her decision: I was given custody. Sheldon would have therapy. George would pay for it. . . . George was to be in the presence of his mother during visitation; if she could not be there, a substitute monitor was to be approved by me.

Here we have, it seems to me, a striking lack of clarity.

Does the Judge think George does molest Sheldon, and that he therefore should be watched by his mother? Does the judge think Sheldon needs therapy because he is being molested? Because he isn't being molested? Because the therapists recommended it?

We went back immediately asking for reconsideration—that molestation was continuing as Grandma wasn't a good monitor. The Judge indicated with a temper display that she was not going to change her decision, that she had heard the evidence and that we did not prove our case at that point. . . . We're scheduled to go back in Court next month to reconsider the visitation issue.

In the meantime, Sheldon has not started therapy and the molestation continues. According to Sheldon, Grandma once walked in while George was molesting Kim and slapped his face. George slapped her face back and she never bothered him again. Or Grandma goes outside. Or she is driven home by her other son, [who is a prominent member of the community], although she appears at the door when the kids are picked up and returned. I have verified that George had the kids at someone else's home one weekend without Grandma—and Sheldon says they sometimes see another of George's friends without Grandma. Sheldon says that George doesn't molest him so much anymore, but does molest Kim a lot.

Remembering George Gilder, I am thinking that on some level, the judge's decision tells us that, if Jan Samuels has failed to socialize her ex-husband within the home; and if he is perfectly well socialized outside the home; and if Jan doesn't choose to continue her socialization work on him any more—then the thing to do is return him to the custody of his mother. And give her another shot at it.

Both children told the babysitter about their abuse, and about their father's threats to remove them from their rooms by means of a tall ladder, while Jan was sleeping.

Jan says:

> Kim is talking a lot about being molested. Upon seeing a screwdriver, she said Dad put that in her " 'gina and tushy" (—as Sheldon once petrifiedly responded to the sight of a screwdriver). Kim saw a picture of a gun in a catalogue and said her dad put one in her " 'gina."
>
> Will it take a perforated organ and 8 × 10 glossies to convince the Court? Will they continue to order me to make the kids available for further abuse—what they *convict* other mothers for under Section [state statute number]?

Enclosed with her letter are four depositions submitted to the court by her attorney. Both Jan's and her neighbor's date back to shortly after the first hearing, and detail Sheldon's saying his father had told him he'd kill everyone in the house if he told anyone about what his father did to him; his fear at not seeing the neighbor's car; Sheldon's not wanting to visit his father, and saying he was worried about his baby sister, and his father's molestation of her, and his saying, "You can't stop me, the police can't stop me, all the doctors can't stop me, and your mother can't stop me." Sheldon also stated his father told him he didn't love him any more because he told his mother; and that his father said he would shoot him dead if he woke up the grandmother.

The neighbor corroborates as much of that as she was witness to.

The other two depositions speak to events which took place more recently. One, from the babysitter, speaks about a time four months after the trial, when she was babysitting and Kim had an "accident" in her training pants.

I took her upstairs to try to change her. I had her bend over so that I would be able to wipe her completely. She started crying hysterically and kept pushing my hand away as I attempted to wipe her, pleading with me not to stick my finger in her "tushy" like her daddy did and asking me not to hurt her like he did.

When Sheldon heard her crying, he came upstairs and begged me not to hurt his sister like Daddy did and tried to pull my arm away from her.

Later, when trying to get Sheldon ready to change his underpants precedent to getting ready for bed, Sheldon started crying. He begged me not to take his pants off. When I asked him why he said that he was afraid I would pull on his penis like Dad does. He indicated that it hurt.

After getting the children calmed down, I put them to bed. Sheldon got out of bed and went into his mother's wardrobe closet. He was hiding, scared. He said, when questioned, that he was hiding from his dad. He said that his dad told him that he gets a tall ladder and brings it at night when his mother is asleep and watches Sheldon and Kim. Sheldon wanted all the shutters and drapes shut because he was afraid his father could see them. Also, he was afraid to go to sleep because his dad further told him that he would take Sheldon and Kim far, far away from his mom by means of the ladder when his mom was either asleep or still downstairs and that they would never see their mom again. . . . I had to convince him that this could not happen as long as I was present before Sheldon would consider going to sleep.

I declare under penalty of perjury that the foregoing is true and correct. . . .

And about a more recent event:

> I supervised Sheldon and Kim Samuels in their home
> . . . On that date, Sheldon related the following informa-
> tion: Sheldon advised that his grandma is supposed to
> be with him and his sister when he visits his father. How-
> ever, after Sheldon and Kim are picked up, sometimes
> his uncle takes Grandma home and they are alone with
> their father. Sometimes his father takes his grandmother
> home. However, Sheldon says, Grandma is brought back
> so she is with them when Sheldon and Kim are brought
> back to their own house, so that his mom will think that
> Grandma is with them to protect them from their father.
>
> Sheldon further related that, one time, Grandma
> walked into the room when his father was doing 'one of
> those bad things' to Kim. Grandma slapped his father
> in the face. Then his father slapped Grandma in the face
> very hard so she left the room and closed the door behind
> her.
>
> On the day this information was related, when their
> father picked them up for a visit, Sheldon was very solemn
> and depressed when he had to leave with Mr. Samuels.
>
> I declare, etc. . . .

Doctor Summit writes:

> Did the father molest the child? It is impossible to
> know or to predict on theoretical or statistical grounds.
> But the child and a passionately protective parent must
> have some right to literal credibility. It is at least as logical
> to believe that a child overstimulated by his father would
> try to test the meaning of his experiences through re-
> enactment with maternal figures as that he fantasized
> experiences with his father out of a projected lust for
> his mother.

The more Jan Samuels presses her case, trying to protect
her children, the more likely it is that the custody of Sheldon
and Kim will be removed entirely from her and given to the
calmer, and increasingly more rational-seeming (by comparison) George.

She says:

> It struck me that how I present myself would very much determine how effective I would be in protecting the kids—just another fucking way of holding me responsible. And it was pretty scary thinking that if I made a bad impression, my kid wasn't to be safe. That made me really angry, and I was always scared the anger showed. And I knew I was so enraged by the whole thing—start to finish—that it had to show.

Not only has she been blamed for oversexualizing Sheldon, for "stealing" his fantasies, she blames herself. "There was the overriding conviction—perhaps still is—that if it weren't for my choice of partner, none of this would have happened." Yet George is normal. And anyone can marry a normal male. The fact that Jan was herself sexually victimized as a child is now evidence against her. Proof either of her tendency to make these things up, or proof that she chose a molester on purpose (on some level).

The visits go on and she waits for—injury.

Do you teach the kids how to lie still so they won't get hurt by the screwdriver? Or do you hope they get hurt just a little so you will have proof?

"Can you imagine looking at your one-and-a-half-year-old daughter, thinking she might have gonorrhea? Can you imagine? Even worse—can you imagine *hoping* your baby has gonorrhea so it might be over? Or be injured *just a little?* And, in fact, knowing gut level that this is what it really takes."

Jan's been advised—by professional colleagues—to take the kids and split.

She's been advised not to.

"If I knew I could get away with it," she says, "I probably would."

But if she did not get away with it, George would get the kids for good.

"And you'd be surprised," she says, "how many people have suggested I have him killed—and how many have suggested someone who could get this done for me. And I mean *responsible* people suggest this."

Much is made of, and deplored about, the passivity, the helpless dependency of the battered wife; the ignominy of the mother of a father-abused child, too weak to protect the children. A good deal has been invested in this stereotype—because without it, we would have to focus attention and censure on the offender—something neither Freud nor the new understanding seemed or seems willing to do. And something which would cast a harsh light on the fact that the permissions for these behaviors have long been an overt or tacit part of the bargain struck with men by the state.

And so a collusion of interests takes place—with medicalization serving state interests, using methods which might otherwise be open to question. And our individual fears make us want to collude too.

Battered wives are passive?

Good. *I'm* not passive.

Sexually abusive men's wives always know?

Whew. *I'd* know. And boy, I'd kill him the minute I found out.

In a small, wealthy community, scandal strikes. One of the leading male citizens—friend to all—is tagged as the neighborhood child molester. Child after child comes forward to testify.

His wife is in shock.

The neighborhood is sympathetic to her—even those whose children were molested by him. What a terrible thing for her to find out suddenly. After all these years of marriage. You understand, they say, *we* understand. He is "sick." He needs "help."

He is actually charged. Actually indicted. Actually tried. Actually found guilty. Actually doing some jail time. (It was the children of other prominent people he was molesting, after all.)

His wife stands by him. She has been married to him for thirty years. They have raised three children. She now waits for his release—having moved from that neighborhood, but not too far.

Her old neighbor visits.

How terribly brave, she says, to stand by him.

Oh well, says the prisoner's wife, what would *you* do?

A sharp intake of breath. Then, "But *my* husband would never do anything like that!"

Meaning, he's healthy. Meaning he's normal.

Forgetting that so was the convicted offender perceived to be, by everyone in that community and by his wife, for the thirty years before six months ago.

We all have a pretty strong interest in colluding as well. How else could we continue to enlist?

Uncle Sam needs you.

6
The Front Lines

". . . does the 'cruel and unusual' formula operate on something called 'treatment' as well as on punishment? Does the constitution know about cruel and unusual cures? The call for a 'Therapeutic Bill of Rights' based on the view that '(t)he greatest danger . . . results from the shaky philosophical underpinnings of our therapeutic programs' indicates as much."

Sanford J. Fox, "Principles of Punishment in Juvenile Court" in The Youngest Minority II, p. 171.

The most important word in child welfare is—not child—but turf. (This is equally an issue in the battered wife response, where "existing programs were sometimes less than hospitable to [battered wife] programs due to fears regarding the potential of overlap in service provisions and competition for the same client population.") It is a business for the management of the maltreated, with some definitions of what constitutes maltreatment so vague as to be arguably legal. Overworked, even glutted, it is staunchly protective of its territory.

In talking negatively about any "social welfare" system these days, it's important to be clear. I am not against protecting abused children. I just think we ought to consider doing it under the due process principle, rather than the "oh good, somebody's doing something about it" principle.

I think we ought to be clear about the potentials for abuse in the system as chosen. Clear about the real meaning in action of the language of help. Clear about whose interest is being served, and at what expense.

The present civil subsystem has an all-but-infinite potential reach into homes—based on allegations of neglect, emotional neglect, moral, and religious neglect. When it offers you "help," it is not an offer you are empowered to refuse.

Some places have more agreeable regulations than others—more checks and balances.

There are good, caring people at all levels of the helping system. Just as there are good and caring individuals who are foster parents. But just as the system set up for foster care encouraged the keeping of children in foster care, rather than returning them home, or freeing them for adoption, the protective services/civil court system lends itself to abuses. Indeed, the system itself may be an abuse.

It's important to keep in mind, as well, that the criminal law, while a way of punishing crime and criminals, is also a means of containing government power. That power, where child protective services are concerned, is limited only by the limitations of the system itself. If funding is cut, so is the system's reach, temporarily: an ameliorating effect, for a hapless reason.

That psychology and social work were wedded to the juvenile court from its inception is not surprising. It was a necessary alliance if one was to give credibility to the fact that this system was legitimately something "other" than the regular justice system. Something which, just twenty-one years after passage of the Fourteenth Amendment, in 1868, sought to circumvent that amendment.

The absence of protections, the absence of representation for the pre-delinquent child or the dependent child, the absence of any visible way to appeal a decision, were for the child's benefit. The court was not there to punish. The intervention that brought the child before the court was a "service." A service, as I've said (and they said) to the state.

The official romance between government, juvenile court, and psychology/social work took place with the Social Security Act of 1935, which provided federal monies to states for the protection and care of homeless, dependent and neglected children.

Neglect remained the primary focus. The poor remained the targeted "clientele." Discovery of the Battered Child *Syndrome*, in 1962, placed child abuse firmly in the medical domain, and led to legislation requiring that physicians and other professionals report suspected cases of child abuse and neglect to local social services. By 1963, however, "gross physical abuse" was seen to be "only one segment of a much wider problem of parental neglect. The unloved child, the emotionally traumatized child, the socially and emotionally deprived child" were all seen to be part of a problem requiring intervention.

In 1969–1970 legislation established a separate Child Abuse part in Family Court, and added child neglect as part of public protection responsibility.

The triadic relationship was official with the Child Protective Services Act of 1973, which mandated that states establish child protective service agencies, and allowed them to set up a central register for reporting.

The National Child Abuse *Prevention* and *Treatment* Act of 1974 established the goal of intervention in its title. (My italics)

Presently, all fifty states have child protective service agencies. Thirty states, the District of Columbia and one territory have purpose clauses in their law which contain preserve-the-family statements.

Forty-six states have Central Registries (plus D.C., Guam, and Puerto Rico).

Central to the agreement is that Supermom, the caseworker, will take care of the problem kids (the parents of the Children of the State). If they do not cooperate, she will say, "Wait till your father hears this." If they still do not knuckle under, she will march them to Superpop's office, the court.

What are child protective services?

In Colorado, "Child Welfare Services mean the provision of necessary shelter, sustenance and guidance to or for children who are, or who, if such services are not provided, are likely to become 'delinquent,' 'neglected or dependent' or 'in need of supervision.' "

How likely to? How are you likely to become neglected? What means this "in need of supervision"? Of 1,355,490 delinquency cases disposed of by juvenile courts in the country in 1977, 392,930 were "status offense" cases—otherwise known as "incorrigibility" or "beyond control" or "in need of supervision:" running away, truancy, curfew violations, ungovernable behavior, or "other" (other than homicide, forcible rape, robbery, assault, burglary, auto theft, weapons, drugs; other, in short, that would be crimes if committed by an adult).

Are likely to: Pre-delinquent.

In Connecticut:

> Protective services is a specialized agency service extended to families in behalf of children who are neglected, abused or abandoned. It is distinguished from other services provided by the Department and other community agencies in that it is involuntary, that is, the parent or guardian of the child has usually not asked for help, and the Department cannot leave them free to decide whether they want help or not. . . .

Yet, "The child neglect procedure is designed to minimize or eliminate the traditional accusatory nature of judicial proceedings which focus on guilt or blame."

So we have an involuntary state intervention based on no accusation that you have committed "neglect."

What is this "neglect" that Supermom and Superpop are such sticklers about? That's tricky. Often defined as "an act of omission or commission," juvenile law experts Martin Guggenheim and Alan Sussman say, "Generally, it covers situations in which parents do *not* do something that should be done, thereby placing the health and safety of their child in danger." That would include the provision of adequate food, clothing, shelter, medical attention, proper supervision. However, in some states "failure to send a child to school is considered neglect, as is a parent's 'moral unfitness,' use of drugs. . . ." Some states define neglect as "failure to provide a child with 'proper' parental care or commission of an act which endangers a child's 'morals.' In some states there is intervention based on 'psychological harm' which, in Idaho, for instance, is "the condition of a child who has been denied proper parental love, or adequate affectionate parental association, and who behaves unnaturally and unrealistically in relation to normal situations, objects and other persons." Where there has been alleged psychological harm, there is nothing to prevent the court, taking wardship of the child, from placing it "voluntarily" in a mental institution for an indefinite period of time—as we shall see. The best interests of a child sometimes know no bounds.

Additionally, neglect can include "unfit home" or "unstable moral environment." And the concern extends not just to the child's (or the parent's) moral existence, but to spiritual existence as well.

Because of the vague definitions and ambiguous meanings of any of the words within the definitions, it is no wonder that it is said that the "caseworker has to have a high tolerance for ambiguity and an ability to live with responsibility for acting decisively while uncertain as to aims and outcomes." What skills should equip her for this? "Skill (in social work) is the capacity to set in motion and control a process of change in specific material in such a way that the change that takes place in the material is effected with the greatest degree of consideration for and utilization of the quality and capacity of that material."

That, certainly, should numb her to ambiguity.

Because the system is imperfect, because few caseworkers are qualified, many are untrained, and there is no uniform notion of when to intervene or how to—perhaps it's best to turn to the literature meant to tell the caseworkers what, optimally, they are meant to be and do.

That is, if we could fix the machine, what would it look like? How would it run?

One pamphlet, entitled "Fundamentals of Child Protection," states blatantly: "A: Child Protective Services are Involuntary."

It recognizes that the situation is inherently adversarial (directly contradicting the more popular presentation of juvenile court intervention as non-adversarial).

As for the question of who their clients are or should be—there simply cannot be a broad enough definition. Here:

"Perhaps a 'Geiger counter' device for casefinding—for locating neglected children—or a door-to-door canvass would surely bring to our attention the children who need our services. That certainly would 'reach out' to the limit." Are they kidding? They are not. "Probably that kind of application of child protective services would truly prevent neglect and the consequent individual and family maladjustments."

It seems mild to suggest that an idea like this needs watching. Particularly when it is closed, "confidential."

The literature wants us (the Caseworkers) to learn of the constructive use of authority (also known as the therapeutic use of authority). This is "in situations where the danger to the health, welfare, morals, or emotional well-being of the child is so acute that it becomes imperative to remove the child from such extremely hazardous surroundings."

We encounter also the "lateral investigation"—something which I, for one, had not thought of (perhaps because it borders on the unthinkable). A "lateral investigation" means they can go to your neighbors, your doctor, your employer, your landlord, and so on. Now about this they do evidence some qualm, deciding that, "Ideally lateral investigation is not made without the client's knowledge. However, there are exceptions."

For instance: "The client herself may say, 'Why don't you ask the neighbors?' Regardless of what psychological motivation may actually prompt that remark—the worker is entitled to take that for consent."

This, surely, is the creative use of ethics?

Now we encounter something odd.

The most frequently propounded reason for using the juvenile court in cases of child abuse is that the standard of proof is lower. You need a "preponderance of evidence," rather than "proof beyond a reasonable doubt," as in the criminal courts.

Yet, we are told here that all the while You the Caseworker are on the trail, you should be making notes because "it is the protective agency's responsibility to resolve *any* doubt with respect to the possible existence of neglect." (Italics mine)

Well, never mind. What is the evidence? What should we write down?

First, about the neighborhood.

"Good neighborhood, tenement district, slum area, neat, orderly, well-kept, dirty, insanitary, verminous, in bad repair, freshly painted, in need of paint, light and airy, dark and gloomy, unventilated."

There. Now we have Investigated. It is time to Diagnose.

"It is generally accepted that conditions of neglect fall into three broad categories: physical neglect, emotional neglect, and moral or spiritual neglect."

What do these mean?

"Physical neglect includes overcrowding, lack of furniture, bedding, chairs, tables, cooking facilities."

Emotional neglect is if you find a child moody, withdrawn, hostile, antisocial, school difficulties, stammers, stutters, or has temper tantrums."

And the last? Moral and spiritual neglect?

Here, they are somewhat less specific—but considerably more urgent.

"Find a cause," they say "and use it to spell out the possibility of damaging effects on the child. This, theoretically, will help with the difficult areas of showing moral and spiritual neglect."

What are we to look for?

"Disrespect for authority, disregard for the property rights of others, immorality, licentiousness, obscenity, profanity, and possible sexual deviations are highly contagious and communicable parental patterns which too readily and too often contaminate children exposed to them at home."

This is really starting to feel quite old-timey isn't it?

> This is equally applicable to attitudes toward religion. The parent who does not attend any church or who flouts religion sets a pattern of irreverence for his children to follow.
>
> We cannot stress sufficiently the deleterious effect of a home climate polluted by a smog of crime, immorality or irreligion.

I like the smog of crime. I saw a TV show on child pornography which made reference to the "iceberg of smut." That was neat too.

From there, they go into the causes of all this sinfulness: inability to cope with personal-family problems; immaturity; mental deficiencies; marital problems, and a host of other mental, emotional, inadequacies. The logic is relentless. For example, they say, "inadequate housing may well be a cause for neglect. In this context, however, we have thought of it as an end result of some deeper problem, possibly a lack of sufficient finances."

Now the mighty Caseworker "must bear the heavy burden of evaluating which way the scale tips by asking: is change possible? Will it be sufficient to bring the level of child care to acceptable standards and can it occur soon enough to halt further damage to the child?"

If the answer is no, she must then turn to the court authority. All this, we are told, is casework: the agency's "non-punitive, non-judgmental and purely helping role." It's a matter—not of parents' rights, or of children's rights—but of the caseworker's "right to intercede for the children."

Okay. Suppose nothing avails. The scale clunks. What will you (the Caseworker) find when you go to court? That varies. However, one thing is constant: the public is excluded. What will you need in court? Proof. "Proof," we are told, "is the result of evidence." We are then told about various categories of evidence. Direct evidence is good. Hearsay evidence is bad. And, we are told, opinion evidence is the most important to a caseworker/petitioner. "This kind of evidence includes things like identity, handwriting, equality, value, weight, measure, time, distance, velocity, form, size, age, strength, head, cold, sickness, health, state of emotions—temper, anger, fear, excitement, rational, irrational conduct, intoxication. . . ."

The employ of which might lead, one presumes, to this kind of non-judgmental testimony: "In a drunken fury, this great 6-foot, 300-pound, sick-looking, fortyish woman with the strength of a buffalo, ran fifty miles an hour at me, hurling furious abuse, for forty minutes in her damp, smelly apartment."

Brooding about (among other things) moral and religious neglect featuring so heavily in a pamphlet dated 1978, I picked up the telephone and called the pamphlet's producer, the American Humane Association.

How could the emphasis be so prominent? Since child protective service is a service to the state—its employees are civil service employees—whatever happened to separation of church and state? And so on.

Well, I was told, that was really an old book, in an updated version (by old, they were guessing 1960's, not 1860's).

Well, then, but it *is* updated?

Well, yes, but not necessarily . . .

But if caseworkers took it seriously—are there any safeguards against intrusions on moral and religious grounds?

No. There really are no safeguards.

Well, all right. Would they please send me their brand newest, most up-to-date training book? Yes.

It is called *Helping in Child Protective Services.* It is, I'm assured, the latest word in the mental high wire act which is involved in training workers to function in this unholy alliance, where an adversary situation has been placed outside the accepted adversary process (and due process). Once more, the question would seem to be: is the situation adversary, or is it not? And the answer (once more) comes back: it is adversary, *but* it is not.

This pep talk for You the Caseworker asserts promptly, "Child protective services are necessary and right."

They assert this because they anticipate the qualms you might have when you see what you're about to encounter.

First and foremost, "You will encounter hostility, which is hard for anyone to deal with effectively (For more detail see the chapter on Hostility, Resistance and Cooperation)." Okay.

And what are the reasons (in that chapter) for a client's hostility and resistance?

• "Anger, hostility and resistance *may be a result of your intervention into the client's life.*" (Theirs italics.)

Client? Isn't that a euphemism here? According to my dictionary, a client is "one leaning on another for protection," "a dependent person under the patronage of another," or "a person or company in its relationship to a lawyer, accountant, etc. engaged to act in its behalf . . ." In what sense is this person who is angry, hostile, and resistant—and who didn't invite you in in the first place, who senses very well the double edge of "protection" you offer—a "client"? This person in whose behalf you are acting only if she does what you tell her or else? Or else you are acting directly against what she sees as her behalf.

• "Your very presence suggests the client has done something wrong—that the client is guilty of hurting the child."

Guilty? What happened to non-judgmental?

• "You are invading the client's privacy."

Well, that's nice and clear.

• "You are proposing that the way the client treats the child is 'wrong.' "

Wrong? What happened to non-judgmental?

• "There is the chance that you may take the child away from the client."

• "There is the chance that the client may be subject to court proceedings as a result of your intervention."

It is worse than that. The "chance" that the client may be subject to court proceedings as a result of your intervention depends entirely on your non-judgmental judgment.

Well then—what is your first task in the face of this Hostility? It's ". . . to dispel the client's negative expectations. Be accepting and authentic rather than judgmental and authoritarian."

How do you do that?

"Reflect the client's feelings." How? Like this:

CLIENT: Who are you to barge in on my life like this?

INAPPROPRIATE WORKER RESPONSE: You wonder who I think I am to barge in on you.

APPROPRIATE WORKER RESPONSE: You're furious that I dare to violate your privacy, like I'm some kind of big shot.

I must confess I find the difference there somewhat indistinct. Except that the appropriate worker response is liable to escalate tempers rather more quickly. In any case, if being a big shot gave people a right to violate other people's privacy, one would wind up evaluating the big-shotness of the burglar, rather than the act of burglary.

In interviews, You the Caseworker are told, you should be non-judgmental and avoid a detached attitude.

How? "Try to show approval or disapproval of what you see and hear." (Non-judgmental approval or disapproval, one supposes.) You are told how to use probing techniques for "purposes of clarification." (There are two kinds of clarification, by the way: immediate and retrospective. Immediate goes like this: "You just said that you hurt Johnny with the broomstick. Tell me, what did you do when you saw Johnny bleeding?")

Now this hostility you're going to encounter can take two forms. It "may be expressed aggressively or passively. Likewise, you are likely to encounter two kinds of resistance: it may be directive, or it may be manipulative.

"Directive behavior is open and visible and tends to encourage a battle between the family and yourself. Directive behaviors include:

- Aggressions directed at you, the worker, or others.
- Open resistance
- Projection of blame
- Trying to find allies: e.g. lawyers [sic], friends and other professionals.

On the other hand, the *failure* to confront you or argue with you or set up battle lines is equally suspect. It is *"manipulative* behavior." The approaches of people who try this are "subtle and may even be cunning, with the intent of rendering your intervention meaningless." This skulduggery includes:

- Admittance of guilt, establishing a 'poor me' approach in which individuals do not intend to be responsible for their actions or themselves.
- Acquiescence.
- Direct verbal acceptance, e.g., "I'm so thankful you're here."
- Stated intentions to cooperate.
- Avoidance—either verbal or physical.

In other words, if the "client" opens her door to the scrutiny based on an allegation of neglect and says she didn't do it, she is hostile. If she says she did do it, she is manipulative. This is almost enough to induce nostalgia for the good old days of ordeal, or the hue and cry.

Nor does this fearless manual shirk a dilemma when it finds one. For instance, "in terms of balancing your expression of help vs. control or help vs. the expression of authority . . . It *could* happen that you see the parent as a perpetrator." No problem, they say. "These two roles appear to be in direct conflict and may result in frustration. However, both roles are important, and they are compatible."

So there. They face the dilemma squarely and, rather than resolving it—they dissolve it.

"While law and policy define your responsibility in terms of the expressions of authority, authority can be invoked humanistically (see the chapter on the Use of Authority)." Okay.

Here we find a situation where they call the alternatives Therapeutic and Non-Therapeutic. I think *we* can call them Manipulative and Hostile.

Their Therapeutic (our Manipulative) goes like this:

A worker went to a home to advise the parents of a petition and court hearing. He informed them of their

right to be represented by legal counsel and offered to
assist them in obtaining representation. He explained the
legal process of custody and the reasons why he believed
this action was necessary. He reviewed the circumstance
which brought the child to the attention of the agency.
He discussed the efforts made to improve the situation
for the child and the results of these efforts. [So far, he
sounds like a school principal who makes house calls.]
He told the parents of his role in the court hearing—
the questions he probably would be asked and the responses he would make. He indicated he would have to
say some unpleasant things about the family situation.

He provided the parents with the opportunity to ask
questions about the entire process [not to mention the
opportunity to come at him with an axe]. At the court
hearing, he sat with the family. After the judge rendered
his decision, the worker expressed his understanding of
the parents' feelings and reassured them that he would
continue his efforts to help them provide adequate care
for the child.

Even if the kid was in foster care? Or in a residential treatment
center?

Understand. His testimony was the primary and weightiest
evidence presented at this court hearing which he petitioned
for in the first place because the victim of his proferred help
was either hostile or manipulative or otherwise rotten beyond
his coping and he thinks the child should be remanded to state
care. And that is what his testimony is going to be.

The Non-T way (our Hostile) to deal with the situation goes
like this:

A worker filed a petition for the temporary custody
of a child and notified the parents by letter of the date,
time and place of the hearing. He advised them of their
right to be represented by legal counsel.

When the parents arrived at the hearing, the worker
nodded to them and remained seated across the aisle with
the agency attorney. After the judge ruled in favor of

the agency and placed the child in temporary custody, the worker went to the family and told them he would pick up the child that afternoon and asked them to have the child's personal items packed.

For me, there is a clear breath of candor in the non-T (Hostile) approach. I like him sitting on the side of the aisle where he belongs. And notice this: in the Therapeutic use of authority, the child is mentioned three times. In the non-Therapeutic, the child is mentioned four times. And the kid gets to take his clothes.

Since the goal of this whole therapeutic use of coercive non-judgmental intervention is *rehabilitative,* perhaps we should look next to what this manual calls THE CPS WORKER AS TREATER. It won't help much, but it's worth a look. What is a treater? It's a " 'counselor' or 'therapist' which refers to being available to really listen to a client, to being a sounding board for his problems and their possible solutions."

You may also be an "enabler" or a "facilitator" or a "helping agent." "Treatment consists of all these activities."

Under THE ROLES OF THE CLIENT, we find "The helping relationship implies that two sides are involved—the caseworker and the client. The client has roles just as the caseworker has roles. In fact, unless the client fulfills his roles, there is no way you can fulfill yours. The client serves as your 'primary information source' and as a 'participant in the helping relationship.' "

So TREATER gets pretty short shrift, and the client can blow the whole game by not understanding her part. What of THE CPS WORKER AS ASSESSOR THROUGH THE CASEWORK PROCESS?

What you do to assess is this:

• You assess at intake (see the chapters on Intake and Initial Assessment) in a logical and orderly manner. You collect the data that defines the problem.
• You also assess during subsequent contacts with the client in order to develop a deeper understanding of his feelings, relationships, environment, special prob-

lems, assets, and liabilities, and the interrelationship among these factors.

[And then?]

• You assess the assessments.

Getting through CPS WORKER AS A PROFESSIONAL ("We sometimes think of 'professionals' as only those who have obtained advanced academic degrees, such as doctors, lawyers, and psychologists. The truth is that *a professional is a member of any profession*"), and through CPS WORKER AS SUPERVISOR, to CPS WORKER AS ADMINISTRATOR, we find that throughout it is imperative to attend to:

"Organized and accurate record keeping. Very often CPS workers get frustrated and discouraged with all the 'paper work' they must complete."

"Unless you recognize the importance of paper work, it seems like a waste of time."

Frighteningly, CPS intervention is directed almost entirely toward mothers—even when it is the male in the house who is abusive. According to our manual:

"Starting the client in therapy before she has been able to convince her husband that she needs it may result in his abusing the child again, just to show her who is boss. The abuse may result in the child's removal and the mother may then retreat from what was becoming a good working relationship because 'I thought you understood about my husband but you really didn't.' "

This would be no more than silly, were it not scary.

The system is empowered to intervene coercively, to mandate cooperation and treatment—not only where no crime has been proven, but where none has been alleged. Physical assault and sexual assault are nominally criminal behaviors. Neglect, however—and however it is defined—is not.

There is little fair warning. The intervention-triggers are vague, so vague that none of us can be fairly said to know all the reasons we might—depending on the place where we live, and the standards of the caseworers—be said to be "neglectful."

Nor is there much protection in the court proceeding, "While the right to notice of charges and counsel are afforded the parents, the right to confrontation and cross-examination of witnesses [in Pennsylvania] and the privilege against self-incrimination required by *Gault* in delinquency proceedings have not yet been extended to dependent-neglect hearings."

And what of, if not entrapment, then what could at least be called the garden path? The caseworker is saying, "Trust me. I am your friend. Tell me about it." Yet she is the very person who—should she decide to petition the court for your child's removal—will be the major witness against you. And her testimony will include (her version of) everything you have told her.

Where the male is abusive, the intervention is directed at the mother. And her failure to prevent his behavior can lead to the child's removal from her.

If this is the way the civil subsystem sees the "therapeutic use of authority," how, I wondered, do the higher legal fathers see adversarial issues arising in the family? How do they respond when confronted with the language of help vs. the liberty-interest, and due process interests of law?

7

Taps for Jackie

Jackie is a landmark kid.

But Jackie will never know that. Jackie is dead.

Even his landmark status has a strange twist: in achieving it, Jackie lost—not just his life—but even his name.*

For history, he is known only as J. L.—in the 1979 Supreme Court decision, *Parham v. J. R. and J. L.*, 442 U.S. 584.

If Child Protective Services, social work as an arm of the law, leads us to the suspicion that *parens patriae* is a legal fiction—is really police power in a social work suit—the final decision in Jackie's case would seem to put a stamp of approval on legal falsehood, with, once again, medicalization as the legitimizing prop.

This is how it began for Jackie:

He was born, illegitimate, on October 1, 1963. When he was eight hours old, he was adopted by a Georgia couple, Dr. Jackson Larrabee and his wife.

The next three years of Jackie's life are dark. However, in 1966, the Larrabees divorced. Jackie's adoptive mother took custody.

Shortly thereafter, she remarried. And became pregnant. With the birth of that child, one account says that she "no longer had a place in her new marriage for him."

Another account, the later testimony of a psychiatrist, says

* His name has been changed here, as have others, excepting the Gorens, and those of the two lawyers arguing before the Supreme Court.

149

"I think he [J. L.] was, in a sense sacrificed for that marriage to be preserved. It's [scapegoating] rarely seen in that kind of clarity, but it happens in more subtle fashion frequently . . ."

Another account says Mrs. Larrabee "really cared for Jackie and it was a painful, traumatic decision to give him up . . ."

Give him up? To where?

To Central State Hospital in Milledgeville, a mental institution. Jackie was six years old at that time.

So, at six, he entered Central State where he was to remain for the next five years and five months of his life. His commitment is the kind legally termed "voluntary."

Jackie, of course, did not volunteer.

He was labeled "hyperkinetic" and as having an "adjustment reaction to childhood." Neither the social worker, nor the lawyer, nor the psychiatrist who were to know Jackie during his hospital stay, ever recorded seeing the alleged hyperactive behavior. What they, uniformly, saw and testified to was a child who was extremely needy, who wanted more than anything else to have a home, to be loved.

Just past his seventh birthday, Jackie was offered a document entitled "Notice to Voluntary Patient on Rights of Discharge." This notice "informed" the child of his rights to release providing his parents or guardians consented. Providing the people who had "volunteered" him to the institution in the first place consented. He printed his name on the form. They did not consent.

People who worked with Jackie during those years described him in similar language: attractive, with "light colored hair that seemed to have a mind of its own." A hungry child— hungry for love, acceptance, attention. Hungry for some personal value.

It was David Goren, a young lawyer then working for Georgia Indigent Legal Services (GILS) who "discovered" Jackie in 1975, and began what was later to become truly a federal case.

David says to me: "I was working at the hospital representing all the patients at the hospital who wanted representation.
And of course the adults were more able to articulate that
they wanted to get the hell out of there. And then one day
Jackie was referred to me by his social worker. And I met
him. And he was a sweet little kid whose parents didn't want
him.

"The administration said, well, they tried to get him a place,
but couldn't. My initial reaction was—well, what's going to
happen? There's nothing that can be done for somebody in
this situation. A little kid nobody wants.

"And so my thoughts became, well, there have been no
cases in this area. But something's wrong with this case. I'm
going to have to look at it.

"But I have people screaming they want to get out right
now, who don't deserve to be there. And then, quite naturally,
my reactions were, well, I'm going to deal with them and try
to get back to this case. So some time went by. And I would
stop back. And then the issue seemed to be the custody issue
at first. If the custody were changed over—from the adoptive
parents to the state—the state thought it could more easily
deal with him, and place him.

"That was very difficult because the adoptive mother didn't
want to face—didn't want to think about Jackie any more. So
getting her to go into the custody proceedings, to give up custody, was something that was very painful for her to do, so
she kept avoiding it. And as the time dragged on, and I saw
nothing was being done—something was wrong. This can't stay
this way indefinitely.

"At which time, we started to look more deeply into how
he got there, and what the procedures were, and what was
so incredibly wrong with this kid who desperately wanted to
be out of the hospital, but who was there 'voluntarily' according
to the law. Which led to the filing of the papers."

The papers were filed, and on November 5, 1975, the Middle District Court of Georgia convened a three-judge panel

to hear Jackie's case. The case was a class action suit on behalf
of Jackie (J. L.) and J. R. (a child who, placed in Central State
by the state as guardian, had also been there over five years),
and 44 other members of their "class"—children in Georgia
mental institutions unnecessarily. At that time the entire child
population in Georgia's institutions was 150. Therefore, those
whom the Department of Family and Child Services admitted
were now confined without cause represented nearly one-third
of the whole.

Oddly enough, this was not really news. Two years before,
in 1973, a Georgia Study Commission on Mental Health Ser-
vices for Children and Youth issued a report which said, "IT
IS THE OBSERVATION OF BOTH HOSPITAL PERSON-
NEL, AND THE COMMISSION THAT MORE THAN HALF
OF THE HOSPITALIZED CHILDREN AND YOUTH
WOULD NOT NEED HOSPITALIZATION IF OTHER
FORMS OF CARE WERE AVAILABLE IN COMMUNITIES."
And advocated that, "ADMISSION GUIDELINES FOR CHIL-
DREN AND YOUTH TO STATE HOSPITALS NEED TO BE
MORE SPECIFIC." And stated that, "THE MENTAL
HEALTH LAWS OF GEORGIA SHOULD BE REVIEWED
WITH SPECIFIC REFERENCE TO THE RIGHTS OF CHIL-
DREN AND YOUTH."

Nor was the issue limited to Georgia. A similar class action
suit was proceeding in Pennsylvania. And in Tennessee, not
long after, a physician testifying in yet another such case said
that ". . . 70% of the children at Lakin State Hospital do
not need to be there and would benefit from outside placement."

As of October 31, 1975, the average time of commitment
for children in Georgia was 456 days. The maximum time,
the record as it were, was 2,035 days. Some of the children
had been placed by their parents or stepparents. Some had
been placed by the state as guardian, when it was unable to
find other care arrangements. Most, like Jackie, had been
placed "voluntarily."

What is "voluntary" commitment of children? Like "non-judgmental, coercive intervention," it is nothing at all. Like "mandatory voluntary" therapy, it is nothing at all. It is best defined by what it is not. It is not commitment by court order. That is termed "involuntary."

So we have, once again, language stood on its head to effect a cosmetic appearance on a practice which might otherwise seem less than tolerable. A mental institution is, after all, a rather drastic environment. And the majority of children are placed there based on "diagnoses" which—even if accurate— are zones away from anything acute.

Indeed, nearly half (43%) of the 441,429 children trafficking in and out of mental institutions or other psychiatric facilities in 1975 were diagnosed as having adjustment reactions to child-hood or youth. And these behavior disorders of childhood were most likely to result in a longer length of hospitalization. 64% of all children were in on non-psychotic charges—including personality disorders and neuroses, and behavior disorders of childhood and youth.

What, after all, is an "adjustment reaction to childhood"? Should there, or should there not, be protections for these kids? Shouldn't they be accorded the rights and protections that the 1967 Supreme Court decision, *In re Gault* 387 U.S. 1 (1967) established for kids accused of crimes? In *Gault*, the Court held that "neither the Fourteenth Amendment nor the Bill of Rights is for adults alone." It gave kids charged in a delinquency proceeding the right to notice, the right to coun-sel, the right to cross-examine witnesses—the rights, excepting that of jury trial—accorded adults charged with criminal behav-ior.

Don't children placed "voluntarily" in a mental institution indefinitely sometimes have a visible conflict of interest with those seeking to place them? Shouldn't there be, at the very least, clearly intelligible definitions of the boundaries of "ill-ness" that make a child "suitable for treatment" in a full-fledged mental institution? Shouldn't there be some provision for ini-tial outside review? For, at minimum, periodic review? (Be-cause if those who "volunteer" you in do not choose to volunteer you out, you are truly out of sight; in fact, as well as by allegation, out of mind.)

Hospital personnel reports began showing recommendations that Jackie be placed in specialized foster care as early as 1973. Why was he still there in 1976—on Ritalin, amphetamine sulphate, and other drugs, developing into ". . . an insecure child who feels he must have your attention with his endless requests"? Or, as David Goren put it, a kid "who needed love incredibly."

When a loss of liberty of these considerable proportions is at issue—an indeterminate sentence of confinement, a lifelong label—there'd seem to be a strong case that the system should outfit a person fully with the protections due any citizen under the Fourteenth Amendment. Even if that person is a child-member of a family. Or a child-ward of the state.

When Jackie's case went to the District Court, it emphatically agreed.

However, when it went, on appeal by the Department of Human Resources to the Supreme Court, it said, effectively, no.

During Jackie's hospital stay, David's wife, Debby Goren, asked him how he would feel about a chance to go into foster care. What he said to her then was that he'd "rather have someone kill him than have no place to go."

In the end, there was no foster care for Jackie.

In the end, Jackie had some place to go.

It was a place where he felt forced to kill himself.

It was Dr. Larrabee's house.

We are sitting in the upstairs study of David and Debby Goren's townhouse. Files, copies of the case's decisions, depositions, newspaper clippings, are strewn on the floor.

I am feeling lowly. It's a brutish business, probing old hurts, inevitably raising what-might-have-been's. David says, "You're forcing me to dig back into parts of my memory that are all so painful."

During the time the case was being prepared, Jackie spent

occasional weekends with the Gorens. And a full two weeks during the summer of 1975. Debby and David were then just recently married. Debby was working as a teacher in special education.

"I was one of two teachers who didn't come to school with some kind of strap or something to hit the kids with," Debby says. "Everybody thought I was crazy."

Were the kids hard to control?

"Oh, no. They were fine. They used to like hanging around my classroom. Whenever they could, they'd come in and talk."

And Jackie? What was it like having him visit?

"Well, it was the first time we'd had a child around us 24 hours a day," Debby says. "But he was real interested in everything. He certainly was no problem."

David says, "I mean he needed love incredibly. He wanted a whole lot to be hugged and to be with us. That was the most prevalent thing I saw. Other than that, he was just an eager, curious, happy kid. Happy in the sense that he was happy when we saw him at our house. Happy to be out of the hospital."

One day David remembers especially clearly:

"We were sitting on the hammock. Looking at the lake in front of the house. He was—a real nice kid. He needed so much. But he was over for the weekend. And it was the second day.

"And he said, 'Are you goin' to adopt me?' Just so blunt. I mean it's hard for me to imagine—a kid—being that blunt. About the reality of life.

"It goes back to adults' misconceptions of what children can perceive. Because they perceive it all. So I just told him what the truth was—which was that we weren't ready for kids. We had not been married that long ourselves, and it wasn't something that we were prepared to do. But that we liked him, and we wanted him to visit with us. And I think he understood that. I mean I wasn't going to say 'maybe.' Because that wasn't realistic.

"But that was his hope. It must have been his hope every day of his life in the hospital. 'Somebody will get me

out.' And it was—it was tempting. Debby's work, her concern
for children, and her teaching career. And my work in the
hospital. I mean you get to the point where you see how adults
have really messed over their kids and you know you're a really
different sort and you could make life different for them. . . .

"Obviously, you can't adopt every kid who comes by. But
you know you can have second thoughts, and say, 'if we'd done
that, Jackie would be alive today.' Obviously, you can't let that
haunt you because that's not realistic. Because that just happens
so often—that you don't know if it's true.

"Maybe it's true."

The specter of what-might-have-been.

Probably true.

An ironic side-fact in this case is that most of the psychiatrists
at Central State Hospital were Spanish-speaking. If the rural
southern children had, as they did, trouble understanding
Debby and David's northern speech, it must have been sore
comedy when those being interviewed for psychiatric commitment tried to answer questions put to them in a heavy Spanish
accent.

The state's main expert witness at the trial did speak English, but it was "expert" English. He, too, you will find, is in
some need of an interpreter. (Still, we must go with what we've
got.)

The Director of the Office of Child and Adolescent Mental
Health Services, Atlanta Division, was asked, at the trial, when
he thought hospitalization was the appropriate treatment for
children. He said:

"It can be quite a variety of circumstances that can make
it appropriate for a child to be hospitalized. One would be a
very acute, severe degree of disturbance. The child's behavior
is quite out of control, and he needs to be in a contained environment until some stabilization is achieved through medication, through program therapy and so on that brings about a
greater degree of capability on the child's part to function
within normal controls."

He continued:

"Other situations, due to social circumstances the child's interaction with his parents may be in sort of a vicious pattern where it's getting worse and worse; and the parents are not able to change or interrupt this vicious circle and a disturbance builds. It may be appropriate to hospitalize the child as part of breaking the cycle and achieving a more stable relationship. . . ."

He was then asked whether the standard, often applied to adult involuntary commitment, was pertinent to children: that of dangerousness to self or others.

"More characteristic [of] what we see is a very aggressive, intense, aggressive response, withdrawn response, a variety of different behavioral patterns. In effect the statement is a *prognostic one.* [*Italics mine.*] It's an effort on the part of the diagnostician to say, 'As far as I can judge, putting all this picture together, the behavior I see and the history I gain, the evidence I see of the parent-child interaction and so on, this is a condition that I predict will clear up with not too much intervention.' "

He has, I think, just asserted that the "diagnosis" of adjustment reaction to childhood is really a prediction that it will all be okay with "not too much intervention." How does one take a *prognosis* that this is a transient problem, and turn it into a prescription for indefinite commitment?

"I think again it's somewhat hypothetical to say that when a condition like this occurs a variety of outcomes can follow. And, intervention at that time is intended to see that the outcome is a reasonably healthy, progressive one. It may be an acute manifestation of the adjustment reaction [which] may disappear with the child settling into a more fixed behavioral pattern of overt rebellion or of submission or something of that sort, which probably would not be a healthy or as healthy an outcome. So, intervention is designed to try to assure when the expected resolution occurs, what comes out will be a reasonably good one for the child's continuing development."

And this diagnosis, then, of adjustment reaction to childhood, does it tell you how severe the symptoms are?

"No, unless that's qualified."

But when the diagnosis is made—adjustment reaction to childhood—that basically means the symptoms are not fixed and will probably go away?

"That's a prediction that's made looking at the whole picture. Whereas diagnosis of personality disorder would be because the history indicates that this has been persistent through a variety of circumstances over a period of time and it looks as though it's likely to keep on characterizing a personal functioning."

So Jackie, at six, was diagnosed as having a "mental illness" that was, by the state's own witness's definition, a prediction that, whatever the problem was alleged to be, it was a mere passing phenomenon; which diagnosis cost him five years of his life, perhaps even his life.

The C & A Director is asked: Another psychiatrist, Dr. (A), has testified here that these diagnoses—adjustment reaction of childhood and adolescence and hyperkinetic reaction—are kind of benign, common diagnoses. Does that upset the hospitalization applecart?

"No, depending on the total judgment of the circumstances and the sort of condition are grounds for hospitalization. There's no reason why it shouldn't be appropriate for hospitalization; some of the time the diagnosis is not that important in the hospital decision. It's the judgment of the total circumstances."

Certainly, for Jackie, a significant part of the total circumstances was that his adoptive mother and new stepfather "volunteered" him out of the home. There are other ways to accomplish this, of course. One way is to go to juvenile/family court and declare the child "unruly" or "incorrigible." Parents doing just this account for one-third of the total juvenile/family court proceedings. And these petitions by parents "virtually always result in an adjudication of wardship." Those kids are then remanded to training schools, to detention homes and, sometimes, to mental institutions. (Of the 812 Georgia children admitted to mental institutions in 1974, 515 were admitted by a parent, guardian, or the Department of Human Resources under the "voluntary" admissions procedure. 297 were involuntary, or court committed.) But that is a quasi-formal proceeding. There is a chance you will lose, have to keep the child, and get a social worker visiting your home all the time in the bargain. And maybe that route would be especially risky when you have a six-year-old child who is eager, curious, and hungry for love.

Back to the Director: How about when two psychiatrists put different labels on the same symptoms? Does that count for anything?

". . . I don't think it should be too important. Certainly, we ought to be trying to standardize diagnoses so we can arrive at better judgments, where we can be more consistent. That will be the millennium when we can do that, when we know what these things are all about so well that we can put a clear common label that has meaning in terms of what we do and so on."

Can he really get away with this? Saying diagnoses are arbitrary, meaningless? That the experts are without expertise? Watch.

"Unfortunately, I think we've been overfocused on the medical model as the only consideration. . . . But it's increasingly apparent that the conditions we're talking about are ones that have multiple factors involved and complex reaction patterns to a total somatic, social, psychological context. And we probably haven't gone far enough in adding diagnoses of family or action patterns or other things to our categories, ways of characterizing as we see them. If family interaction pattern is really side-tracked; and the overt manifestations are relatively mild in the child, that can be a very serious circumstance, although the label itself looks relatively benign."

Even illness, then, does not allow enough latitude. The Director thinks we'd be better off using the label "disorders." Disorders would allow for even wider outreach. One could have a TV disorder, or a cooking disorder. . . . This would certainly expand the kit-and-caboodle "continuum" of reasons you could hospitalize a child. Why, he has just said, the *milder* the symptoms, the more worried we should be.

He was then asked: "One of the contentions that's been made in this case is that parents sometimes attempt to scapegoat a particular child as mentally ill and everybody else in the family is healthy. In your experience is that a phenomenon you've seen?"

He replied, "I'll qualify the way you worded it by saying or taking out the words, 'parents try to.' Parents certainly do. . . ."

Often?

". . . it's probably fairly common in terms of families in general of patients we see in child psychiatry. . . ."

Does the same thing go on in private hospitals?

"There would be a parallelism. . . . The parents may come in saying, 'I can't handle it any more; do something.' And, they say at the hospital or it might be the psychiatrist who says, 'I think hospitalization is indicated.' The parents would agree, and that would decide it."

Okay. If adjustment reactions to childhood is really a prognosis, a prediction of what might happen in the future, a label describing behavior that some Significant Other now finds socially unacceptable, doesn't that depend on the person doing the labeling?

"It certainly would have to be true, yes, that the person would agree that the intensity, the level, the extent of his behavior was socially unacceptable. What social unacceptability means; it means that the social group is not accepting; and that's why they brought them there in the first place."

He was then asked, "And the Department of Family and Children's Services? When they volunteer a child, what happens when that child is all better? When hospital personnel think he should be released?

"The problem here in part is the history and tradition of mental hospitals which have been dumping grounds in the past. As we try to move out of this, there are a lot of people who still treat them as dumping grounds. There are juvenile court judges who say, 'I want this kid to be kept in a hospital from here on out until he's grown.' The DFCS takes the child to the hospital and says, 'Now it's off our hands.' "

"Dumping grounds," then, were the Director's own words. And they were far from unfamiliar ones to be used about mental institutions and children. In 1972, an Illinois Court decision stated: "It is common practice of employees of the Illinois Department of Children and Family Services to place many minors into a State mental institution when they consider no other facilities available. The DCFS does not conduct permanent placement facilities for its wards but relies on foster homes and private institutions. If a foster home is inappropriate for a child and private insitutions which are appropriate charge more than Department of Children and Family Services will pay or if these institutions will not accept a child, then DCFS employees often employ a technique referred to as 'dumping.' "

Attorney David Ferlerger writes: "Furthermore, when children are 'dumped' into mental institutions by child welfare agencies, they often have a difficult time getting out. There are questions as to who has jurisdiction over a committed child. The court, the hospital or the welfare agency. And once the welfare agency places a child in a mental institution it may forget about him entirely."

The C & A Director is now asked: And when parents refuse to take their kids back?

"I think probably the more appropriate thing the hospital would do would be to seek to have custody removed from the parents, if the parents are inflexible in their attitudes that they're not going to take the child back. Probably also the hospital staff ought to be in some cases sizing parents up and saying it would be disruptive to send this child back to the parents . . . it might at times be appropriate for the hospital to raise the issue and initiate proceedings to have custody removed. . . .

"This is a new issue, because of the history of where the hospitals have been and so on. A conservative view about disrupting family relationships which has been promoted by the courts and all sorts of people, mental health people have not been in the forefront of perhaps coming out and saying, 'We ought to break up families.' "

No, no. Leave the child in the hospital. At all costs, preserve the family.

The Fourteenth Amendment to the Constitution of the United States says:

> Section 1: All persons born or naturalized in the United States, and subject to the jurisdiction thereof, are citizens of the United States and of the state wherein they reside. No State shall make or enforce any law which shall abridge the privileges or immunities of citizens of the United States; *nor shall any State deprive any person of life, liberty, or property, without due process of law; nor deny to any person within its jursidiction the equal protection of the laws.* (Italics mine)

Adults who "voluntarily" commit themselves to mental institutions are now guaranteed the right to un-volunteer themselves: to sign themselves out after notice. If the hospital attempts to counter that, and change their status to "involuntary" patient, they are entitled to a hearing, to legal counsel, to contest.

For children committed "voluntarily" by their parents (or by the state), there are no such recourses. The only people who can "volunteer" them out of the hospital are the people (either parents, guardians, or the state as guardian) who "volunteered" them in.

For all the legal language that was to ensue, the fundamental question became—within the context of a drastic liberty deprivation—are children due the rights and protection of "persons" under the Constitution?

Where a due process question arises, the general rule seems to be that it triggers three questions:

First, has a constitutionally recognized liberty been infringed?

Then, if so, is that infringement attributable to state action?

Third, if both of the above ring in a yes answer, then what procedures are required by the state? And what kind of a burden will that place on the state?

The Supreme Court had decided in favor of children having a liberty interest within the juvenile court/delinquency context. However, protection for children in a delinquency proceeding is protection for the child against an action by the state. Not against an action by the child's parent, involving the state. And not in an allegedly "medically indicated" procedure either. The only major ruling that entered that mined area was a ruling for children's liberty interest in cases of abortion: a ruling that said children did not need their parents' permission to seek an abortion. There, they did not find "any significant state interest in conditioning an abortion on the consent of a parent or person in loco parentis that is not present in the case of an adult." Would that, logically, extend in principle to Jackie's case? Would there be found to be a significant state interest in continuing permission for parents to commit their children?

Could one place hope in the fact that the Supreme Court had repeatedly expressed doubts about psychiatry? In 1956, it said that "the only certain thing that can be said about the present state of knowledge and therapy regarding mental disease is that science has not reached finality of judgment."

In 1968, Justice Burger in a dissenting opinion, said, "Lawmakers in recent years have been sensitive to the need to make civil commitment difficult recognizing the danger of relatives farming out their kindred into mental institutions for motives not always worthy."And in 1975, he wrote:

> There can be no doubt that involuntary commitment to a mental hospital, like involuntary confinement of an individual for any reason, is a deprivation of liberty which the State cannot accomplish without due process of law

(cite omitted). Commitment must be justified on the basis
of a legitimate state interest, and the reasons for committing a particular individual must be established in an appropriate proceeding.

Would these previously stated attitudes—toward commitment of adults—help in the case of children?

For opening innings, Jackie's side was in good form.

In the Middle District Court, their claim was that the admission of the kids by parents or guardians was unconstitutional;
that it violated the Fourteenth Amendment. They claimed that
due process required "initial and periodic consideration for,
and placement in the least drastic environment necessary for
proper treatment."

(The uh-oh in there, which we discover later, is the underlying assumption that the kids did in fact need some form of
treatment, rather than that they were well until proven sick—
which is what the hearing was meant to be for.)

They effectively countered the defendant's claim that the
procedures presently operative were adequate; and that there
was "insignificant stigma" involved in putting a kid in a mental
hospital. And they certainly demolished the defendant's attitude that there exists in the world a kind of psychiatric infallibil-
ity (which should have been obviously decimated by the fact
that each side was able to come up with three perfectly respectable—and inalterably opposing—psychiatric experts).

They pointed to the vagueness of the psychiatric labels,
the resulting contradictory diagnoses.

"For Jackie," Dr. (A) said, "it was hyperkinetic disorder
and adjustment reaction of childhood. These are two different
kettles of fish—one is not the same as the other. . . ."

For the other child, J. R., "one diagnosis was borderline
mental retardation and literally on the next page in the documents . . . which I examined, had the psychiatrist check off
'not mentally retarded.' "

They presented plentiful evidence that the children at hand
were there without any reason pertinent to the children them-

selves or their condition—(i.e., had been "dumped"). And they made use of the lovely experiment conducted by Dr. David L. Rosenhan in 1973. Rosenhan had eight normal people (himself included) trundle off to "volunteer" themselves as mental patients at twelve different hospitals. They all spoke truthfully about themselves, with one exception. They claimed they had auditory hallucinations. They heard words like "hollow," "empty," and "thud." Every one of the twelve were admitted, diagnosed as schizophrenic—and when they were finally released, the record read, not better or doing fine, but "schizophrenia in remission."

(As a follow-up, Rosenhan alerted the hospitals that more "pseudopatients" were loose and might try to get themselves admitted. In the next months, 44 "pseudopatients" were identified by the hospitals. Rosenhan had, actually, sent none out.)

Jackie's advocates also pointed out the inescapable fact that adults support adults. That the child, although the alleged client or patient, is not the one paying the bills; that children are not believed; that, in particular, a child who has been brought to a clinician by an anxious (or frantic) parent seeking the child's admission (and therefore exaggerating the child's misbehaviors) is automatically given a biased glance. That, where there is a difference between the child's assertions and the adult's, the psychiatrist will believe the adult. For instance, as Dr. (A) said, "Jackie was described as rebellious against authority, yet he was cooperative with the psychologist. Further Jackie was described as hyperactive, but no hyperactivity was noted at the time of admission."

The opposition countered by simply continuing to talk about "medically indicated" procedures.

From their very inception, mental institutions have offered a simple way of warehousing (or "dumping") inconvenient relations. As with most institutions in this country which stand on a liberty-threatening flaw, every now and then someone has noticed.

In 1860, Mrs. Dorothy Packard's husband, a Calvinist

preacher, had her committed for daring to publicly disagree
with his theological views. When released,

> she became an energetic crusader for the rights of asylum
> inmates. She won passage of statutes providing jury trials
> for every patient already committed (in Illinois), recogniz-
> ing the right to express insane-sounding opinions without
> fear of resulting commitment (in Massachusetts), and es-
> tablished visiting committees, including female represen-
> tation, to inspect insane asylums (in Iowa and Maine).

Additionally, she wrote *Modern Persecution or Insane Asylums
Unveiled*—in seven volumes. All of which stirred up a splash
of concern over people being railroaded into mental hospitals
by relatives with doubtful vested interests in eliminating their
inconvenient presence.

But public concerns fade. And as psychiatry got an ever-
greater power grip as a profession, it was able to effectively
suggest that people who thought mental institutions were
dumping grounds were victims of delusions that were less than
sane. By the 1940's and 1950's, they were able to posture enor-
mous insult at the idea that judicial hearings and judicial safeguards were necessary to keep "sick" people from their ministrations. Such safeguards for individuals would be traumatic.
Would be humiliating and counter-therapeutic. (So the argument here—as in juvenile/family court matters—is that it is
a civil matter not needful of due process protections because
it is medical, benign, curative.) It was argued then, as it is
now, that crazy people could only find a formal, impartial hearing hideously upsetting. That someone who was emotionally
ill would only be made more so by delaying incarceration
("treatment").

In other words, the very thing the safeguard was to check
on—*whether* the individual in question was mentally ill, or
sufficiently so to be confined indefinitely in a loony bin—was
the thing taken as a given, as pre-determined. These experts
do not discuss, they diagnose.

In 1975, the discharges from mental hospitals of children
under eighteen showed:

- 2,992 labeled neuroses
- 3,407 as personality disorders
- 4,598 as childhood disorders
- 11,479 as *transient* situational disorders
- 2,558 were loaded under something called "other."
- Fully 26.7% of the 42,690 children were in for transient situational disorders.

In the Pennsylvania class action suit, *Bartley v. Kremens,* similar to *Parham,* the children had been hospitalized for these reasons:

- Runaway, incorrigible
- Runaway
- Runaway, truancy, delinquent behavior
- Aggressive behavior toward family. Refusal to attend school. Excessive demands on attention at home.
- "Father out of household in the military."
- Interim placement while family was on vacation
- Hyperactivity interfered with routine of household and disturbed family members
- Family problems
- Family conflicts
- Began to have trouble handling anger and hurt feelings toward his parents. Took these feelings to school with him.
- Runaway conflict with parents
- Because argumentative and wanted to stay out of school. Patient's mother overdosed and was hospitalized. Patient then had to be.
- Neglect. Social deprivation.
- Sometimes hyperactive. Illegitimate.

Debby Goren, with a master's degree and years of experience working with children, says: "Jackie was not hyperkinetic.

I've worked with many hyperkinetic kids. Jackie could sit for a period of time and watch TV. He could sit and read. He went everywhere with us. We went camping. We went to parties. We went to restaurants. And he was never a problem. Jackie was there with me during the summer. While David was working, Jackie and I used to walk, to go swimming. Almost a mile away. And he would go out and play with the other kids at the pool. We would walk back, and he'd help me fix dinner."

I ask what it's like for a normal kid in a mental hospital. David says, "Dreadful. Especially the time Jackie was there. One of the attendants was found to have taken one of the kids and killed him. When Jackie was much younger. And he was always frightened of that. He had whole lots of stories about those kinds of things happening."

Debby says, "He was real scared at night."

David says, "And it's cold. I mean it's cold emotionally. It's a hospital. Obviously, it's not a home. The walls are cold. And the social workers at times may be nice and friendly. But they leave and they go home. You stay there alone at night, afraid that the attendants are coming to get you."

In November, 1975, just as the Middle District Court three-judge panel was being assembled, DFCS was scurrying to place Jackie. They pressed for a hearing in the county court which would rule that Dr. Larrabee had to pay toward Jackie's support.

Meanwhile, Dr. Larrabee was seeking custody of Jackie.

David says: "He was the one who appeared, and said, 'I'll take him.' He was very eager. He came to me and he said, how could he get Jackie back? And he was very eager to do that. And I also met his wife. They described their lovely home, their eagerness for Jackie. And at this point in time, the hospital people were looking for someplace to put him. They wanted to get him an appropriate placement, and the taker was Dr. Larrabee.

"It's just interesting in hindsight, when you look back—

there were the requirements of doing a home study which takes sixty days at least. And of course Jackie, who's so close to getting out he's just tasting it, and—'When are they going to let me out? When are they going to let me out?' I tried to explain to him you have to do this home study.

" 'When are they gonna be finished?' 'We don't know. It's going to take a while.'

"So finally they spent all the time allegedly studying Dr. Larrabee and his home, and said, 'Fine. This is the right place for him.' "

The money thing is interesting all around. Kids or no kids, funds were a consideration the courts would have to take into account.

Twenty-four of the forty-six children in question had been recommended for special group home placement. DFCS was claiming that a major obstacle in effecting that was the state of the economy. The necessity of adopting an austerity budget. The inability of the state to afford new programs. But here are the numbers involved:

It was costing $40,000 a year for each of the twenty-four children in the hospital. That comes to $960,000 a year.

It would cost ($7,500 a year for each child) around $60,000 a year to run three group homes for the same twenty-four kids, with eight in each home. Or $180,000. What the state/ defendants were saying was that they could not afford to *save* $780,000.

I am wondering about Jackie's mother. Did Jackie, I ask David, ever mention her?

"That was real hard for him to talk about. He didn't want to talk about it. That was very painful for Jackie to deal with. He didn't really want to talk about her at all."

This was reportedly included in a psychological evaluation in July, 1975:

"Jackie expressed considerable anxiety about his relationship with his parents. He stated, 'I know their names, but I don't want to know them. I don't talk about them anymore.'

"When asked about his father, Jackie said, 'I've never seen my real father.' He then hid his head and began to cry."

Did he—one thrashes around, looking for *something*—did he have any friends in the hospital?

"It was fleeting. Some of the kids left."

So he'd watch other kids going home, going to some home. . . .

"He also knew that, as he got older, the chances were less and less that anyone would want him," Debby says.

David adds: "The rejection factor. Again, adults, a lot of adults don't have any real conception of what kids feel. He knew he was being screwed over. He knew he was given the ultimate rejection with nobody wanting him to live with them. He knew these things. And nothing remedied that. He just stayed in the hospital year after year. Continually, what you saw in this case was the buck being passed from one agency or from one person to another. Who didn't want to take responsibility. And each party along the line, the state agencies or the state people involved would just say, "Well, he doesn't fall into our categories. So we can't do anything for him." And then that led to people just forgetting about him. And so he was at Central State Hospital, and he was just going to stay there."

As, quote, hyperkinetic, unquote?

"They have to justify. They have to justify why he's still there."

Debby says, "And once he's called hyperkinetic—foster placements are difficult to find. So why bother? You really don't have to if you can find a reason not to."

But a sweet, nice-looking kid. . . .

David says, "I know. But a 'mental case.' No matter how much you want a kid—no matter if he's got blond hair and blue eyes—he's been in a mental hospital."

Debby says, "And he's been on medication. Medication scares people to death."

J.L., 12, ID #172–897.

In a fit of lucidity—given the surrounding logical lunacy—
the Middle District Court of Georgia ruled clearly for Jackie
et al on February 26, 1976.

In effect, it ruled that Jackie was a person.

It held:

> This case raises the most important question of every
> child's constitutional right to liberty, not only the liberty
> that includes freedom from bodily restraint (cite omitted)
> but also the liberty that includes the freedom of an ordi-
> nary, every-day child in these United States of America—
> the freedom to live with mothers, fathers, brothers and
> sisters in whatever the family abode may be; the freedom
> to be loved and to be spanked; the freedom to go in and
> out the door, to run and play, to laugh and cry, to fight
> and fuss, to stand up and fall down, to play childish
> games; the freedom to go to school and to frolic with
> schoolmates; the freedom to go to Sunday school and
> church; the freedom to watch and listen or not to watch
> and listen to television; the freedom to buy candy at the
> corner store; the freedom to be a normal child in a normal
> household cared for by normal parents.

It went a bit overboard. As one witnesses so often where
brutalities against children are at issue, there's a marked tendency to skid from the base to the lofty, without ever stopping
at minimal decency. To go from Dickens to Disney; from the
cruel to the impossible.

But they did establish that, "Unfortunately, as the evidence
indicates, there are some parents who abuse . . . authority
and who under the guise of admitting a child to a mental hospital actually abandon their child to the state." And, without
indicting the entire psychiatric profession, they declare that,
since psychiatrists are capable of making mistakes, they
shouldn't be given "the power to confine a child in a mental
hospital without procedural safeguards being imposed to guard
against errors in judgment and/or the arbitrariness that the
best of us humans exhibit from time to time." Both parents

and the Department of Human Resources as Custodians, the court observed, have, at present an "unchecked and unbalanced power over the essential liberties"—of the children in question.

Yet next, surely, the ruling contains an interesting slip. It suggests the trap door through which the state will achieve its later reversal. The language suggests that the children involved both are and are not emotionally disturbed. Listen:

> *A child is alleged to be emotionally disturbed.* The child is admitted to a mental hospital where he may be detained and restrained of liberty for years. It is of no constitutional consequence—and of limited practical meaning—that the institution to which he is admitted and in which he is detained is called a hospital. The fact of the matter is that however euphemistic the title, a regional hospital named Central State Hospital or Georgia Mental Health Institution is an institution known by all as one for the confinement of mentally ill children and adults, in which the child is confined for a greater or lesser time. His world becomes a building with locked doors and windows, regimented routine and institutional hours. Instead of mother and father and sisters and brothers and friends and classmates, his world is peopled by psychiatrists, psychologists, social workers, state employees and *children who are to a greater or lesser extent also emotionally disturbed.* (Italics mine.)

Two months after that decision was handed down (giving the Department of Human Resources sixty days to begin to place the children), in April, 1976, Jackie was ensconced with Dr. Larrabee, his wife, their three children. For the Gorens, a wall of silence began descending.

Debby says, "We never saw him after he went to live with Larrabee. He called us a few times when he first went there. Mainly to say that he missed us and things were okay. And he was glad to be out of the hospital."

Visits were planned, but, the Gorens say, they were always canceled by Dr. Larrabee.

"I don't know," David says. "It's difficult. Our involvement was a professional one, with me representing Jackie. But it was also personal. I mean, he came and stayed with us. And we cared about him as a human being. And you know—we were going to get together. And in fact one day—we were going to go over, to go to his home with Dr. Larrabee, and they said no, they weren't going to be there."

Debby says, "They did that a couple of times, and at the time we never thought anything about it. That it was so hard for him to set up a time when we could come. And Dr. Larrabee wanted to be there while we were there."

Meanwhile, the Department of Human Resources had entered a motion to "stay order and judgment" pending their appeal to the Supreme Court. One of the major criteria for granting a stay is that the applicant must establish a strong likelihood of success on the merits of their case. In other words, it has to look like they've got a shot at winning a reversal.

The Georgia Court denied the motion to stay "since defendants failed to establish a strong likelihood that they would prevail on appeal. . . ."

But they did prevail, of course. How?

Justice William O. Douglas wrote, "Not long after my appointment, [former Chief Justice Charles Evans] Hughes made a statement to me which at the time was shattering but turned out to be true: 'Justice Douglas, you must remember one thing. At the constitutional level where we work, 90 percent of any decision is emotional. The rational part of us supplies the reasons for supporting our predilections.' "

That being the case, it is useful to listen in on their decisions, to better learn what the Higher Fathers' predilections are.

The case was argued twice: that in itself was unusual. The first time, December 6, 1977, two of the Justices were absent, Brennan and Blackmun. However, although Blackmun opted out, Brennan listened to the argument on tape. One probability for the re-argument, then, is that initially the eight participating Justices were evenly split.

In the ring, as it were, were John L. Cromartie, executive director of Georgia Legal Services for Jackie et al. And R. Douglas Lackey, assistant Georgia attorney general, for the opposition.

Cromartie was urging the justices to uphold the Georgia ruling that kids were entitled to a hearing before an impartial examiner and were due other procedural rights before they could be popped in a mental institution either by their parents, or by a guardian.

Lackey was arguing that in American society "we have determined that children cannot make certain decisions for themselves. One of these is in the area of selecting medically indicated treatment."

Since they are works of non-fiction, after all, it probably makes the most sense to "review" the written briefs presented to the Supreme Court. In any case, if we are dealing with the justices' emotions and predilections, these are apt to be affected as much by tone and style as by logic and content.

Two Views of "Voluntary"

The first briefs under consideration are entitled *Brief for Appellants* (T. M. "Jim" Parham, Individually and as Director of the Division of Mental Health and W. T. Smith, Individually and as Chief Medical Officer of Central State Hospital) dated August, 1977, and *Appellants' Reply Brief,* dated November, 1977.

One is struck by a tone of self-assurance in this work that borders on the smug. Their theme, however, while not creditable to this reviewer, is canny and deserves a grudging respect.

What the authors glommed onto was the Middle District Court's failure to find in so many words that the children in question had been wrongfully committed in the first place.

Certainly, there was plenty of testimony on record to indicate the possibility that the commitments had been wrongful from the start. The state's own witness, the C & A Director, stated that a parent might just come in saying they couldn't handle it any more and the psychiatrist would agree and that would more or less be it. Another psychiatrist testified that the diagnoses were often contradictory, and in any case were common and benign. The lay person, at least, reading this brief in light of later events, will regret that the catchall vagueness of the admittedly non-serious (indeed, "transient") "diagnoses" or "prognoses" such as adjustment reaction to childhood did not come under attack in the ruling. The failure to explicitly criticize them, or to explicitly find that the children had been falsely committed initially—the very reason why hearings were being advocated—left a door wide open through which the authors of this work could make a loquacious and lawyerly exit.

That omission allowed them continually to reiterate the phrase "medically indicated decision." To liken the parental right to commit a child to any other "medical" procedure. A tonsillectomy. And later, more (melo)dramatically, to cancer of the leg.

It allowed them to repeat and repeat the phrase "mentally ill children." In what is surely a breathtaking stretch of language, they put forth as the central issue "whether parents may, *with the advice of a physician,* determine that their children will receive treatment for mental illness in a state mental health facility." (italics mine) One must admire the phrase "mental health facility." It sounds no worse than a physical fitness facility.

But even they don't play that "advice" game twice. Later, on the same page, they modify, correcting the reference to read "concurrence" of a physician. However, by hammering away at the presumptive phrase "mentally ill children," they effectively obliterate the basic connection: the formal hearings, the due process safeguards called for, are to determine *whether* a child is indeed mentally ill; or (unfeeling phrase) "suitable for treatment."

(What standard would make any of us not suitable for treatment? Couldn't our children, on cranky days, be found "suitable for treatment"?)

The authors posture a kind of barely patient restraint. They seem irked at having to explain what they consider so obvious.

> The State is merely fulfilling a proprietary function similar to that of a private hospital, and it is fundamentally unfair to require that parents be subjected to adversarial hearings and confrontations with *their mentally ill children* simply because the parents happen to select a State mental health facility for their children, rather than costly private facilities. [Italics mine.]

In other words, they should not be penalized for mere thrift.

Further (obviously) ". . . any additional procedures would merely add unwarranted impediments to the hospitalization of children and . . . such impediments, in the form of adversarial hearings, would frequently prove harmful to *mentally ill children.*" (Italics mine.)

They take on the argument for the "less drastic means" doctrine—that is, really, in this case, isn't there something less drastic one could do with these children than put them in a mental institution for an indeterminate period of time?—and sweep it away, saying ". . . the application of this constitutional doctrine to the present case is entirely inappropriate, not only because the children are voluntary patients, but also because the "less drastic means" doctrine wrongly presupposes that children possess the same right to liberty as adults, a conclusion which is unsupportable in fact or law."

Very pretty. The "same right to liberty" is a grandstand play to any father's (or grandfather's) heart. It equates the right not to be placed in a loony bin "voluntarily" against your will, with the right to choose your bedtime, or raid the fridge. Give them this right and the next thing you know they'll want the right not to do their homework.

The authors seem much in a hurry to get done with this silly business so they can get back to important issues. So much so that they don't notice when their own citation works contrary to their case. Reciting Blackstone in his *Commentaries,* they call forth his statement that, "The duty of parents to provide for the *maintenance* of their children is a principle of natural law; an obligation. . . ; laid on them not only by nature herself, but by their own proper act, in bringing them into the world. . . ." But, in placing their children in a state institution, isn't it to be considered that parents are turning said maintenance of their children over to the state?

They refer to previous Supreme Court hymns to "a private realm of family life which the state cannot enter," and to the "sanctity of the family." This, riding roughshod over the fact that the parents in question have directly sought state intervention.

They bat halfheartedly at the arguments presented about the reliability of psychiatric diagnoses, or their inconsistency. But, wherever possible, they make sure to refer to psychiatrists as "physicians" and to repeat "medically indicated treatment." They assert the district court was unable to conclude that even a single child had been not mentally ill or not suitable for treatment when initially hospitalized.

"Unable" or not, they unfortunately *did* not.

Further, it is (they imply) perfectly clear (and why do we not understand it?): "The Superintendent [at the hospital] does not decide that the child will be hospitalized; he merely decides whether the hospital *will be made available* for a particular placement." (Italics mine.) The state "simply makes available an alternative, which parents or guardians are free to select, if appropriate, or reject. It is the parents' or guardians' initiative and their decision, that result in the hospitalization of the child, rather than the actions of the State."

That does seem to say, does it not, that the state makes itself available as a participant when a parent chooses to dump a child in one of its institutions? What happened to the "advice" of a physician? According to this document, there is simply no problem at all.

Why, when a kid is accepted, when this institution is made available to him, he is classified as voluntary and has all the rights of any voluntary patient. Except for one thing: " . . . if the voluntary patient was admitted upon the application of his parent or guardian, the patient's discharge prior to his becoming eighteen years of age may be conditioned upon the consent thereto of his parent or guardian." What, "may be"? It is.

But that is nothing if not a good thing because "children cannot be treated as adults with respect to receiving *medical treatment.*" (Italics mine.) They might fail to understand that placement in a mental hospital is good for them. That the state here is simply "rendering . . . medically indicated treatment upon the request of the person, or one legally responsible for the person." That the hospital "acts as a provider of medical services, not as a prison."

And over and over, the Sesame Street drill phrase, "mentally ill child."

Appellees [that is, Jackie's side] in their complaint, in essence, asked for a hearing replete with all the trappings normally associated with an adversarial proceeding, including the right to counsel, the right to subpoena witnesses, the right to cross-examine the person seeking the hospitalization of the child, and a host of other rights more compatible with a criminal proceeding than with the hospitalization of a *mentally ill child.* [Italics mine.]

". . . the adversarial nature of the hearing would detrimentally affect the *mentally ill child.*" (Italics mine.)

And, most astonishingly, this: "Who would argue that J. L. and J. R. at the ages of six and seven, should have had the freedom to do as they pleased." (They do not use a question mark; it is, to them, beyond question.) "These children, like most children [sic], undoubtedly did what their parents or guardians directed them to do. They got up in the morning when they were told, they ate when they were told, they went to bed when they were told." And *these* are your "mentally

ill children"? Your "adjustment reactions to childhood" who
are "suitable for treatment"?

These are the mentally ill children who, if the recommended safeguards existed for them, would "necessarily be
denied treatment" for lack of the "most appropriate setting"
for that treatment?

Indeed: "The result of applying the concept created by
the district court is that mentally ill children will be the victim
of discrimination, which they do not deserve and cannot avoid."
Were it necessary, as the District Court ruled, for these "mentally ill" children to be placed in "the most appropriate setting"—the inevitable result would be that "some mentally ill
child must be denied treatment"—and this "will be as tragic
in practice as it is unsupportable in theory."

And so we have, at the highest level, the legal state confronting the therapeutic state.

This brief is slick. Summary. Bold, impatient, decisive. A
fatherly dictum issued when Daddy is already late for the office.

Now we come to the *Brief for Appellees* (J. L. and J. R.,
Minors, Individually and as representatives of a class of persons
similarly situated), dated September, 1977.

In contrast with the previous brief, this document is thorough and considering—but cautious. Some of its most moving
points are relegated to footnotes. The footnote on page five
reads: "Pending review by this Court, J. L., one of the named
plaintiffs died. The Court was informed of his death by letter
in August, 1976. The death of J. L. does not moot the instant
action. . . ."

It is a document that anticipates an assumed bias on the
part of the reading justices. It makes obeisance to that bias,
pulling punches. It lacks the arrogance of the former brief;
seems a bit self-conscious about Going Before the Supreme
Court.

J. L.'s case was surely tragic in practice. And a system which
permits the totally unnecessary incarceration in a mental institution of even one child for five years seems unsupportable

in theory. (At least as unsupportable as that "some mentally ill child must be denied treatment"?) Yet (and perhaps this is hindsight, after all: we know what happened), this sincere effort fails quite to prove it. Perhaps, given the decisive tack taken by the opposition and adding the court's "predilections" into the equation, the issue was foregone. Still, those of us rooting for Jackie's team might have liked to see a bit more stern conviction, a bit more pep.

After all, the greatest pathology anyone directly perceived and attributed in the record to Jackie was the description given by Dr. (A), after visiting with him:

> One of the things that I noticed about Jackie is that he was—he latched onto whoever seemed to offer him what I would call a feeding experience, a nurturing experience, giving experience, at that moment. . . . (I)n an institutional setting because one doesn't have the mother and father . . . whom one can rely on for nurturance over an extended, really indefinite period of time, one has to make use of whoever is available at the moment. Also, one learns that the good guy or the good woman who might be available today might not be available on the next shift or . . . the next week or month, so one takes what one can when one can. I saw a great deal of that mentality in Jackie.

In other words, the kid tried to survive, given what was.

Dr. (A) further described Jackie as "obviously clamoring for a home life and [he] asks very explicitly to be taken care of in a family setting . . ."

The authors here present a reasonable case, but a worried one. They double back on their points. They say, for instance, that:

> It is beyond dispute that a significant number of the families involved with state mental institutions are dysfunctional families, and thus there are inherent conflicts of interest between parents and child. Thus, even though it is certainly unfortunate and one can wish it were not

so, the fact remains that in these situations the interests
of family solidarity are minimal. . . .

Well, that's *okay* (although did we really need the euphemism "dysfunctional" to describe a family which simply wants
one of its children taken by the state?)

But then (damn it) they backtrack, saying, "The interest
of the family is not to be free of the child, but in the solidarity
of the family and in assuring that needed and appropriate mental health services are provided which meet their child's therapeutic needs. . . ."

But again: the question was whether there should be protections and safeguards to determine whether a child even *had*
"therapeutic needs," or, if he did, for some "treatment disorder" whether these were such as to require indefinite incarceration.

It was, as the authors do state, unarguable. These kids were
dumped. By the state's witness's own testimony, "the state
may act to institutionalize simply because a social worker deter-
mines that foster care is unavailable or unworkable . . . (a decision to institutionalize by DFCS is not subject to review within
the agency or guided by any state policy)."

One authority at the C & A Unit of Central State Hospital
noted that "J. L.'s commitment was initiated by his adoptive
mother in order to save her second marriage. J. L.'s stepfather
had delivered an ultimatum; that she must choose between
J. L. and himself. She chose the latter." One child was institutionalized due to a "lack of community resources." Another
was in because the community mental health center was unable
to pick him up "due to work pressures. . . ."

David says, "What really, really bothered me about the Supreme Court was—in their opinion the record did not indicate
that in essence kids were dumped into mental hospitals. In
spite of the C & A Director's flat out statement that kids are
dumped in mental hospitals."

The C & A Director had said, "The problem here in part

is the history and tradition of mental hospitals which have been dumping grounds in the past. As we try to move out of this, there are a lot of people who still treat them as dumping grounds. . . ."

David says, "It was right there. In the C & A Director's own words."

Debby says, "Burger just said there's no way to believe that parents don't have the best interests of their child at heart. Who could believe that parents would just dump their kids?"

David says: "And the Supreme Court refused to accept, and it was incredibly the state's opinion all along, and they even had experts testify—that there's no such thing as a stigma in mental hospitalization. And I can't believe that you say to anybody, 'This is my friend, she was a mental patient,' and they don't react to that. That they don't perceive the person differently than if you say, 'This is my friend,' period."

Well. There's always that old saw about how a hearing would be so upsetting to a mentally disturbed person.

David says: "Yeah, as opposed to its not being upsetting if the kid's okay and doesn't need it and he's committed.

"And what's interesting also from Burger's perspective is he wrote a very strong concurring opinion in the *Donaldson* case—the very big recent commitment case of an adult.

"The issue was, are you being deprived of your liberty if you're put into a mental hospital? Especially if you're not dangerous. If it's not for the police function but for the *parens patriae* function. And in that case, in Burger's concurrence, he says we have to look at criminal safeguards, because doctors can't tell us that they can fix things, or that they can treat people. We have to be very concerned about what procedures you use.

"He very strongly rejected the original idea—in the *Donaldson* case—which was that an individual if they're committed to a mental hospital—has a right to treatment. And if those individuals don't get their treatment then they ought to be released.

"Burger disagreed, saying what is this treatment? It's too nebulous a term. And we have to look at it in deprivation of liberty and due process safeguards. But you turn around and talk about a kid and his opinion is all of a sudden very different. And he can't see that there's any—in essence—a deprivation of liberty that we have to worry about for a kid, because the kid's parents are looking after him and after all he's only going to a hospital.

"The analogy they chose here is the kid having a tonsillectomy. And the parents made that decision and the kid's not going to have a right to refuse to have his tonsils out. And it's the same thing with wanting him to go to a mental hospital.

"It was very frustrating sitting in the Supreme Court during the arguments. You wanted to get up and scream."

Debby says, "I wanted to scream, '*But Jackie's dead!*' "

One can easily see why.

The oral argument before the Supreme Court of the United States took place at 10:00 A.M., on Tuesday, October 10, 1978. It was all over at 11:10.

Mr. Lackey, for the state, went first.

He set up the issue as the constitutionality of the Georgia statute which allows ("recognizes the rights of") parents of *mentally ill children* to make application for those children to state mental health facilities. And he sets up Jackie et al's argument as being that children have a constitutionally protected liberty interest here and that the kids have a right to treatment in the most appropriate setting.

What he's leaning on, to begin with, is that we as a society have decided there are "certain decisions" kids can't make—among them, those which are "medically indicated." He says, "That is, it is our position that in our society parents, with the advice of a physician, routinely make decisions which range from whether a child is to have a tonsillectomy to decisions which have life and death consequences for the child."

He says:

> One example, which I would like to use, is the situation where the parent is faced with the child who has a heart defect, a young child, and a doctor says, "Of course, the

child can live without an operation. The child will be
an invalid for his or her entire life. I can operate. If the
operation is successful the child will lead a normal life.
If the operation is not successful, the child will die."

That kind of decision, that kind of decision-making
process occurs in the family *routinely* [italics mine], yet
no one has ever suggested that that kind of a decision
which clearly could have the consequences which are
much more adverse than what we have here—no one
has ever suggested successfully except in a few recent
district court decisions, that that kind of decision-making
process is required to be subjected to an adversarial proceeding. . . .

QUESTION [The transcript does not tell me which justice
   is asking which question]: I want to be sure I understand
   you, Mr. Lackey. Are you suggesting that the Constitution of the United States would prohibit the intervention by the state in that sort of situation?

MR. LACKEY: I believe, sir, that it would prohibit it to
   the extent that the state did not have a compelling
   state interest to interfere—

QUESTION: Or are you suggesting that it is constitutionally
   permissible for a state to leave that decision to the parent? Those are two quite different propositions, aren't
   they? Which are you suggesting?

MR. LACKEY: It would be our position that it would not
   be constitutionally permissible for the state to interfere
   with the family in that situation, absent the demonstration of a compelling state—

QUESTION: You don't need to go nearly that far in arguing
   this case, do you?

QUESTION: You need stand on only the second leg, don't
   you?

MR. LACKEY: I certainly could. I believe I could. Perhaps
   I don't understand your question.

Arguing before the Supreme Court could be seen to be
lessons in arguing the Supreme Court, evidently.

QUESTION: I think it is rather important, because those
   are two quite different propositions. First, the claim

. . . that a state would be constitutionally prohibited from intervening in the parent-child relationship. That's one proposition.

MR. LACKEY: Yes, sir. I understand.

QUESTION: Another is that a state may constitutionally leave such a decision to the parent, but need not constitutionally do so.

MR. LACKEY: I see that the second point would be easier and—

QUESTION: Well that's all you need in this case, isn't it?

MR. LACKEY: Yes, sir, that would resolve this case from that standpoint.

QUESTION: If you rely on the first point, I suppose it would be unconstitutional for a state to say an operation has to be performed by a doctor. Parents could use self-help on a heart operation. You don't really maintain that.

MR. LACKEY: No, sir, I wouldn't maintain that. . . .

QUESTION: Your position here is that the Constitution of the United States doesn't require any more than what Georgia hasprovided.

MR. LACKEY: That's absolutely correct, sir. Either for the reason that the child does not have a liberty interest or if the child does have a liberty interest in this particular situation, because of the process which we provide him, meets all the basic requirements that the Constitution would mandate.

In other words, he'll take it any way he can get it.

QUESTION: Of course, the whole procedure has as its end result the confinement of the child. Do you suggest that doesn't involve a liberty interest?

MR. LACKEY: No, sir. It is our position that the confinement is secondary and a necessary incident—

QUESTION: That wasn't my question.

MR. LACKEY: I'm sorry, sir.

QUESTION: The question is: Are you suggesting that the child does not have a liberty interest at stake?

MR. LACKEY: Yes, sir, my first position is that in this case, where the parent makes the decision and there is confinement as a necessary result of that decision, that the

child does not have a liberty interest. It is our position
that constitutional rights arise out of relationships and
the relationship that is here is between parent and child,
not between the child and the state.

QUESTION: But it is the child who is locked up, not the
parent.

MR. LACKEY: Yes, sir, that is correct.

QUESTION: You are not, surely—or are you—suggesting
in answer to my brother, Brennan's, question that there
is not a deprivation of liberty?

MR. LACKEY: Not in the constitutional sense. Certainly
the child is restrained to the hospital.

QUESTION: Are you saying that it is the same kind of deprivation involved—different in degree only—as having
an appendix operation, heart bypass or confinement
for smallpox?

MR. LACKEY: Yes, sir, that was my whole point, exactly,
in response to Mr. Justice Brennan. I evidently wasn't
answering his question. The confinement in the hospital
is just a necessary incident, incidental to the treatment
itself.

QUESTION: Mr. Lackey, if I understand you correctly, it
would be constitutional for a state to say to a parent,
"If you want to keep your child in the basement for
the next three years because you think it would be
healthy to keep him out of the sunlight," or something
like that, that would be perfectly constitutional. We
just have to rely on the wisdom of the legislature not
to pass such statutes, but you say if they did there would
be no constitutional objection to it.

That's a rather difficult position to maintain.

MR. LACKEY: It is a difficult position to maintain. I don't
believe I could maintain it.

It goes on like this. For anyone with the actual kids involved
on their mind, it get worse.

What Mr. Lackey says, eventually, is that because rich parents can dump their kids in private institutions without all
this legal folderol, to offer due process protections to poor chil-

dren simply because they are dumped in state institutions discriminates against poor parents.

Mr. Lackey rings in one more time the grievous liability it would be if the Fourteenth Amendment were to be invoked every time a child has a heart bypass. However, if that doesn't hold up then—fallback position—the progression of events for a "voluntary" admission in Georgia is perfectly all right as is.

A question specifically challenged Mr. Lackey on his use of the word *"admitted"* vs. *"committed."* It is *admitted,* he assures us. Then, several minutes later, discussing the provision for children's access to the courts after incarceration, he is asked at what stage they have that access.

MR. LACKEY: At any stage, sir. Let me explain, and I want to be careful about this.

We have a state statute that requires the Department of Human Resources to see that all patients have access to counsel for maintenance in legal matters in which they are involved. We have statutes that provide three courts that these children can go to. I hadn't thought of it as being at any stage of their *commitment. . . .*" (italics mine)

Sic.

He wasn't careful enough.

But no one caught it.

QUESTION: In our hypothetical, how would it occur to the youngster involved to go to court? At whatever stage?

MR. LACKEY: That is, perhaps, the most difficult question you could ask.

His answer is that either a lawyer would stumble on them—randomly, accidentally, as David stumbled on Jackie—or, "We have a pamphlet that every patient receives. It is a handbook on patient's rights. . . ."

QUESTION: If you have a child five or six years old, is that a very practical thing?

MR. LACKEY: I don't know whether it is or not, sir. . . .

Where the questions directed to Mr. Lackey seemed to help
him get where he wanted to go, the questions to Jackie's team,
to Mr. Cromartie, seemed to keep leading him away from his
points.

It is more than halfway into the confrontation when we
finally get anywhere near the point:

> MR. CROMARTIE: . . . We rely very heavily, in this case
> on the magnitude of the child's interest. The magnitude
> is simply enormous. We are talking about children being
> locked within the sterile walls of institutions, where—
> QUESTION: That's also true when an adult voluntarily ad-
> mits himself to a mental hospital, isn't it?
> MR. CROMARTIE: But an adult can turn around and say,
> "I want out:" and he must be let out or involuntarily
> committed. A child does not have that option.
> QUESTION: The same option that put him in can take him
> out, i.e., the desire of his parent, isn't that correct?
> MR. CROMARTIE: That is a disagreement that, I think that,
> we had in the last oral argument about whether the
> placement of a child in an institution is truly voluntary.
> QUESTION: Well, Georgia has said that it is voluntary. And
> the question is whether or not Georgia can, agreeably
> to the Constitution, adhere to the centuries-old Com-
> mon Law rule that a parent speaks for his child, and
> the Common Law presumption that there is a commu-
> nity of interest between child and parent. That's the
> basic question in this case, isn't it?

As Nicholas Kittrie has remarked, sometimes it is one's family from whom one most needs protection.

Indeed, the very idea of common interest, in Jackie's case,
in the case of other kids dumped in institutions—defies all reason. The non-legal mind, at least, can only quiver in bewilder-
ment, looking at Jackie's story, the testimony about other children not needing institutionalization, at how "community of
interest" can be any sort of "basic question" in this case.

What is being suggested here is that there is a "constitutionally based independent parental power over children" which
"creates a sphere of personal domination which, at least for-

mally, resembles the relationship of the early Roman father over his children."

> MR. CROMARTIE: Well, I find absolutely no authority for the proposition that a parent has ever been able to institutionalize a child in a state mental institution. I find no authority to support that proposition.

That's not right, unfortunately. The evidence is that parents were *traditionally* able to do just that.

> QUESTION: What about tuberculosis? How is it developed in tuberculosis or smallpox?
> MR. CROMARTIE: The child would be carried to a doctor or to a hospital and treated there and we—
> QUESTION: Well, confined—
> MR. CROMARTIE: It is not my understanding that tuberculosis treatment is confined in the same sense that you are confined in a mental institution.
> QUESTION: What's the difference, in the sense, if he is placed there by his parents and the parents say to the doctors, "Keep him here until he is well"—or she is well—and they go to see him twice a week?
> MR. CROMARTIE: Well, for centuries, the courts have treated physical care and physical treatment different from mental commitment.
> QUESTION: Who has treated it differently?
> MR. CROMARTIE: The courts have. The Georgia courts have. In *Morton v. Sims,* and other cases, they have said mental commitment is by its very nature coercive. It is coercive by nature, plus it is not—there are not commonly accepted medical norms—
> QUESTION: On your first point, that mental care is coercive by its nature, it is surely no more coercive than to put a child in a hospital and have his leg amputated because he has the kind of cancer that might spread. Would you agree with that?
> MR. CROMARTIE: I would agree to that, yes, Your Honor.

Why? Should we really have agreed to that? Did we need to? When adjustment reaction to childhood is, by the state's own expert witness testimony, a prognosis of something transient—something that's going to go away all by itself? Well. Whatever. We are now firmly set on the garden path; reduced to quibbling over whether all cases of medical treatment for bone cancer in children should be subject to judicial scrutiny. Until:

> QUESTION: Now, once an adult voluntarily gets himself admitted to a mental hospital, he is locked up there, isn't he?
> MR. CROMARTIE: He can get out.
> QUESTION: And a child can get out on the wish of his parents.
> MR. CROMARTIE: Yes. In the case of J. L. and J. R., they wanted out right after they got in. They didn't want to go in. If they had been an adult, they could have requested of the superintendent that they be left out and the superintendent would either have had to let them out—
> QUESTION: If they had been an adult and didn't want in, then they would not have voluntarily gotten themselves admitted to the hospital, would they?

And more. The court wonders: after all, most states force kids to attend school, isn't that so? Is that unconstitutional? And how about a military academy? Suppose the parents decide their kid is borderline incorrigible and send him there? Where there are a whole lot of restraints? And what's the difference between that and a tuberculosis sanitarium?

Nor is it that the justices do not get the point:

> QUESTION: I had thought a good deal of your case depended upon evidence, of which the record contains a good deal, that because of the relative unreliability of psychiatry, as contrasted with the more conventional forms of medical practice, a hearing was appropriate because of the consequent risk of incorrect decisions. And that, therefore, you would distinguish the tuberculosis situation on that basis.
> MR. CROMARTIE: That is a part of our argument.

QUESTION: I thought it was.

MR. CROMARTIE: I think that the more basic argument we have is that when there is a deprivation of liberty as extreme as right here, that, traditionally, our courts have regarded at least notice and a hearing to the person involved, and that—

QUESTION: That would require, I would suppose, logically, for you to contend that the Constitution requires notice and a hearing with respect to a leg amputation or admission to a tuberculosis sanitarium.

MR. CROMARTIE: I think I would concede the tuberculosis sanitarium, that it would probably require a hearing there. We don't feel like in the leg amputation that the elements involved that we have in this case, distinguishing it in terms of family autonomy and breaking into the family autonomy, would be present in the leg amputation situation, where they are here. The potential conflict of interest, the request by the family itself that the child be taken out of the home—we feel like those are different for those reasons.

QUESTION: Mr. Cromartie, don't you have a lot of difficulty trying to distinguish on the basis of the magnitude of the deprivation? I thought your case rested on the point Mr. Justice Stewart made earlier that the Common Law presumption rests on the notion that there is a community of interests between the parent and the child, where there would be in the tuberculosis case, the leg amputation, and all the rest. But your point, as I understood you in your brief, was in part that you can't be so sure there is that community of interest in the mental institution context when the parent is asking that the child be placed . . . because there well may be a family conflict as the source of the problem.

So isn't the scope of your argument limited to the case in which the basis for the Common Law presumption is no longer applicable?

MR. CROMARTIE: There were several points that we made. That was one of them. . . .

Now. Isn't it possible that a child could be so emotionally disordered that he is not competent to participate? What about psychotic children? Very disturbed, psychotic, psychopathic persons? What about, what about . . . ?

> MR. CROMARTIE: . . . Getting on toward the end of my argument, we feel that the cases of J. L. and J. R., very dramatically, illustrate how some sort of hearing process, informal though it may be, could have prevented both of them from spending over five years of their lives in a mental institution. In the case of J. L., his primary out-patient therapist had recommended only a month or so before that he not be institutionalized. And yet, [her] recommendation was not even considered when J. L. was placed into that mental institution. Of course, also the evidence shows that J. L. was placed in the institution—the decision was made three days before he ever showed up at the institution.
>
> QUESTION: Assuming that I agree with what you say, what's going to happen if we end up with a hearing with three psychiatrists on one side and three on the other? Then what does the court do?
>
> MR. CROMARTIE: Somebody is going to have to make a decision. That is typical—
>
> QUESTION: Have you ever tried to make one with three psychiatrists on one side and three on the other? If you ever try it, you will be committed.

And with that, we leave the justices to decide 6–3: "*Held:* The District Court erred in holding unconstitutional the State's procedure for admitting a child for treatment to a state mental hospital, since on the record in this case, Georgia's medical factfinding processes are consistent with constitutional guarantees."

This is their balancing act:

> First, the private interest that will be affected by the official action; second, the risk of an erroneous deprivation of such interest through the procedures used, and the probable value, if any, of additional or substitute procedural safeguards; and finally, the Government's interest, including the function involved and the fiscal and administrative burdens that the addition or substitute procedural requirement would entail.

To the first point they say there is no such thing as considering the child's interest as separate from the parents'. They are "inextricably linked"—combined, welded, merged. What they simply don't believe is that "the likelihood of parental abuse is so great" that there need to be adversarial protections for the child.

> Our jurisprudence historically has reflected Western Civilization concepts of the family as a unit with broad parental authority over minor children. Our cases have consistently rejected any notion that a child is "the mere creature of the State" and, on the contrary, asserted that parents generally "have the right, coupled with the high duty," to recognize and prepare [their children] for additional obligations.

And that high duty includes recognizing illness and taking medical advice.

Nor do the justices insist that their decision meshes with reality:

"As with so many other legal presumptions, experience and reality may rebut what the law accepts as a starting point; the incidence of child neglect and abuse cases attests to this." This, however, "is hardly a reason to discard wholesale those pages of human experience that teach that parents generally do act in the child's best interests. . . . The statist notion that governmental power should supersede parental authority in *all* cases because *some* parents abuse and neglect children is repugnant to the American tradition."

How about that. And I thought the Constitution read: "Nor shall any State deprive *any* person of life, liberty, or property without due process of law; nor deny to *any* person within its jurisdiction the equal protection of the laws." Funny.

And here it is: ". . . there is no finding by the District Court of even a single instance of bad faith by any parent or member of appellee's class . . ."

Oh well. I suppose the District Court couldn't have had future-glasses.

David says, "You wouldn't have lost anything to say without all the strict cold legal arguments—kids are dumped in the mental hospital. They're dumped there without any regard for their rights. Without any regard for whether they need it.

"The state's own witnesses admit that kids are dumped there. That wasn't said like that. I don't know if it would have made any difference—to just hit that point. And get the Court talking about that, instead of these convoluted discussions on how many psychiatrists should make the decision on who should admit a kid, and don't all psychiatrists disagree with each other, and, you know, isn't it the same as going to get your tonsils out. That's the only thing I felt about it—that it just should have forced the Court to deal with the dumping problem. Because it was the state's own expert witness's term, kids are dumped. And that's the essence of the case. And they just didn't really deal with that."

David holds up a copy of the Voluntary Release form Jackie signed when he was seven years old. "How could the Supreme Court ignore a seven-year-old kid signing his name to this document?"

On Wednesday, August 4, 1976, "a 12-year-old boy who spent five years in a state mental hospital even though psychiatrists said he was not mentally ill, was found hanged in the closet of his bedroom."

Jackie's body was found by Dr. Jackson Larrabee. Jackie was hanging by a jumprope tied together with another rope.

His body showed bruises. The end conclusion was that Jackie had hanged himself.

According to newspaper accounts, witnesses recalled they'd seen Jackie forced to run and ordered to fall from his bicycle on command, etc.

On February 10, 1977, a jury of nine men and three women decided that Larrabee was guilty of child abuse.

He was sentenced to five years in prison for the child abuse he had committed.

Funny. Jackie did five months more than that—just for being committed.

Debby says, "Jackie had said to us and had said to other
people that he just wanted out, and he would never go back
no matter what happened to him. He would never go back.
I mean he had no alternative when he got out. He knew nobody
would believe him, either."

David says, "It was probably a combination of Larrabee's
treatment of Jackie, and maybe a threat to put him back in
the hospital. Might have led to what happened." Frustration:
"You can't close your eyes to what happens. You can't take
a very upright position like the Supreme Court and say there's
nothing in the record to indicate there's any dumping children
in the hospital. That's bullshit. The state's own witness, the
C & A Director, admitted kids get dumped in the hospital,
admitted they get tangled up in all this bureaucratic mess,
and procedures, and they stay in the hospital, live there. I
mean that's how the state's own witness . . ." Frustration.

I'm clumsy gathering my stuff together to leave their house.
Or *feeling* clumsy.

Debby says, "The thing is how much Jackie cared about
other people. When he was with us, we'd take him shopping,
to the shopping mall. And there was, in the middle, this kind
of merry-go-round. And we'd give him some money, he'd always want something—candy, whatever. And when we were
done shopping, we'd find him—buying rides for the other kids."

8

Family Covenant

"I have now come to believe that the ideology of Blaming the Victim so distorts and disorients the thinking of the average concerned citizen that it becomes a primary barrier to effective social change."

William Ryan, Blaming the Victim, p. xv

I propose that it is more, not less, serious to do severe harm to those toward whom you stand in a relationship of trust—than to do similar harm to a stranger. Obviously, there are more kinds of harm—emotional, psychological—devisable among intimates. But I am speaking only of harm which would be seen as criminal outside the home. That is the only kind we can make rules about: it is the only harm we can legislate against, and effectively enforce that legislation.

Nor is this concept unfamiliar in law. Professor Kittrie says, "This concept of special relationship, or trust relationship, exists in other areas of the law. It is called *fiduciary*. It tells you that there are relationships the law considers arms-length relationships. And relationships it considers fiduciary—involving a special duty to protect the people with whom you share the relationship. For instance: a partnership. That is not considered the same as a stranger relationship. If I have a shop, and you have a shop down the street, you don't owe me anything. But if you and I have a shop in partnership, and you find out there are troubles in the business and you don't tell me, that violates our fiduciary relationship. You have a special duty to tell me. If the president of a company knows something which will adversely affect a stockholder, the same thing applies. The concept exists in the law primarily in partnerships, in corporate

196

law, as a civil concept, but it could move into the criminal area."

If men, and not animals, "seldom let their defeated enemies escape and often treat their helpless victims with the utmost cruelty," then a societal consensus is needed to bring us to the level of civilization existing in animals: we must act to ensure that the loser be allowed to go free.

We must ensure that Americans, tortured or sexually assaulted in their "homeland," can go to America for justice: for protection of their person—of their life and basic liberty.

Professor Kittrie says, "What you are saying is in the Constitution. The basic concept you are talking about is there."

I say, "Yes." And meaning no disrespect, I add, "That's what Susan B. Anthony said."

Beginning with "We, the people, . . ." continuing with the inalienable rights to life, liberty and the pursuit of happiness, including the Fourteenth Amendment "nor shall any State deny to any person within its jurisdiction the equal protection of the law," Anthony used the "Constitutional Argument" to vindicate the call by women for the right to vote.

One hundred and ten years later, the Constitutional argument can be brought forth again. The only question (still) left to be settled: are women—(once they are wives and mothers)—and are children—persons?

Anthony wrote, "I scarcely believe any of our opponents will have the hardihood to say they are not. Being persons, then, women are citizens, and no State has a right to make any new law, or to enforce any old law, which shall abridge their privileges or immunities." Can one not add "or to *fail* to enforce any law" protecting their liberty or person—simply because of their female/familial status?

Also, she warns:

"It is a poor rule that won't work more ways than one. Establish this precedent, admit the States' rights to deny suffrage, and there is no limit to the confusion, discord and disruption that may await us. There is and can be one safe principle of government—equal rights to all." And the very *first* of those

198 THE HOME FRONT

equal rights, the very most basic, is equal protection under the law, for all.

It is a matter fundamental to our form of government.

Our form of government represented a drastic departure from the hierarchical form of social organization. It was based on the concept of self-government, autonomy, with each unit bound not to decrees from above; with government requiring the consent of the governed. "Our Declaration of Independence," Professor Kittrie says, "is based on the concept of social contract." It involves a balance of rights and duties, and basic unabridgeable protections for every citizen. One need not even approach the utopian—concepts of children's "rights" beyond the most basic, for instance—to request or require that the protections of life and bodily integrity be extended to all within the smallest social unit. To require that, where crimes are at issue, the family be regarded as within the jurisdiction of the State, should the victim have no recourse but to seek that protection.

If, as Charles Rembar writes, "civilization hangs on the habit of obedience to the criminal law," it is time to be missionaries, and civilize the last outpost of sanctified savagery—the home. If we choose to be serious, the legitimate vehicle is the criminal justice system of law. Rembar says:

"The kind of law to which this habit of obedience is directed is usually the criminal law. It carries a higher charge of moral sanction than the civil law. We have one sort of accustomed response where conduct is declared a crime, another where its only consequence is a civil liberty." And certainly, one might add, a far different one where the only consequence is a counseling liability either directed exclusively toward the victim, or implicating the victim.

About treating wife-assault as a crime, Law Professor Raymond Parnas writes:

> Simply put, we must go with what we know. And we know that we cannot ignore or condone acts or threats of imminent violence. We know that the police are best

equipped to protect others and themselves. We know how to punish, whether by fine, incapacitation, other denials of full liberty, embarrassment, inconvenience, etc. And we know punishment is a clear statement of the personal responsibility of the offender and the condemnation and retribution of society. We also know that where punishment is to be imposed, the criminal process provides the best safeguards that such punishment is imposed on the appropriate person under the most adequate circumstances. We know that incapacitation prevents repetition during the period of incarceration. Finally I submit that we are increasingly coming to believe that punishment, quickly, fairly, proportionately and appropriately imposed, may deter or reduce the quality and quantity of some kinds of bad conduct as least as well, if not better, than attempts at speculative therapy. . . .

Surely this is a meaningful consideration where we largely have men who have no *other* criminal proclivities; who would not in any *other* way risk social censure.

There is no question that there are real procedural and evidentiary problems to be addressed. But the fact that they exist (and can probably be solved—as well as most evidentiary problems are solved) should not be used to obscure the fact that the substantive issue—the issue of the rights we possess, once within the family, and the duties each must accept, once within the family—remain to be decided. Are crimes in the home crimes? Or are they not? Is it one's right to be protected from bodily harm and physical intrusions by those with whom you share the home? Is it a mother's duty to protect her children from her husband? Or his duty not to assault and invade them? If the former, is it a mother's right to expect society's support in that protection?

Or not?

Licensing systematic viciousness or sexual assault in the smallest unit of society has to be a danger to *our* whole society. It threatens the credibility of that unit as an institution in a country which strongly professes entirely other ideals for the society as a whole.

One does not need more evidence that many household victimizers were themselves victimized as children, or saw their mothers victimized; nor do we need more evidence that juvenile delinquents and adult criminals often come from violent homes (or cruel institutions) to show danger to the public from the private. When a child receives massive and ongoing firsthand evidence that permissions or justifications exist for brutality even toward those who are meant to be special, by those who are meant to be trusted—why should that child believe in sanctions against violence where the victimized are "only" unknown strangers?

I believe that we can re-design and re-negotiate the family covenant—the compact among intimate individuals and including the state. I believe we have the leverage to do so—if we choose. Indeed, I believe that doing so may be the only way to preserve the integrity of "the family." To maintain its credibility as a social unit deserving of commitment.

I believe, as well, that—once we understand the nature of the state's interest in "the family," and understand that, as individuals, we have a parallel but dissimilar interest in the family—there is both reason and room for bargaining. Once we understand what is served by the therapeutic "understanding" which blames the wounded, and seeks rehabilitation to get them back in the abusive home—and once we understand that all women, marrying, having children, all children being born, share the risk of victimization commonly—we can make an informed choice. And I suggest that we must do so in order to preserve any semblance of credibility about the sanctity of "the family."

I realize I have spoken only of the nuclear family. It seems to me that unless we decide about the rules governing the most commonly accepted trust relationship, there is no chance of securing protections for those with other forms of life-arrangements, other kinds of trust ties. If "prior links," "prior relationship" even within the recognized family structure constitute an exception to citizenship and its protections, then obviously so will exceptional or less-accepted forms of relationship.

Jail.

Am I suggesting that these otherwise good citizens—who are *only* criminal toward those related to and dependent on them—go to jail with the nasty people?

Oh, yes. (I know that only *some* will. Just as only some wives and mothers will choose to prosecute—either when all else has failed, or in order to secure a fact-finding sufficient to ensure their continued custody of abused children following divorce. But oh, yes.)

That, presently, is how we treat criminals (albeit very unevenly). A good re-socializing program while they're in jail would be fine in the name of preventing recidivism, in the name of our finer feelings. But not in the name of family harmony. That, where crimes have been committed, and where the only safe recourse seen by the victim is criminal justice, is bunkum. When you put a married bank robber in jail, you are certainly disrupting his family's harmony.

Crimes.

Or not crimes.

Not, however, crimes *but* not crimes. Not "sick." At best, this is a prettied-up evasion. At worst, it's an atrocity for victims and the mothers of victims.

Doctor Summit says, "The choice to use diagnosis has proved dangerous. The psychiatric examination punishes the ones with the most to lose. The one seeking help is the more cooperative partner. She goes in hoping to protect the child. She's entirely willing to confide in the psychiatrist. And she winds up being punished." Being punished *again,* and again for her trust.

I am not saying that the availability of psychological help is a bad thing—for those seeking it voluntarily—nor that practitioners collectively have evil designs on our society. Merely that its ideologies and language have become overempowered.

Chief Justice David L. Bazelon, United States Court of Appeals for the District of Columbia, has written:

Psychiatrists are also asked by institutions (communities, schools, the military, the courts, prisons and industry to name a few) to administrate, label and sometimes treat individuals for institutional purposes—for example, to suppress deviance which is detrimental to the institution. This perversion of the traditional medical model of patient care raises conflicts for the psychiatrist between the individual's and the institution's interests, and often carries him beyond his acknowledged expertise. This cannot be blamed on the psychiatric profession. Rather, it reflects society's reluctance to create adequate social or legal mechanisms to deal with the problems we dump in psychiatry's lap. We prefer to assume that by labelling the process "medical" and its results "treatment" we can convert coercion into benevolence and deprivation into help.

"Sick," then, also sets up some open-ended machinery for circumventing civil protections which need not be confined to matters of family.

An open declaration of expectations must be made to women. What will gain a mother praise and support from society and the law, should her husband prove to be unsocialized or unsocializable; should he abuse her, or abuse their children? What do we *expect*? That she leave? That she stay? That she go into therapy? That she kill him? (If the law will not help her, if she is outside its borders—is it legitimate to condemn her for what she does to help herself or her children?)

If we despise a woman who would choose a man over her children, then the system must support her in making the alternate choice.

Why did she stay? Why did she let him? Why did she provoke him? Why didn't she stop him? Why did she trust him? This leads, by implication, to why did she marry him? And—given that there is no telling in advance which individual may take advantage of the tacit permission to physically abuse or sexually assault within the home—it leads then to why did she marry? Better to ask why, presently, normal and otherwise law-abiding men are not held accountable by society for gross injury in the home. And consequently do not see themselves as accountable. And (consequently) see the behavior as justifiable.

Faced with the fact that, marrying, women become liable for a male's unpredictable behavior in the home, and even in the face of conscription, I would choose to go to Canada. If there were a Canada for women, or for children.

There is now an attempt to shift from therapeutic control to religious control. We face, however, not a dramatic change, but rather one of style and language. The language of repression is simply less agreeable than the language of scientific, psychologized enlightenment.

A resurgence of interest in the doctrine that children are born sinners, with wills that need to be broken, testifies to the fact that these moral values could be quickly and cost-effectively re-tooled to religious values. The Family Protection Act (S 1378, H.R. 3955) was introduced in the Senate by Senators Jepsen, Laxalt, Garn, and Hatch (and in the House, by Representatives Siljander, Dannemeyer, Jeffries, Dan Crane, Hansen, McDonald, and Phil Crane) in the summer of 1981. Section 104 (c) would change the definition of child abuse to specifically exclude discipline or corporal punishment of a minor or any person designated by a parent with authority over the child. Section 501 is headed, "No Federal Regulation of Religious Institutions." In capsule:

> This section prohibits the federal government from imposing on any church-related child care center, orphanage, foster home, social action training program, shelters for abused spouses or children, or juvenile delinquency or drug treatment center any requirements with respect to admission, policies, instructional or methodological hiring or selection of employees, or staff or operating procedures.

God knows what the agenda is for "abused spouses." But there are already 3,000 establishments, profit or non-profit, handling an estimated 300,000 American kids; the abused, the neglected, the runaway-status offender, the unplaceable, the unwanted. . . . Any one of them could become church-related overnight without missing a beat, or—for those already so inclined—changing a beating.

These institutions represent incarceration, often forcible incarceration—with no escape, and no appeal. The founder of one such establishment said on TV (ironically, in light of Jackie's case),

> If you go into a hospital and you don't want to stay there, all you have to do is make an aggressive gesture at a nurse and you're kicked out. All you have to do is light your bed on fire and you're kicked out. So consequently kids learn how to get out of treatment. At Elan the first thing they learn is, you're not gonna get out of here. . . . You know, no matter how many times you run away, we will go and get you. . . .

Called residential treatment facilities, group homes, therapeutic communities, private schools, boys' and girls' ranches, those that are secular can justify any regimen as therapeutic or as teaching or enforcing "moral values." A simple repositioning from the (for instance) behavior-mod/therapeutic, to the religious would entirely exempt them, under the new legislation, from guidelines and scrutiny.

And, of course, some religious institutions are already in place. Periodically, war stories emerge: allegations of beatings or one sort of torment or another. These are rebutted with the claim that they are necessary to the teaching of spiritual values.

It can be quite a challenge, then, to distinguish the traditional from the innovative and therapeutic sometimes, certainly where both feel licensed to use brutal force, and both are licensed to incarcerate children indefinitely, and both do so in the name of a higher moral or spiritual good.

We face the literal de-criminalization of child abuse (so long as it is called discipline or corporal punishment). The open dismissal of the plight of the battered woman (by alluding, for instance, to a victim who flees as a "runaway wife"). We face the explicit legitimization of the family as an appropriate arena for barbarism. The open declaration that a victim's rebellion is insurgency.

About the current "pro-family" forces, Wes McCune, Director of Group Research, a Washington, D.C., organization that has been following the activities of the right wing for years, said at a meeting of Planned Parenthood in February, 1981, "The alliance between right wing single-issue anti-abortion groups has become an effective coalition. That coalition has pre-empted the right to use the term 'family.' They stole it right away from you. They got it. And I don't know how you will ever get it back."

Well. Perhaps by calling for law and order in the home. (Odd, isn't it?) Calling for rules against criminal behavior, and enforcement of those rules; and—where no viable parent remains to a child-victim—making that child's care and placement a priority; assuring that child protection of his most fundamental rights, with a vigor commensurate with his greater vulnerability—in order to restore credibility to "the family."

Failing the introduction of serious bottom-line rules, and failing that respect for individual rights is triggered by the infraction of those rules, present efforts to define a "person" as human life from the moment of inception are bitterly comical. In light of what is, this means that the fetus will have rights as a citizen of the womb, most of which it will lose immediately upon becoming a citizen of the home.

The fetus's life and well-being are protected. His property— that is, his mother—is also secured. On birth, the rules change. All kinds of restrictions, rejections, abuses, and punishments may be heaped upon him by those who hold his care in trust, and his rights in escrow. Legally, on his own, he has no property, or even right to life. He can be dumped on the state as beyond control, or placed in a mental institution, should a parent or the state as guardian volunteer to do so. Not dumped, he can be maimed or sexually molested. The most he can effect is his own stigmatizing removal to another home, or to an institution. The problem he has, becomes the problem he *is*.

He will not recover any kind of comfortable control of the

physical integrity of his person, or simple protection of his rights again for eighteen to twenty-one years.

If our young fertilized-egg-citizen gets wise, he will hire lobbyists to work for legislation to protect his right to remain in the womb for eighteen to twenty-one years.

There is a difference between tender-hearted and tender-minded. There are limits to "mine," as in "my" husband, "my" wife, "my" child, and "my" parent.

Abuse and abandonment are not part of a perfect childhood. Assault and rape are not part of a viable marriage. Emotional, religious, and moral neglect have no business triggering state intervention. Psychological abuse is scarcely definable and about as legislatable as bickering or the withholding of affection. What needs protecting in serious instances is not family harmony, but the person and the rights of the victimized individual.

In criminalizing household felonies, vengeance, retribution, and even offender-rehabilitation are negligible factors. The major goal is to restore the victim's individual identity, and activate due protections.

> . . . the most important role of the criminal law and its most important business, is to protect individuals from unconsented to and unjustified physical invasions of their persons (to protect each of us from forcible physical harm by others) by preventing such conduct. Crimes like intentional and reckless homicide, forcible rape, aggravated assault, and robbery are our most basic crimes. These are crimes that threaten our safety and security.

I would add sexual molestation of a child.

It is certainly true that the criminal justice system is dominated by centuries of male bias in its standards. It is also true that it is subject to public scrutiny and public pressure to change.

In 1977, when a storm of protest arose because Wisconsin

circuit court Judge Archie Simonson said that a teenage boy
accused of rape was only "reacting normally" to temptation—
the judge was ousted in the next election. More recently, another Wisconsin judge described a rape victim as "an unusually
sexually promiscuous young lady." As the *Washington Post*
reported, "The young lady was 5 years old." The assailant in
this case, the mother's boyfriend, was alleged by the judge
to have been victimized by the child. He "just did not know
enough to knock off her advances." Ultimately, the judge imposed a 90-day sentence only because the offender had tried
to lie to him. The judge said, "I think if he would have come
in and admitted to me that he did this thing, he would have
walked out that very day on the street under probation."

This stirred the citizens to outrage. It stirred groups to move
to recall the judge.

Most district attorneys are elected.

Most judges are elected.

The police are subject to public pressure and outcry. They
take seriously what is popularly and politically taken seriously.

Assistant District Attorney Jeanine Pirro has been running a one-of-a-kind Domestic Violence Unit in Westchester
County, New York, since 1978. She has done extensive prosecuting and extensive police training on both wife abuse and child
abuse. She says, "The cops are victims of society's prejudices.
If they get no backing in the justice system, what are they
supposed to do? If they get the message that, 'The D.A.'s not
going to take the case,' they won't bother."

The police, D.A.'s, judges, and politicians can be made re-
sponsive to a decision on the part of the public to seriously
censure felonious household behaviors. And the criminal justice
system, unlike the socio-legal system, is open to scrutiny.

But.

Arguments are piled up against criminalizing household violence like furniture piled to a door against an intruder. Sometimes it seems like all the furniture in the house. Some are
the old arguments defending the "progress" represented by

the therapeutic state. The "inappropriateness" of punishment. The inadequacy of sanctions, etc. Some border on the absurd, the "psychological injury" which will be done to the offender, the "counter-productiveness" of jail-time to family harmony.

Some, if they are flatly so, as presented, are enough to subvert any credibility lingering in the institution of "the family," or the home as a place where you're still in this country.

For example: In "inter-spousal violence," the law "has met its match." The law, as this one paper argues, has known for ages that these things were so common as to represent an inevitability. Hence, the author says, "the allegation that a particular spouse was physically abused" made the phrase "he beat me on and about the head" a trite pleading, because it was encountered so often.

The argument continues that apart from police and prosecutorial reluctance, prosecuting will bring further violence, loss of income by the incarceration (as though divorce would ensure a continuation of income). And anyhow, you only get light penalties, and civil protection orders don't work. Also, short of homicide, who's to say violence is not an appropriate way of dealing with "the strains of daily living?" Nor does treatment work because batterers are unmotivated and there's no leverage. What we have here, according to this line of thought, is a social problem of such stunning intransigence that nothing can be done criminally, civilly, or therapeutically. Hang out the sign: Pass At Your Own Risk.

Other arguments are contradictory:

The offending provider will do jail time—vs. you'll never get a conviction.

The criminal justice system is cumbersome, ham-handed, ineffectual, and women won't prosecute. Followed by—they'll prosecute falsely, out of spite and vengeance.

Children won't testify, or the system will traumatize them— followed by: they'll make up stories in their eagerness to go to court with their "fantasies."

And then, of course, you get, *but:* it will cost money.

I've got a good idea.

Suppose, in keeping with present theory and sentiment, we appeal to the private sector.

If, as I suggest, lending dignity and support to individuals who chance to become victims while performing service as a member of the family, is to the greater good of preserving the image of "the family"—why not encourage private contributions? Make these *very* beneficially tax-deductible.

A contribution to a battered woman's refuge, for instance, would then give you a substantial tax advantage. So, for donors, as well as for victims, we would be providing battered wife "shelters." (The logic of current economics is difficult, but I think I am learning.)

There are arguments which are not just piled-up defenses against the bogeyman. One, put forth by lawyers who would keep child abuse within the juvenile justice jurisdiction, is the higher standard of evidence necessary in criminal court—the need for proof beyond a reasonable doubt, rather than a preponderance of evidence.

I take this as deserving of serious and skilled attention (should we decide to pay such attention), not, however, as an ipso facto roadblock.

> Under our criminal justice system, the state accepts the burden of proving beyond a reasonable doubt the guilt of one accused of crime. In civil litigation, on the other hand, it is generally accepted that the verdict may rest upon a preponderance of evidence.
>
> We make this distinction because, whereas in civil litigation the effect of error in fact-finding ordinarily is of no greater severity to either party, in a criminal prosecution the accused ". . . has at stake an interest of transcending value . . ." i.e., his liberty.

The bizarre result of not threatening the liberty of the *offender* in child-assault or child-sexual-assault, is that what is presently threatened is the liberty of the *victim*. And certainly it can be argued that the severity of an error in fact-finding in both wife-assault and child-assault, where the non-offending parent seeks divorce is very great indeed where she risks losing partial

or full custody; where the child may continue to be at part-
or full-time risk.

Another argument raised against prosecuting child abuse
is the absence of criminal intent. This is somewhat circular
unless the criminality of child abuse is defined. One lawyer–
author comments on a case where a five-year-old child was
held down on a bed and his genitals were burnt with a red
hot screwdriver. The trial court convicted the custodian of
"assault with the intent to inflict grievous bodily harm." On
appeal the verdict was reversed to "common assault" since
the intent to inflict grievous bodily harm was not shown. With
respect, the nature of the weapon and the place of injury hardly
left room for doubt as to the intention.

A considerable number of wife-batterers and paternal child
molesters say they did not know they were doing anything
wrong. Does this correspond to a plea of insanity under the
M'Naughten rule that "at the time of the committing of the
act, the party accused (must be) labouring under such a defect
of reason, from disease of the mind, as not to know the nature
and quality of the act he was doing or if he did know it, that
he did not know he was doing what was wrong." Or would
it make more sense to plead that it was not common knowledge—that there was no fair warning—that such things were
criminally, seriously wrong?

There is, as I've said, no question that there are problems—
the solving of which depends, I believe, on our general will
to do so.

One way, or the other.
Jan Samuels says:

> At the final court hearing recently, my ex- was granted
> unsupervised custody. The last psychiatric expert called
> in by the court decided George probably wasn't abusing
> the kids because he was normal, although he might be
> doing it. But it was more likely that I was over-stimulating
> them—because I was normal. He concluded that—since

I was normal—if George was really abusing the kids, I
would have done the normal thing. I would have taken
them and run. Or I would have killed him.

(Curious. That the two "normal" solutions to the discovery of
ongoing molestation are both seriously against the law.) She
continues, "In any case, I must add that if I were to kill at
this point, it would be mass murder."

Under our present management-policy toward crimes in
the home, a certain murderousness, a certain madness, is an
appropriate response.

I suggest, current trends notwithstanding, we will have a
chance to choose again. And I hope then we will not allow
ourselves to be diverted by benign language and others' interests, or stymied by the "horizon effect." The horizon effect,
as described by scientists interested in computer programming
of backgammon, is where "the program searches deeply
enough to discover a difficulty in the play but then acts as if
the difficulty did not exist."

It notices the difficulty, but it postpones it by taking another
tack, doing something else, setting up moves which are irrele-
vant to the solution of the problem. "Since all the branches
are investigated to the same depth, the search is terminated
before the problem is discovered in that particular branch.
As a result the program acts as though it has permanently
avoided the difficulty."

Liberal goals, like equal rights, equal parenting, children's
rights—as well as conservative ones like restoring faith in "the
family"—cannot achieve a solid rest without a decision for, a
commitment to, something more basic: the right, within the
context of the family—as well as outside it—of each individual
to Equal Protection under the Law.

Notes

Preface: Some Preliminaries

P. xii. ". . . tip of the iceberg." Murray A. Straus, Richard J. Gelles, and Suzanne Steinmetz, *Behind Closed Doors, Violence in the American Family* (New York: Anchor Press/Doubleday, 1980), p. 4.

P. xii. "between one in four and one in three." Straus, Gelles, and Steinmetz, *Behind Closed Doors*, p. 32.

P. xii. "3.4 and 4 million children." Straus, Gelles, and Steinmetz, *Behind Closed Doors*, p. 62.

P. xii. "1.4 and 2.3 million children . . . 'beaten up.'" Straus, Gelles, and Steinmetz, *Behind Closed Doors*, p. 62.

P. xii. "900,000 and 1.8 million children . . . knife or gun." Straus, Gelles, and Steinmetz, *Behind Closed Doors*, p. 62.

P. xii. "half . . . abused in some other way." Jeanne M. Giovannoni and Rosina M. Becerra, *Defining Child Abuse* (New York: The Free Press, 1979), p. 222.

P. xii. "or had their hair pulled out." "Intimate Victims: A Study of Violence Among Friends and Relatives; A National Crime Survey Report," SD-NCJ-N-14, NCJ-62319 (U.S. Department of Justice, Bureau of Justice Statistics), pp. 1, 13, 45.

P. xii. "or play bondage games." Roberta Thyfault, "Childhood Sexual Abuse, Marital Rape, and Battered Women: Implications for Mental Health Workers," paper for Colorado Mental Health Conference, Keystone, Colo., October 24, 1980, p. 3.

P. xiii. ". . . divorce and moved out." "Intimate Victims," p. 16.

P. xiii. "neglect . . . 'unfit parent' . . . 'depravity.'" "Child Sexual Abuse, Legal Issues and Approaches," A Monograph by the National Legal Resource Center for Child Advocacy and Protection, American Bar Association, Young Lawyers Division (Washington, D.C., September 1980), p. 7.

P. xiii. "and the abuse continues." Roland Summit, M.D., "Recognition and Treatment of Child Sexual Abuse," from a chapter to be published in

213

Preface: Some Preliminaries (*Cont.*)

Providing for the Emotional Health of the Pediatric Patient, ed. Charles E. Hollingsworth (New York: Spectrum Publishers), ms. p. 30: "Mothers who leave a sexually abusive husband may go bankrupt trying to buy testimony that will challenge the father's demands for child custody." Also, Helen Singer Kaplan, M.D., Ph.D., with Terri Schultz, "The Gravity of Incest," *Savvy,* March 1981, p. 91: "Some fathers homosexually molest little boys, their own sons, as well. In a custody case that recently came to my attention, the mother wanted protection for her son because each weekend when the boy saw his father, the father made him have oral sex! The child was about six years old and the father's attorney tried to say there was no harm in it!"

P. xiii. ". . . remarries or moves away." "Intimate Victims," p. 16.

P. xiii. "greater and sometimes deadly force." E.g., "Homicide is a last resort, and it most often occurs when men simply will not quit. As one woman testified at her murder trial, 'It seemed like the more I tried to get away, the harder he beat me.' Gloria Timmons left her husband, but he kept tracking her down, raping and beating her; finally when he attacked her with a screwdriver, she shot him. Patricia Evans filed for divorce, but her husband kept coming back to beat her with a dog chain, pistol-whip her, and shoot at her." Ann Jones, *Women Who Kill* (New York: Holt, Rinehart, and Winston, 1980), p. 298.

P. xiii. animals let enemies go free. Anthony Storr, Introduction to *Family Violence: An International and Interdisciplinary Study,* ed. John M. Eekelaar and Sanford N. Katz (Toronto: Butterworths, 1978), p. 5.

P. xiii. ". . . threaten her with a wrench." "Intimate Victims," p. 16.

P. xiv. ". . . and charged with his murder." Angela Brown (Battered Women's Research Center, Denver, Colo.), "High Risk Lethality Factors in Abusive Relationships," paper presented at the Colorado Mental Health Conference, Keystone, Colo., October 25, 1980, pp. 4–5.

P. xiv. ". . . in the stomach again." Sue E. Eisenberg and Patricia L. Micklow, "The Assaulted Wife: 'Catch-22' Revisited," *Women's Rights Law Reporter* 3, (1977), p. 139.

P. xiv. "more acute during pregnancy . . . first pregnancy." See Straus, Gelles, and Steinmetz, *Behind Closed Doors,* pp. 43, 44, 176, 187; Lenore E. Walker, *The Battered Woman* (New York: Harper & Row, 1979), p. 105; Eisenberg and Micklow, "The Assaulted Wife," p. 144; Vicki D. Boyd and Karen Klingbeil, "Battered Women: The Everyday Crime," paper presented at August 1977 National Meeting of the Psychological Association's panel on Domestic Violence, p. 4. Some researchers have referred to this phenomenon as "pre-natal child abuse." It sounds as much, if not more, like sibling rivalry.

P. xv. ". . . all socioeconomic lines." E.g., Straus, Gelles, and Steinmetz, *Behind Closed Doors,* p. 31.

P. xv. "he *was* the household." For father's total ownership of children

Preface: Some Preliminaries (*Cont.*)

see, e.g., Mason P. Thomas, Jr., "Child Abuse and Neglect, Part I: Historical Overview, Legal Matrix and Social Perspectives," *North Carolina Law Review* 50 (1972), pp. 293–300. For total ownership of wives, see, e.g., R. Emerson Dobash and Russell Dobash, *Violence Against Wives* (New York: The Free Press, 1979), pp. 36–47.

P. xv. ". . . chastise her the harder." G. G. Coulton, *Medieval Panorama: The English Scene from Conquest to Reformation* (New York: W. W. Norton and Co., 1938), p. 615.

P. xv. ". . . unto Christ his head." Coulton, *Medieval Panorama*, p. 615.

P. xv. ". . . private law of Rome." Monroe L. Inker and Charlotte Anne Peretta, "A Child's Right to Counsel in Custody Cases," in *The Youngest Minority I: Lawyers in Defense of Children*, ed. Sanford N. Katz (American Bar Association, 1974) p. 33 (citing 8 *Harvard Law Review* 39, at 41, 1894).

P. xvi. "father, cattle, mother, children." Patrick R. Tamilia, "Neglect Proceedings and the Conflict Between Law and Social Work," *Duquesne Law Review* 9, no. 573 (1971), p. 579.

P. xvi. "it didn't count." See Florence Rush, *The Best Kept Secret: Sexual Abuse of Children* (Englewood Cliffs, N.J.: Prentice-Hall, 1980), pp. 17–19.

P. xvi. "copulation had taken place." Rush, *The Best Kept Secret*, pp. 32–33.

P. xvi. "restraining her by domestic chastisement." Sir William Blackstone, quoted in Dobash and Dobash, *Violence Against Wives*, p. 61.

P. xvi. "conected with a Tyrant." Mary Beth Norton, *Liberty's Daughters: The Revolutionary Experience of American Women, 1750–1800* (Boston: Little, Brown and Co., 1980), p. 44.

P. xvi. "condemned by statute." Elizabeth Pleck, "Wife-Beating in Nineteenth Century America," *Victimology* 1 (1979), p. 63.

P. xvi. "immigrants and blacks." Pleck, "Wife-Beating in Nineteenth Century America," pp. 65–66.

P. xvii. "failed to cook his breakfast." Carl N. Degler, *At Odds: Women and the Family in America from the Revolution to the Present* (New York: Oxford University Press, 1980), pp. 170–71.

P. xvii. "committed to an insane asylum." Because it is focal to the remainder of the book, I emphasize here the convenient role of "mental illness" in disposing of victims of household offenses. "Both in England and in the colonies where Blackstone's prestige was even higher than in his own country, wives were deprived of almost all rights. In the United States, it was easy to get rid of a troublesome wife by having her committed to an insane asylum." Amaury de Riencourt, *Sex and Power in History* (New York: Dell Publishing Co., 1974), p. 307. "The 1851 Illinois commitment statute, for example, provided that married women and infants who, in the judgement of the medical superintendents of the state asylum at Jacksonville, are evidently insane or distracted 'may be entered or detained at the request of the husband or the

Preface: Some Preliminaries *(Cont.)*

guardian of the infant, without the evidence in other cases.'" Nicholas N. Kittrie, *The Right to Be Different: Deviance and Enforced Therapy* (Baltimore: The Johns Hopkins University Press, 1971), p. 64.

P. xvii. "kidnapped . . . and returned to the father." Pleck, "Wife-Beating in Nineteenth Century America," pp. 68–69.

P. xviii. ". . . away on a distant journey." Coulton, *Medieval Panorama*, p. 614.

P. xviii. ". . . mistress of every house." John Stuart Mill, *The Subjection of Women* (1869; reprint ed., London: Dent, 1955), cited in Dobash and Dobash, *Violence Against Wives*, p. 69.

P. xix. ". . . 55 percent . . . were males." Giovannoni and Becerra, *Defining Child Abuse*, p. 235 n.

1. The Combat Zone

P. 2. "convinced their wives mean to leave them." See, e.g., Del Martin, "Battered Women: Society's Problem," in *The Victimization of Women*, (vol. 3 in *Sage Yearbooks in Women's Policy Studies*), ed. Jane Roberts Chapman and Margaret Gates (Beverly Hills: Sage Publications, 1978), p. 123. Also, "National Evaluation of the LEAA Family Violence Demonstration Program, First Interim Report: History and Development" (San Francisco: The URSA Institute, January 1980), p. 19: "All programs reported difficulties in enforceing (sic) diversion directives regardless of when and by whom (DA vs judge) these are issued. Difficulties stem, in part, from the fact that divertees often refuse to participate in the program. Staff noted that abusers often disclaim responsibility for domestic violence and therefore see no reason to participate in counseling."

P. 2. ". . . my wife and my daughters." Kee MacFarlane, "Sexual Abuse of Children," in Chapman and Gates, *The Victimization of Women*, p. 90. . . . doing her a favor." Phil Donahue, transcript #11099, November 9, 1979, WGN-TV, Chicago, Ill. Also see "The Police Perspective in Child Abuse and Neglect" (Gaithersburg, Md: International Association of Chiefs of Police, September 1977), p. 8: "Incest usually has taken place over a long period of time, from six months to several years. According to one study, fathers confronted with detection frequently deny the incest or if they admit it, attempt to minimize their guilt, and often express surprise that incest is punishable by law. They frequently insist that they have done nothing wrong; some fathers believe sexual access to be one of their parental rights."

P. 3. definition of aggravated assault. Sir Leon Radzinowicz and Marvin E. Wolfgang, eds., *Crime and Justice, Vol. I: The Criminal in Society*, 2nd Rev. Ed. (New York: Basic Books, 1971), p. 77.

P. 3. child abuse "de-criminalized." Douglas J. Besherov, "The Legal Aspects of Reporting Known and Suspected Child Abuse," *Villanova Law Review* 23, no. 3 (1977–78), p. 493: "The handling of child maltreatment now has been almost completely de-criminalized."

Preface: Some Preliminaries (*Cont.*)

P. 3. "criminal justice system . . . inappropriate." Susan Forward, M.S.W., and Craig Buck, *Betrayal of Innocence: Incest and Its Devastation* (Los Angeles: J. P. Tarcher, 1978), p. 145.

P. 3. "keep the abusive family intact." Forward and Buck, *Betrayal of Innocence*, p. 145.

P. 3. "The Battered Child Syndrome." Kempe, Silverman, Steele, Droegmoller, and Silver, "The Battered-Child Syndrome," *Journal of the American Medical Association* 17 (1962), 181.

P. 3. "medical aspects . . . emphasized . . . legal aspects . . . played down." For an excellent political analysis of the response to child abuse, see Barbara J. Nelson, "Setting the Public Agenda: The Case of Child Abuse," in *The Policy Cycle*, ed. Judith V. May and Aaron S. Wildavsky (Beverly Hills: Sage Publications, 1978), pp. 17–41.

P. 3. "emotional neglect." Michael F. Sullivan, "Child Neglect: The Environmental Aspects," *Ohio Law Journal* 29, p. 103 n.: "In addition to the usual catch-all clauses, general moral catch-all clauses are found in 40 state statutes, and many states have more than one. Under these a child is neglected who is in a situation or environment injurious to his morals (Alabama, Alaska, Arizona, Georgia, Indiana, Minnesota, Mississippi, Nebraska, New Hampshire, North Carolina, North Dakota, Ohio, Pennsylvania); whose home by any reason of depravity on the part of the parent is an unfit place (Alabama, California, Colorado, Florida, Hawaii, Indiana, Michigan, Montana, New Hampshire, New Mexico, North Dakota, Oklahoma, Rhode Island, South Dakota, Texas, Vermont, and Washington); whose parent is unfit by reason of immorality or depravity, to care properly for him (Maryland, South Carolina, Tennessee); who is without proper moral care (Connecticut, Idaho, Kansas, Massachusetts, Minnesota, Mississippi, New York and Wisconsin); whose parents are immoral or depraved (Connecticut, South Dakota, Texas, and Vermont); who is found in a disreputable place (Arizona, Delaware, Mississippi, New Hampshire, Ohio, and Oklahoma); or who is found living with vicious, immoral or disreputable people (Alaska, Arizona, Colorado, Delaware, District of Columbia, Iowa, Mississippi, New Hampshire, New Mexico, and Ohio)." This paper also tells us (p. 108) that a study of neglect referrals in Minneapolis–St. Paul over a two-month period "found that the problems most frequently cited in neglect complaints in order of frequency were: excessive drinking, inadequate housekeeping, illicit sex relations of parents and leaving children unattended." All this, however, was not new, but rather a further institutionalization of "justified intervention" begun in the late 1800's. (See Chapter 6.) Also Jeanne M. Giovannoni and Rosina M. Becerra, *Defining Child Abuse* (New York: The Free Press, 1979), pp. 10–11. A 1977 checklist of "things to look for" put out by the American Humane Association includes "demoralizing circumstances," "lack of dental care," "dirty, ragged (clothing) and generally in terrible disrepair." Also "denied normal experiences that produce feelings of being loved, wanted, secure, and worthy." Also "values in home conflict with society." Also "immature parents . . . failure to individual children and their needs."

Chap. 1. The Combat Zone (*Cont.*)

See also Vincent De Francis, "The Fundamentals of Child Protection: A Statement of Basic Concepts and Principles" (Englewood, Colo.: The Child Protective Division of the American Humane Association, 1978), pp. 25–27.

P. 3. "crimes in the home . . . domestic violence." See "National Evaluation of the LEAA Family Violence Demonstration Program, First Interim Report: History and Development," p. 19.

P. 4. "International Classification of Diseases." Kathleen J. Ferraro (Arizona State University, Department of Criminology), *Processing Battered Women*, unpublished study of the help provided battered women in shelters.

P. 4. "Symptom of 'family dysfunction.' " Michele Tipple, Lenore Fox, and James Downey, "Boulder County Child Sexual Abuse Treatment Program: A Community-Based Approach to Intervention and Treatment with Incestuous Families," in *Innovations in the Prosecution of Child Sexual Abuse Cases*, (Washington, D.C.: American Bar Association, National Legal Resource Center for Child Advocacy and Protection, November 1981).

P. 4. "preserve the family." E.g., "Polk County Intra-Family Sexual Abuse Program, Des Moines, Iowa," *Innovations in the Prosecution of Child Sexual Abuse Cases*, p. 89; "Boulder County Sexual Abuse Treatment Program," *Innovations*, p. 121; etc. A number of incest programs make use of the criminal justice system to gain leverage over the offender so they can coerce him into treatment. This use of the criminal justice system raises a host of other issues which cannot be covered within the scope of this book. However, with rare exception their stated goal is to preserve the family as well.

P. 4. "one divorce . . . 'normal.' " More than one-third of first marriages among the recently married are likely to end in divorce. Over one-third who divorce once and remarry are likely to divorce again. "By adding married couples who separate but never divorce to these statistics, it is likely that nearly half of all recent American marriages may be disrupted by divorce or separation." Graham B. Spanier and Elaine A. Anderson, "The Impact of the Legal System on Adjustment to Marital Separation," *Journal of Marriage and the Family* 41, no. 31 (August 1979), p. 605.

P. 4. "parents can . . . dump their children." Lee E. Teitelbaum and James W. Ellis, "The Liberty Interests of Children: Due Process Rights and Their Application," *Family Law Quarterly* 12, no. 3 (Fall 1978), p. 162.

P. 4. "retribution: criminal prosecution." E.g., Bernard M. Dickens, "Legal Responses to Child Abuse," *Family Law Quarterly* 12, no. 1 (Spring 1978), p. 7: "Sexual abuse of children by their guardians is particularly difficult to assess dispassionately. Particular instances may so outrage normal sensibilities as to trigger public, institutional and judicial reactions of repugnance themselves bordering on violence." Also, Michael Wald, "State Intervention on Behalf of 'Neglected' Children: A Search for Realistic Standards," 27 *Stanford Law Review* 985 (April 1975), p. 985. Also, "Polk County Intra-Family Sexual Abuse Program, Des Moines, Iowa" (*Innovations*, p. 85) presents this contradic-

Chap. 1. The Combat Zone (*Cont.*)

tion: "A notion began to form that the proper remedy for the offender did not always lie in extended periods of incarceration. . . . *Under the past system of handling incest cases the status of the victim as the one to be punished was illustrated by the removal from the home while the offender parent was allowed to stay with the family*" (italics mine). The evidence from the past I have found does not suggest any widespread punitive stance. It suggests, rather, that the victim was regarded as an "accomplice witness" where it did go to court. See *American Law Reports*, Annotated 74 ALR2d, pp. 710–11. For example:

State v. Kurtz (1921): "where the daughter with whom defendant was accused of having incestuous relations was 16 years of age at the time the act charged was committed, and according to her testimony she and defendant had been having illicit relations for a period of about a year before the date of such act, the court stated that she was an accomplice whose uncorroborated testimony was insufficient to uphold a conviction."

People v. Oliver (1941 Co. Ct): "the court, without expressly stating whether the act was with the consent of the daughter who was 18 years or more of age, held that she was an accomplice and her evidence must be corroborated. But it is to be noted, as possibly tending to show some sort of consent on the part of the female that she testified that the father had had sexual intercourse with her during the past 8 years, and the court said that the testimony was absolutely incredible, and that it was of the opinion that the prosecutrix was a wayward girl, and was attempting to 'hang' her father for her own delinquencies."

P. 4. letter from New York State Family Court Judge. Nanette Dembitz, "Assault Cases That Don't Belong in Criminal Court," *New York Times* A-Editorial page, January 19, 1981.

P. 5. "non-violent in all other social situations." Lenore E. Walker, *The Battered Woman* (New York: Harper & Row, 1979), p. 24.

P. 5. " 'appropriate' victim." R. Emerson Dobash and Russell Dobash, *Violence Against Wives* (New York: The Free Press, 1979), pp. 31–47.

P. 5. "71% . . . had been arrested . . ." Lenore E. Walker, "Clinical Aspects of the Battered Woman Syndrome Study," paper presented at the Colorado Mental Health Conference (Keystone, Colo., October 25, 1980), ms. p. 5.

P. 6. "light bulb unchanged." E.g., Dobash and Dobash, *Violence Against Wives*, pp. 98–101.

P. 6. "violence on TV." Lucien A. Beaulieu, "Media, Violence and the Family: A Canadian View," in *Family Violence: An International and Interdisciplinary Study*, ed. John M. Eekelaar and Sanford N. Katz (Toronto: Butterworths, 1978), p. 59.

P. 6. "total and winning contrition." Walker, *Battered Woman*, pp. 55–70.

P. 7. ". . . within manageable bounds." Arnold Gesell, M.D., and Frances

Chap. 1. The Combat Zone (*Cont.*)

I. Ilg, M.D., *Infant and Child in the Culture of Today: The Guidance of Development in Home and Nursery School* (New York: Harper & Row, 1943), p. 179.

P. 7. ". . . desire to please." Gesell and Ilg, *Infant and Child*, p. 179.

P. 7. ". . . condoning the crime." A. L. Goodhart, *English Law and the Moral Law* (London: Stevens and Sons, 1953), pp. 92, 93. Cited in Anthony M. Platt, *The Child Savers: The Invention of Delinquency* (Chicago: The University of Chicago Press, 1969), p. 155.

P. 8. ". . . to declare that stealing is forbidden." H. L. A. Hart, *Punishment and Responsibility.* Cited in Sanford J. Fox, "Philosophy and the Principle of Punishment in the Juvenile Court," in *The Youngest Minority II: Lawyers in Defense of Children*, ed. Sanford N. Katz (American Bar Association Press, 1977), p. 170. Also, Nicholas N. Kittrie, *The Right to Be Different: Deviance and Enforced Therapy* (Baltimore: The Johns Hopkins University Press, 1971), p. 405: " 'The ultimate justification of any punishment,' wrote Lord Denning, 'is not that it is a deterrent but that it is an emphatic denunciation by the community of a crime.' "

P. 8. ". . . absurd." Benjamin de Mott, "The Pro-Incest Lobby," *Psychology Today*, March 1980, pp. 11, 16.

P. 8. " 'positive or beneficial.' " For the positive and beneficial aspects alleged, see De Mott, "The Pro-Incest Lobby"; "Attacking the Last Taboo," *Time*, April 14, 1980, p. 72; and Philip Nobile, "Incest and the Last Taboo," *Penthouse*, December 1977, pp. 117, 126, 157.

P. 8. ". . . no condemnation of the behavior is intended." Michael Wald, "State Intervention on Behalf of 'Neglected' Children," p. 1024 n. 203.

P. 9. ". . . symptoms may not be manifest." Wald, "State Intervention," p. 1025. Nor is this a solitary lawyer's evaluation of sexual abuse of children within the home. See also Dickens, "Legal Responses to Child Abuse," p. 7.

P. 9. "moral condemnation." Wald, "State Intervention," p. 1027.

P. 9. ". . . not very helpful." Wald, "State Intervention," pp. 997–98.

P. 9. ". . . embedded in the social structure." Irving Tallman, "Implementation of a National Family Policy: The Role of the Social Scientist," *Journal of Marriage and the Family* 41, no. 3 (August 1979), p. 471.

P. 9. "the 'law'—as personified by judges and child welfare agencies." Michael S. Wald, "Thinking About Public Policy Toward Abuse and Neglect of Children: A Review of *Before the Best Interests of the Child,*" *Michigan Law Review* 78, no. 5 (March 1980), p. 662.

P. 10. ". . . viewed as excessive." Kittrie, *The Right to Be Different*, p. 384.

P. 10. ". . . compulsory therapeutic realm." Kittrie, *The Right to Be Different*, p. 384.

P. 10. ". . . the exercise of the state's *parens patriae* powers." Kittrie, *The Right to Be Different*, p. 46.

Chap. 1. The Combat Zone (*Cont.*)

P. 10. ". . . limiting state intervention." Kittrie, *The Right to Be Different,* p. 361.

P. 11. " 'non-judgmental' intervention." E.g., "Outrage engendered by parental violence to children is hard to contain within a precise legal formula of assault, and flows over to condemn violence done to a child's reasonable expectations of care and to his need of a protective, nurturing and stimulating home life. Legal definitions of child abuse and of children in need of care or protection have therefore gone beyond mere physical battery and are inclined to include a guardian's physical neglect endangering a child's welfare. They also range from causing positive emotional damage, such as a depressed self-image and sense of worthlessness, to giving inadequate affection or attention, so as to induce emotional deprivation and lack of opportunity to develop relationships." Dickens, "Legal Responses to Child Abuse," p. 4.

P. 11. ". . . mature and responsible adult." Henry H. Foster, Jr., and Doris Jonas Freed, "A Bill of Rights for Children," in *The Youngest Minority I,* ed. Sanford N. Katz (American Bar Association, 1974), p. 322.

P. 11. "the *state* 'should assure . . .' " J. Goldstein, A. Freud, and A. Solnit, *Beyond the Best Interests of the Child* (1973), pp. 5–6. Cited in Wald, "State Intervention," p. 987.

P. 12. ". . . future state of dangerousness." Kittrie, *The Right to Be Different,* pp. 361–62.

P. 12. "unemployment . . . stress of employment." E.g., "Brenner and others . . . think the frustration unemployed or underemployed men experience in the job market explains high assault and homicide rates. Using much the same data, however, Eyer (et al.) . . . identify violence against others with the peak in the business cycle and attribute this correlation to the relative stress in a highly competitive expansive labor market." Evan Stark, Anne Flitcraft, and William Frazier, "Medicine and Patriarchal Violence: The Social Construction of a 'Private' Event," *International Journal of Health Services* 9, no. 3 (1979), p. 479.

P. 12. "overly traditional views of marriage." Diane Hamlin, "The Nature and Extent of Spouse Assault," in *Prosecutor's Responsibility in Spouse Abuse Cases,* U.S. Department of Justice, LEAA, (Chicago: National District Attorneys Association, March 1980), p. 7. Also Barbara Star, Carol G. Clark, Karen M. Goetz, and Linda O'Malia, "Psychosocial Aspects of Wife Battering," *Social Casework,* October 1979, p. 484.

P. 12. "collusive." C. Henry Kempe and Ruth Kempe, *Child Abuse* (Cambridge, Mass.: Harvard University Press, 1970), p. 18; Ingrid K. Cooper, "Decriminalization of Incest: New Legal-Clinical Responses," in Eekelaar and Katz, *Family Violence,* pp. 518–28. Also M. Leahy, *"United States v. Bear Runner:* The Need for Corroboration in Incest Cases," *Saint Louis Law Journal* 23 (1979), p. 750.

P. 13. "allows. . . . to be committed." E.g. S1012 of the Family Court Act, cited in "The Children of the State: Child Protective Services in New

Chap. 1. The Combat Zone (*Cont.*)

York State," report by the Temporary State Commission on Child Welfare, June 1980, p. 14. The phrasing "commits or allows to be committed," or "commits or permits to be committed," is also in the child abuse tradition. In 1968, Michael F. Sullivan, "Child Neglect: The Environmental Aspects," *Ohio State Law Journal* 29, pp. 101–2: "In these excessive discipline or cruelty situations, courts frequently make the cruelty by one parent grounds for a finding that the other parent neglected the child as well, either on the theory that the passive parent failed to give the child necessary care and protection or that failure to intercede on the child's behalf is itself cruelty. This would appear to prejudice unnecessarily the passive parent's chances for custody in a later proceeding if the parent should choose to leave the neglectful spouse." Or see James L. Jenkins, Marsha K. Salus, and Gretchen L. Schultze, "Child Protective Services: A Guide for Workers" (Washington, D.C.: U.S. Department of Health, Education and Welfare, August 1979), p. 1.

P. 13. National Legal Resource Center first-draft recommendation. National Legal Resource Center for Child Advocacy and Protection (a program of the Young Lawyers Division, Washington, D.C.) draft II, of March 1982, "Recommendations for Improving Legal Intervention in Intrafamily Child Sexual Abuse Cases" amends the language to read "non-offending parent," and continues to suggest civil liability for the "non-offending parent" who "knew or had reasonable cause to believe" the sexual abuse was taking place, but recommends that the "non-offending parent" should not be held criminally responsible "unless such parent had actual knowledge of the abuse."

In a May 1982 draft, under Civil Proceedings (p. 3), among the factors to be considered are: "(1) whether the parent knew or had reasonable cause to believe the child had been abused and did nothing to prevent or stop it; (2) what actions the parent has taken to protect, support and care for the child following disclosure of the abuse; (3) whether the parent voluntarily agrees to participate in an appropriate counseling or treatment program." Under Criminal Proceedings (p. 5): "The non-offending parent should not be held criminally responsible when the offending parent commits sexual abuse upon a child, unless such parent participated in committing the abuse, or had actual knowledge of the abuse, and did nothing to prevent or stop it. Where such parent is criminally liable, therapeutic dispositions should be authorized."

P. 13. ". . . specialized treatment program." ABA, Draft I.

P. 14. "naive." Richard Gelles, review of *Violence Against Wives* by R. Emerson Dobash and Russell Dobash, in *Society* 16, no. 6 (September 10, 1980).

P. 14. "zero in the 1960's." "Not one article on domestic violence appeared in *The Journal of Marriage and the Family* between 1939–1969." Evan Stark.

P. 15. "Battered Husband Syndrome . . . finally 12 million men." Ann Jones, *Women Who Kill*, (New York: Holt, Rinehart and Winston, 1980), pp. 300–301.

Chap. 1. The Combat Zone *(Cont.)*

P. 15. "The Woozle Effect." Beverly Houghton, "Review of Research on Woman Abuse," paper presented at the annual meeting of the American Society of Criminology, Philadelphia, November 1979. Cited in Richard J. Gelles, "Violence in the Family: A Review of Research in the Seventies," *Journal of Marriage and the Family* 42, no. 4 (November 1980), p. 880.

2. The Abuse of the Psychological

P. 16. "well-documented." Ralph Blumenthal. "Subtleties in Origin of Master's Theories Sought in Documents," *New York Times*, August 18, 1981, pp. C1–C2; Blumenthal, "Did Freud's Isolation, Peer Rejection Prompt Key Theory Reversal?" *New York Times*, August 25, 1981, pp. C1–C2; David Gelman, "Finding the Hidden Freud," *Newsweek*, November 30, 1981, pp. 64–70; Milton Klein and David Tribich, "On Freud's Blindness," *Colloquium* 2, no. 2 (December 1979), pp. 52–59; Joseph J. Peters, M.D., "Children Who Are Victims of Sexual Assault and the Psychology of Offenders," *American Journal of Psychotherapy* 30, no. 3 (July 1976), pp. 398–432; Florence Rush, *The Best Kept Secret: Sexual Abuse of Children* (Englewood Cliffs, N.J.: Prentice-Hall, 1980), especially chap. 7, "A Freudian Coverup," pp. 80–104; Judith Lewis Herman, *Father-Daughter Incest* (Cambridge, Mass: Harvard University Press, 1981), pp. 9–11; Roland Summit, M.D., "Recognition and Treatment of Child Sexual Abuse," to be published in *Providing for the Emotional Health of the Pediatric Patient*, ed. Charles E. Hollingsworth (New York: Spectrum Publishers, 1982), ms. pp. 24–30.

P. 17. "vengeful fantasies." Summit, "Recognition and Treatment of Child Sexual Abuse," p. 25.

P. 17. ". . . listening . . . to himself." Rush, "The Freudian Cover-up," *Chrysallis* 1, no. 1, p. 39.

P. 17. "not been beaten enough or not at all." Klein and Tribich, "On Freud's Blindness," p. 52.

P. 18. "going mad again." William G. Niederland, M.D., *The Schreber Case: Psychoanalytic Profile of a Paranoid Personality* (New York: Quadrangle/New York Times Book Co., 1974), p. 14.

P. 18. "fleetingly made little men." Niederland, *The Schreber Case*, pp. 16, 17, 19, 25, 78, ff.

P. 18. "miracles." Niederland, *The Schreber Case*, pp. 17, 19, 27, 60, 61 ff.

P. 18. ". . . must be somewhere." Niederland, *The Schreber Case*, p. 82.

P. 18. miracles enumerated. Niederland, *The Schreber Case*, p. 82.

P. 18. ". . . degree unsurpassed by any female." Niederland, *The Schreber Case*, p. 20.

P. 18. ". . . transferred into a woman." Niederland, *The Schreber Case*, p. 24.

Chap. 2. The Abuse of the Psychological (*Cont.*)

P. 18. "unmanned." Morton Schatzman, *Soul Murder: Persecution in the Family* (New York: Random House, 1973), p. 95.

P. 19. "displaced version of Daniel Paul's father." Sigmund Freud, M.D., L.L.D., *Collected Papers*, vol. III in *The International Psychoanalytic Library*, ed. Ernest Jones, M.D., trans. Alix and James Strachey (London: The Hogarth Press, 1953), pp. 436, 437. Also Schatzman, *Soul Murder*, pp. 18–19.

P. 19. ". . . familiar ground of the father-complex." Niederland, *The Schreber Case*, pp. 41, 69. Also Freud, *Collected Papers*, p. 440.

P. 19. ". . . demanding it from him." Freud, *Collected Papers*, pp. 440–41.

P. 19. ". . . soul-voluptuousness." Schatzman, *Soul Murder*, pp. 96–97.

P. 19. ". . . autistic, and ambivalent." Eugene Bleuler (1950) quoted about Daniel Paul in Schatzman, *Soul Murder*, p. 8.

P. 19. "salvation of future generations." Schatzman, *Soul Murder*, p. 15.

P. 20. "he himself used." Schatzman, *Soul Murder*, p. 15.

P. 20. ". . . upon his contemporaries." Schatzman, *Soul Murder*, p. 16.

P. 20. ". . . of their contemporaries." Niederland, *The Schreber Case*, p. 5.

P. 20. ". . . all the 'higher things' of life." Niederland, *The Schreber Case*, p. 63.

P. 20. ". . . live and die for his task." Schatzman, *Soul Murder*, pp. 154–55.

P. 20. "*love* of the people." Schatzman, *Soul Murder*, p. 155.

P. 20. "cooked up as practice in his home." Schatzman, *Soul Murder*, p. 10. Also Niederland, *The Schreber Case*, p. 50.

P. 20. "medically licensed sadist." Niederland, *The Schreber Case*, p. 70: "a father whose sadism may have been but thinly disguised under a veneer of medical, reformatory, religious, and philanthropic ideas." Also p. 57: "strong sadistic components in Dr. Schreber's personality."

P. 20. "breaking the child's will." E.g., "Niederland, *The Schreber Case*, p. 65: "Dr. Schreber's educational principles directed toward radically crushing 'the child's crude nature' from the earliest age, by means of verbal admonishments, mechanical restraints, and bodily punishment" were designed to achieve "a state of complete submissiveness in all children before they reach their fifth or sixth year of life."

P. 21. ". . . submission to government." *Settlements to Society: 1584–1763*, vol. I in *A Documentary History of American Life*, ed. Jack P. Greene (New York: McGraw-Hill Book Co., 1966), p. 306.

P. 21. ". . . train of evil consequences." *Settlements to Society*, p. 306.

Chap. 2. The Abuse of the Psychological (*Cont.*)

P. 21. ". . . the truth from them?" Anita Schorsch, *Images of Childhood: An Illustrated Social History* (New York: Mayflower Books, 1979), p. 156.

P. 21. ". . . threaten the very structure of modern society." Schorsch, *Images of Childhood*, p. 156.

P. 21. ". . . until the child finally obeyed." Robert Sunley, "Early Nineteenth-Century American Literature on Child Rearing," in *Childhood in Contemporary Culture*, ed. Margaret Mead and Martha Wolfenstein (Chicago: The University of Chicago Press, 1955), p. 160.

P. 22. ". . . belongs to the father." Schatzman, *Soul Murder*, pp. 17–18.

P. 22. ". . . immutably planted in him." Schatzman, *Soul Murder*, pp. 21–22.

P. 22. "three times a day." Niederland, *The Schreber Case*, p. 71.

P. 22. ". . . calms down or falls asleep." Schatzman, *Soul Murder*, p. 29.

P. 23. ". . . impure motive is removed." Schatzman, *Soul Murder*, p. 33.

P. 23. "hour of reckoning." Niederland, *The Schreber Case*, p. 56.

P. 23. "actual barbarisms." Niederland, *The Schreber Case*, pp. 74–84.

P. 23. ". . . front of the shoulders." Schatzman, *Soul Murder*, p. 46.

P. 23. "moving in his sleep." Schatzman, *Soul Murder*, p. 46.

P. 23. "hair was pulled." Schatzman, *Soul Murder*, p. 49.

P. 23. "mouth held shut." Niederland, *The Schreber Case*, p. 77.

P. 24. ". . . only through noble battling." Schatzman, *Soul Murder*, p. 22.

P. 24. ". . . if it became erect." Schatzman, *Soul Murder*, pp. 118–19.

P. 24. ". . . or bed." Schatzman, *Soul Murder*, p. 119.

P. 24. "surgical treatment." Schatzman, *Soul Murder*, p. 119.

P. 25. "arm-waving sideways." Schatzman, *Soul Murder*, pp. 82–83.

P. 25. "water enema." Niederland, *The Schreber Case*, p. 19. Daniel Paul also believed in the "miracling-up of the urge to shit."

P. 25. "in cold water." Schatzman, *Soul Murder*, p. 83.

P. 25. " 'miraclings-up' . . . sexual 'miracles' an exception." E.g. Schatzman, *Soul Murder*, pp. 52, 61; Niederland, *The Schreber Case*, pp. 66, 76, 94. Additionally, p. 60: "Many of the divine miracles affecting the patient's body become recognizable, shorn of their delusional distortions, as what they must originally have been modeled on: the infantile regressively distorted image of the father's massive, coercive, as well as seductive manipulations performed on the child's body." And Daniel Paul wrote (p. 155): "hardly any memory from my life is more certain than the miracles recounted in this

Chap. 2. The Abuse of the Psychological (*Cont.*)

chapter. What can be more definite for a human being than what he has lived through and felt in his own body?"

P. 25. "penetrating a child." Schatzman, *Soul Murder,* p. 95.

P. 25. ". . . penetrating . . . a child ten times." Schatzman, *Soul Murder,* p. 100.

P. 25. ". . . may have wished to penetrate children." Schatzman, *Soul Murder,* p. 100.

P. 25. "*Luder* . . . a hussy, or even a whore." Niederland, *The Schreber Case,* pp. 43–44.

P. 25. "*Miss* Schreber." Niederland, *The Schreber Case,* p. 44.

P. 26. ". . . male seed . . . thrown into my body." Schatzman, *Soul Murder,* p. 97.

P. 26. "the purpose of sexual abuse." Niederland, *The Schreber Case,* p. 23; Freud, *Collected Papers,* p. 427.

P. 26. "foul masses . . . lets himself be fucked." Niederland, *The Schreber Case,* p. 17.

P. 26. ". . . common human experience." Niederland, *The Schreber Case,* pp. 13–14.

P. 26. ". . . unfit for print." Niederland, *The Schreber Case,* p. 14.

P. 27. ". . . in the public eye." Freud, *Collected Papers,* pp. 419–20.

P. 27. ". . . seminal incorporation became clear." Roland Summit, M.D., "Beyond Belief: The Reluctant Discovery of Incest," in *Women's Sexual Experience: Explorations of the Dark Continent,* ed. Martha Kirkpatrick (New York: Plenum Publishing Corp., 1982), p. 137.

P. 27. ". . . than where girls are involved." Schatzman, *Soul Murder,* p. 87.

P. 27. "root of his paranoia." This was the Freudian explanation of paranoia: "A homosexual wishful fantasy of loving a man lies at the core of the conflict in cases of paranoia among males." Niederland, *The Schreber Case,* p. 25.

P. 28. "masked castration fear." Klein and Tribich, "On Freud's Blindness," p. 54.

P. 28. ". . . from my observation." Freud, *Collected Papers,* p. 149.

P. 28. "observations on the sexual life of children." Freud, *Collected Papers,* p. 150.

P. 28. ". . . without being intimidated." Freud, *Collected Papers,* p. 150.

P. 28. ". . . widdle with?" Schatzman, *Soul Murder,* p. 125.

P. 28. "naughty." Schatzman, *Soul Murder,* p. 125.

P. 28. ". . . bag to sleep in." Schatzman, *Soul Murder,* pp. 125–26.

P. 28. "Castration complex." Daniel Paul's "intense castration fear" was made much of as part of his "symptomatology" on entering the hospital. Yet

Chap. 2. The Abuse of the Psychological (*Cont.*)

Dr. Flechsig, the medical director of the hospital, describes "the use of actual castration in his hospital as a method to be employed for the cure of serious nervous and psychological ailments." Niederland, *The Schreber Case*, p. 104. And Flechsig castrated at least three inmates and wrote of it as a successful treatment. Schatzman, *Soul Murder*, p. 120. Freud said of Daniel Paul, "His father's most dreaded threat, castration, actually provided the material for his wish-phantasy (at first resisted but later accepted) of being transformed into a woman." But as Schatzman writes, "Where is Freud's evidence? Freud comes to think this about Schreber, I presume, because he holds the dread of castration to be virtually universal. From where does the dread come? Does Freud propose that sons imagine their fathers threaten them with castration, even if the fathers do not?" *Soul Murder*, pp. 111, 112, 115.

P. 29. ". . . does not even require evidence." William Ryan, *Blaming the Victim* (New York: Pantheon Books, 1971), pp. 12–13.

P. 29. ". . . individuals toward Fuhrer figures." Wilhelm Reich, *The Mass Psychology of Fascism* (New York: Farrar, Straus and Giroux, 1971). Cited in Schatzman, *Soul Murder*, p. 72.

P. 30. ". . . Oedipal . . . remains dominant." Florence Rush, personal communication.

P. 30. ". . . dogma of disbelief . . . sophisticated professionals." Summit, "Recognition and Treatment of Child Sexual Abuse," p. 27.

P. 30. fired from the Freud Archives. Gelman, "Finding the Hidden Freud," p. 65.

P. 30. "in some Oedipal drama." John Leonard, review of *The Age of Desire: Case Histories of a Radical Psychoanalyst* by Joel Kovel (Pantheon) in *New York Times*, January 14, 1982. p. C–21.

P. 31. ". . . parents' pleasure instead of his own." Christopher Lasch, *Haven in a Heartless World: The Family Besieged* (New York: Basic Books, 1977), pp. 180–81. I have deliberately chosen an erudite non-psychiatrist's description of the Oedipal theory. It is the informed non-professional's perception of the theory I'm pointing to.

P. 31. "food deprivation, indeed food *teasing*." See, e.g., Niederland, *The Schreber Case*, p. 71.

P. 31. ". . . dreams of taking his place." Lasch, *Haven in a Heartless World*, p. 181.

P. 31. ". . . dominate every other activity." Lasch, *Haven in a Heartless World*, p. 181.

P. 32. ". . . castration by the father." Melanie Klein, cited in Lasch, *Haven in a Heartless World*, p. 181.

P. 32. ". . . aggressive impulses against himself." Lasch, *Haven in a Heartless World*, p. 124.

Chap. 2. The Abuse of the Psychological *(Cont.)*

P. 32. ". . . primacy of the unconscious . . . embraced." Florence Rush, personal communication.

P. 33. ". . . preserve that type of society." Harold Feldman, "Why We Need a Family Policy," *Journal of Marriage and the Family* 41, no. 3 (August 1979), p. 455.

P. 33. "socialized to subjection." See Florence Rush, "Sexual Abuse of Children, A Feminist Point of View," in *Rape: The First Sourcebook for Women,* ed. Noreen Connell and Cassandra Wilson (New York: New American Library, 1974).

P. 33. "excesses on the part of his own father." Sophie Freud Lowenstein, review of *Freud und Sein Vater* [*Freud and His Father*] by Marianne Krull (Munich: Verlag C. H. Beck, 1979) in *Family Process* 19 (September 1980), pp. 307–13. E.g., "Freud felt that he himself and some of his siblings were neurotics and holding on to the seduction theory would have meant that his own father was guilty of some kind of seduction."

P. 33. "tyrannical, brutal . . . murderous." Klein and Tribich, "On Freud's Blindness," p. 53.

P. 33. ". . . brute force of the father." Klein and Tribich, "On Freud's Blindness," p. 53.

P. 34. ". . . good-natured candour." Klein and Tribich, "On Freud's Blindness," p. 53.

P. 34. ". . . violence of his own rage." Klein and Tribich, "On Freud's Blindness," p. 53.

P. 34. ". . . his own mother's destructiveness." See Leon Shaskolsky Sheleff, *Generations Apart: Adult Hostility to Youth* (New York: McGraw-Hill Book Co., 1981), pp. 256–57.

P. 35. "clipping the patient's hair." Sheleff, *Generations Apart,* p. 258.

P. 35. "prepotent determinant . . . not without destructive effect." Joseph C. Rheingold, M.D., Ph.D., *The Mother, Anxiety, and Death: The Catastrophic Death Complex* (Boston: Little, Brown and Company, 1967), pp. 105, 106.

P. 35. ". . . intervenes threateningly." Rheingold, *The Mother, Anxiety, and Death,* p. 131. Maternal seduction, however, is catastrophic. Is, indeed, "a very different story. . . . The pathogenicity of maternal seduction lies not just in the exploitation of the child for the mother's gratification, but in the hostile motive that almost always lies behind it; in fact seduction may be an expression of the mutilative impulse." Whereas daddies, of course, are just doing the kids a favor. (p. 132.)

3. The War on the Ground

P. 37. ". . . the widowed." Evan Stark, Anne Flitcraft, and William Frazier, "Medicine and Patriarchal Violence: The Social Construction of a 'Private' Event," *International Journal of Health Services* 9, no. 3 (1979), p. 472.

P. 37. ". . . troubled marriage." Michael D. A. Freeman, "Wife Le Vice Anglais?—Battering in English and American Law," in *Fathers, Husbands and*

Chap. 3. The War on the Ground (*Cont.*)

Lovers, ed. Sanford N. Katz and Monroe L. Inker (American Bar Association Press, 1979), p. 211.

P. 37. ". . . prior symptoms." Stark, Flitcraft, and Frazier, "Medicine and Patriarchal Violence," p. 470.

P. 38. ". . . breadwinner." Diane Hamlin, "The Nature and Extent of Spouse Assault," in *Prosecutor's Responsibility in Spouse Abuse Cases,* U.S. Department of Justice, Law Enforcement Assistance Administration (Chicago: National District Attorneys Association, March 1980), p. 7. Also, "The Victim Advocate," A Special Criminal Justice Improvement Publication of the National District Attorneys Association (Chicago: The National District Attorneys Association, 1978), p. 7: "Victims of spouse assault may have unrealistic or stereotypic expectations of themselves and their marriages. Often, they have entered the marriage expecting it ought to serve as a panacea for all their problems. Most of these women believe the man should be the head of the house and the major breadwinner."

P. 38. battered wife plays a "crucial role." John R. Lion, M.D., "Clinical Aspects of Wife-Battering," in *Battered Women: A Psychosociological Study of Domestic Violence,* ed. Maria Roy, p. 127. You may be the kind of woman to "fear kind husbands and good men, lest such individuals go away or otherwise hurt them" (p. 132). You may have a "greater tolerance for violence." "International Association of Chiefs of Police Training Key," in Roy, *Battered Women,* p. 147.

P. 38. "Zero Mostel." William Ryan, *Blaming the Victim* (New York: Pantheon Books, 1971), p. 3.

P. 38. ". . . whenever he wishes." Barbara Star, Carol G. Clark, Karen M. Goetz, and Linda O'Malia, "Psychosocial Aspects of Wife Battering," *Social Casework: The Journal of Contemporary Social Work,* October 1979, p. 484.

P. 39. "problem the patient *is.*" Stark, Flitcraft, and Frazier, "Medicine and Patriarchal Violence," p. 473.

P. 39. "mental hospital." Stark, Flitcraft, and Frazier, "Medicine and Patriarchal Violence," p. 476.

P. 39. "insane asylum." Amaury de Riencourt, *Sex and Power in History* (New York: Dell Publishing Co., 1974), p. 307.

P. 39. "1891 . . . false imprisonment in an insane asylum." James W. Ellis, "Volunteering Children: Parental Commitment of Minors to Mental Institutions," *California Law Review* 62, no. 840 (1974), p. 854 n. 78.

P. 39. ". . . custody of the children." Stark, Flitcraft, and Frazier, "Medicine and Patriarchal Violence," p. 475.

P. 40. ". . . GET AWAY." "Battered Women: Handbook for Survival" (Milwaukee Task Force on Battered Women, 1978). Cited in Jennifer Baker Fleming, *Stopping Wife Abuse: A Guide to the Emotional, Psychological, and Legal Implications for the Abused Woman and Those Helping Her* (New York: Anchor Press/Doubleday, 1979), pp. 31–32.

P. 40. "contrary to popular myth . . ." Roland Summit, M.D., "Recognition and Treatment of Child Sexual Abuse," to be published in *Providing*

Chap. 3. The War on the Ground (*Cont.*)

for the Emotional Health of the Pediatric Patient, ed. Charles E. Hollingsworth (New York: Spectrum Publishers), ms. p. 21. Also Summit, "Beyond Belief: The Reluctant Discovery of Incest," in *Women's Sexual Experience: Explorations of the Dark Continent,* ed. Martha Kirkpatrick (New York: Plenum Publishing Corp., 1982), p. 137.

P. 41. "during the 1960's." Richard Gelles, "Violence in the Family: A Review of the Research in the Seventies," *Journal of Marriage and the Family* 42, no. 4 (November 1980), p. 873.

P. 41. "issue . . . devoted to family violence." *Journal of Marriage and The Family* 42, no. 4 (November 1980).

P. 41. "review of the research." Gelles, "Violence in the Family," pp. 873–85.

P. 41. "evolutionary perspective." Gelles, "Violence in the Family," pp. 880–83.

P. 41. "why 'normal men slip rather easily . . .' " Summit, "Beyond Belief," ms. p. 25.

P. 42. ". . . defense . . . child abuse." Michael P. Rosenthal, "Physical Abuse of Children by Parents: The Criminalization Decision," *American Journal of Criminal Law* 7, no. 2 (July 1979), p. 168.

P. 43. "Because they're alone . . . of independence." Florence Rush, personal communication.

P. 43. ". . . They have competition." Judge Ben B. Lindsey and Wainwright Evans, *Companionate Marriage* (Garden City, N.Y.: Garden City Publishing Co., 1927), p. viii.

P. 44. "nationalization of women." Margaret Mead and Elena Calas, "Child-Training Ideals in a Postrevolutionary Context: Soviet Russia," in *Childhood in Contemporary Culture,* ed. Margaret Mead and Martha Wolfenstein (Chicago: The University of Chicago Press, 1955), pp. 180–81.

P. 44. ". . . to the Soviet State." Jessie Bernard, *The Future of Motherhood* (New York: Penguin Books, 1975), pp. 277–78.

P. 44. ". . . Soviet female . . . oppressed . . . never had been before." De Riencourt, *Sex and Power in History,* p. 375.

P. 44. ". . . the child-care state." George F. Gilder, *Sexual Suicide* (New York: Quadrangle/The New York Times Book Company, 1973), p. 59.

P. 45. "by accident." E.g., Lenore E. Walker, *The Battered Woman* (New York: Harper & Row, 1979), p. 16.

P. 46. "Your husband is probably middle-aged." Ingrid K. Cooper, "Decriminalization of Incest: New Legal-Clinical Responses," in *Family Violence: An International and Interdisciplinary Study,* ed. John M. Eekelaar and Sanford N. Katz (Toronto: Butterworths, 1978), pp. 519–20.

P. 46. "with other criminal activities." Lenore E. Walker, "Clinical As-

Chap. 3. The War on the Ground (*Cont.*)

pects of the Battered Woman Syndrome Study," paper presented at the Colorado Mental Health Conference. (Keystone, Colo., October 25, 1980), p. 3.

P. 47. "tends to be positively conservative." Kee MacFarlane, "Sexual Abuse of Children," in *The Victimization of Women,* ed. Jane Roberts Chapman and Margaret Gates (Beverly Hills: Sage Publications, 1978), p. 89.

P. 49. equal rights for men . . . father's rights movement. See, e.g., William K. Stevens, "Congress of Men Asks Equality for Both Sexes," *New York Times,* June 15, 1981, pp. B–9, C–2.

P. 50. "63% . . . never as good as what *could* be." Adele Hendrickson, Esq., and Joanne Schulman, Esq., "Trends in Child Custody Law: What They Mean for Women," September 10, 1981. Available from the National Center on Women and Family Law, 799 Broadway, Rm. 402, New York, NY 10003. 63% custody to fathers, p. 7; "parenting potential," p. 19; "trade her financial demands down," p. 13. Also, see "Custody—Discrimination—Fathers—'Tender Years' Doctrine," 8 *Family Law Reporter* 2202 (2–9–82). For more information and documentation, contact the Child Custody Committee, National Center on Women and Family Law.

P. 50. violence no evidence of father's unfitness. Hendrickson and Schulman, "Trends in Child Custody Law," p. 31.

P. 51. "lose custody altogether." Hendrickson and Schulman, "Trends in Child Custody Law," p. 32.

P. 51. "anxieties in the area of sexuality." Summit, "Recognition and Treatment of Child Sexual Abuse," p. 30.

P. 52. case of Jan Samuels. Summarized in Summit, "Recognition and Treatment of Child Sexual Abuse," pp. 30–35. Material from personal communication, court documents, affidavits, etc.

P. 60. "less trial than tribulation." Charles Rembar, *The Law of the Land: The Evolution of Our Legal System* (New York: Simon and Schuster, 1980), p. 102.

P. 62. ". . . right to a loving father." Roland Summit, personal communication.

4. Storming the Castle

P. 64. "quagmire if the 'facts' are concerned only with who did what." "Adolescent Abuse and Neglect: Intervention Strategies and Treatment Approaches," Executive Summary, July 1979, Urban and Rural Systems Associated, San Francisco (a report prepared for the Youth Development Bureau, U.S. Department of Health, Education and Welfare), pp. 8–9.

P. 64. "scapegoating one family member." "Adolescent Abuse and Neglect," p. 9.

P. 65. ". . . (rejection) with females they had dated." Judith V. Becker and Gene G. Abel, "Men and the Victimization of Women," in *The Victimiza-*

Chap. 4. Storming the Castle (*Cont.*)

tion of Women, ed. Jane Roberts Chapman and Margaret Gates (Beverly Hills: Sage Publications, 1978), p. 36.

P. 65. ". . . frequently the mother." Becker and Abel, "Men and the Victimization of Women," p. 39.

P. 65. "when he did it." Becker and Abel, "Men and the Victimization of Women," p. 39.

P. 65. "went out and raped." Becker and Abel, "Men and the Victimization of Women," p. 40.

P. 65. ". . . overly permissive individual." Becker and Abel, "Men and the Victimization of Women," p. 41.

P. 65. ". . . normal conversations." Becker and Abel, "Men and the Victimization of Women," pp. 45–46.

P. 66. ". . . from contact with women." Becker and Abel, "Men and the Victimization of Women," p. 47.

P. 66. ". . . conducive to their rehabilitation." Becker and Abel, "Men and the Victimization of Women," p. 47.

P. 66. "2.06 of all rape victimizations." Dr. Nicholas N. Kittrie of The American University Law School, paper delivered at the Fifth International Seminar on Methodologies for Research in Serious Criminology, University of Messina (Italy), December 4, 1981.

P. 67. ". . . without further consequence." August 28, 1981 letter from Gene G. Abel, M.D., Director, Sexual Behavior Clinic, Research Foundation for Mental Hygiene, Inc., New York Psychiatric Institute.

P. 68. ". . . the same individual." Nicholas N. Kittrie, *The Right to Be Different: Deviance and Enforced Therapy* (Baltimore: The Johns Hopkins University Press, 1971). For a more complete history of criminal justice, see chap. 1, "The Divestment of Criminal Justice and the Coming of the Therapeutic State," pp. 1–50.

P. 68. ". . . a component of public hygiene." Michel Foucault, *Power/ Knowledge: Selected Interviews and Other Writings, 1972–1977,* ed. Colin Gordon (New York: Pantheon Books, 1980), pp. 204–5.

P. 68. "professionalizing . . . apparatus of boundary defenses." Henry J. Meyer and Sheldon Siegel, "Profession of Social Work: Contemporary Characteristics," in *Encyclopedia of Social Work,* 17th issue, vol. 2 (Washington, D.C., National Association of Social Workers, 1977), p. 1068.

P. 69. ". . . lack of hygiene, or suchlike." Foucault, *Power/Knowledge,* p. 205.

P. 69. ". . . responsibility of those accused." Jacques Donzelot, *The Policing of Families* (New York: Pantheon Books, 1979), p. 126.

P. 70. ". . . detectable, foreseeable—anomaly." Donzelot, *The Policing of Families,* pp. 126–27.

Chap. 4. Storming the Castle (*Cont.*)

P. 70. *"obstacles* to his admission." Thomas S. Szasz, M.D., *Law, Liberty, and Psychiatry* (New York: Collier/Macmillan, 1968), p. 41.

P. 71. ". . . outside the scope of police power." "Developments in the Law, the Constitution and the Family," *Harvard Law Review* 93: 1156, no. 6 (April 1980), pp. 1198–99.

P. 72. ". . . individual's welfare." "Developments in the Law," p. 1199.

P. 72. ". . . security of its citizens." "Developments in the Law," p. 1200.

P. 72. "public's interest is not at stake." American Bar Association Section of Family Law, ABA Press, 1979, p. 202. Cited in Michael D. A. Freeman, "Le Vice Anglais?—Wife-Battering in English and American Law," in *Fathers, Husbands, and Lovers,* ed. Sanford N. Katz and Monroe L. Inker.

P. 72. ". . . normal banking operations." Szasz, *Law, Liberty, and Psychiatry,* p. 183.

P. 73. ". . . stealing 'his own plate.' " Edward Jenks, D.C.L. (Oxon.), *The Book of English Law* (Athens, Ohio: The Ohio University Press, 1967), p. 114.

P. 74. ". . . domestic harmony and romantic love." Doris Klein and D. Crim, "Violence Against Women: Some Considerations on its Causes and on its Elimination," unpublished article (June 1980) which was set to appear in *Crime and Delinquency,* January 1981, ms. p. 22.

P. 74. "A man's home is his castle." John Bartlett, *Familiar Quotations,* 10th ed., ed. Nathan Haskell Dole (New York: Blue Ribbon Books, 1914), p. 24.

P. 75. ". . . valuable incentive for labor." Jamil S. Zainaldin, "The Emergence of a Modern American Family Law: Child Custody, Adoption, and the Courts, 1796–1851," *Northwestern Law Review* 73:1038 (1979), p. 1068. Referring to the case *Mercein v. People ex rel. Barry,* 25 Wend. 65 (New York, 1840).

P. 76. "crucial roles." George F. Gilder, *Sexual Suicide* (New York: Quadrangle/The New York Times Book Co., 1973), pp. 187, 188.

P. 76. ". . . to make himself equal." Gilder, *Sexual Suicide,* p. 14.

P. 76. ". . . giving up the role." Gilder, *Sexual Suicide,* p. 23.

P. 77. ". . . on men's terms." Amaury de Riencourt, *Sex and Power in History* (New York: Dell Publishing Co., 1974), p. 124.

P. 77. ". . . committed ethnic suicide." De Riencourt, *Sex and Power in History,* p. 126.

P. 77. "will fail." Gilder, *Sexual Suicide,* p. 59.

P. 77. ". . . to meaningless but insistent copulation." Gilder, *Sexual Suicide,* p. 105.

P. 78. ". . . offenders against family and children . . . single men." Gilder, *Sexual Suicide,* p. 6.

P. 78. "Male dominance . . . conventional male power . . . male sexual and economic . . ." Gilder, *Sexual Suicide,* p. 24.

Chap. 4. Storming the Castle (*Cont.*)

P. 79. ". . . the man's part in it." Gilder, *Sexual Suicide*, p. 132.

P. 80. ". . . designed to restrict." Gilder, *Sexual Suicide*, p. 133.

P. 80. "Male potency . . . our deepest human experiences." Gilder, *Sexual Suicide*, p. 135.

P. 80. "the sexual constitution. . . . As with guns . . . of female sexuality." Gilder, *Sexual Suicide*, pp. 136–37.

P. 81. ". . . the hope or presence of progeny." Gilder, *Sexual Suicide*, p. 70.

P. 81. ". . . courtesans of those cosmopolitan times." De Riencourt, *Sex and Power in History*, p. 125.

P. 81. ". . . on their femininity." Gilder, *Sexual Suicide*, p. 195.

P. 81. ". . . men . . . submit . . . more happily." Gilder, *Sexual Suicide*, p. 203.

P. 82. ". . . prevent males from mutual destruction." Julia Schwendinger and Herman Schwendinger, "Sociology's Founding Fathers: Sexists to a Man," *Journal of Marriage and the Family* 33, no. 4 (November 1971), p. 792. "Women were conceived chiefly as *instruments* of social control" with an " 'obligation' to properly socialize the present and future members of the labor force, their husbands and children" (p. 796).

P. 82. ". . . mother who feeds and clothes him." Jerome Tognoli, "The Flight from Domestic Space: Men's Roles in the Household," *The Family Coordinator: Journal of Education, Counseling and Services* 28, no. 4 (October 1979), p. 604.

P. 82. ". . . their own chances . . . depended on it." Donzelot, *The Policing of Families*, p. 40.

P. 83. ". . . get the man there too . . . values of civilization." Gilder, *Sexual Suicide*, p. 248.

P. 84. ". . . maintenance of family connections." Gilder, *Sexual Suicide*, p. 142.

P. 84. ". . . commitment to the family." John Kenneth Galbraith, "The Higher Economic Purpose of Women," in *Annals of an Abiding Liberal* (New York: New American Library, 1979), p. 45.

P. 85. "The concept of the household . . . of a composite or collective." Galbraith, *Annals of an Abiding Liberal*, p. 44.

P. 85. ". . . would attract attention." Galbraith, *Annals of an Abiding Liberal*, p. 43.

P. 86. ". . . in civilized society." Gilder, *Sexual Suicide*, p. 247.

P. 86. "total home support." Charlotte Perkins Gilman, *The Home: Its Work and Influence* (Chicago: The University of Illinois Press, 1972), pp. 318–21.

Chap. 4. Storming the Castle (*Cont.*)

P. 86. "occupational options not now open to them." John Scanzoni, "Strategies for Changing Male Family Roles: Research and Practice Implications," *The Family Coordinator* 28, no. 4 (October 1979), pp. 440–41.

P. 87. ". . . requisite behavior." Galbraith, *Annals of an Abiding Liberal,* p. 45.

P. 87. women who killed. From transcript of Phil Donahue Show, #19235, September 23, 1980, WGN-TV, Chicago.

5. A Little War History

The main sources synthesized in this chapter are as follows:

Social History

"The Children of the State: Child Protective Services in New York State," The Temporary State Commission on Child Welfare Report. New York, June 1980.

Cott, Nancy F. *The Bonds of Womanhood: 'Woman's Sphere' in New England, 1780–1835.* New Haven: Yale University Press, 1977.

Degler, Carl N. *At Odds: Women and the Family in America from the Revolution to the Present.* New York: Oxford University Press, 1980.

Douglas, Ann. *The Feminization of American Culture.* New York: Avon Books, 1978.

Ehrenreich, Barbara and English, Deirdre. *For Her Own Good: 150 Years of the Experts' Advice to Women.* New York: Anchor Books, 1979.

Norton, Mary Beth. *Liberty's Daughters: The Revolutionary Experience of American Women, 1750–1800.* Boston: Little, Brown and Co., 1980.

Platt, Anthony M. *The Child Savers: The Invention of Delinquency.* Chicago: The University of Chicago Press, 1969.

Saur, Mrs. P. B., M.D. (with a special introductory chapter by The Celebrated Charles Pusheck, M.D., A.M.). *Maternity: A Book for Every Wife and Mother.* 1896.

Law History

Areen, Judith. "Intervention Between Parent and Child: A Reappraisal of the State's Role in Child Neglect and Abuse Cases." *Georgetown Law Journal* 63: 88 (1975), pp. 887–937.

Kittrie, Nicholas N. *The Right to Be Different. Deviance and Enforced Therapy.* Baltimore: The Johns Hopkins University Press, 1971.

Legislative Manual for the 2nd National Juvenile Justice Legislative Advocacy Conference, St. Louis, Mo., November 11–13, 1979. St. Louis: The National Juvenile Law Center.

Thomas, Mason P., Jr. "Child Abuse and Neglect, Part I: Historical Overview, Legal Matrix, and Social Perspectives." *North Carolina Law Review* 50 (1972), pp. 293–349.

Zainaldin, Jamil S. "The Emergence of a Modern American Family Law:

Chap. 5. A Little War History *(Cont.)*

Child Custody, Adoption, and the Courts, 1796–1851." *Northwestern University Law Review* 73:1038 (1979), pp. 1038–89.

P. 90. "inadequately trained." "The Children of the State," p. 5.

P. 90. "workers promoted into it." "The Children of the State," p. 5.

P. 90. "know what should be reported." "The Children of the State," pp. 28–29.

P. 90. rely on own backgrounds. "The Children of the State," p. 27.

P. 90. "phone call, a visit." "The Children of the State," p. 28.

P. 91. "reduce their workload." "The Children of the State," p. 30.

P. 91. "form is filled out incorrectly." "The Children of the State," pp. 32, 33.

P. 91. "impossible to reach." "The Children of the State," p. 54.

P. 91. "six months or more." "The Children of the State," p. 59.

P. 91. "carbon paper . . . lousy" "The Children of the State," p. 57.

P. 91. "moral and religious neglect." Vincent de Francis, J.D., "The Fundamentals of Child Protection: A Statement of Basic Concepts and Principles" (Englewood, Colo.: The American Humane Association, 1978).

P. 92. "powers of the Star Chamber . . ." Dean Roscoe Pound, Foreword to *Social Treatment in Probation and Delinquency* by P. Young (1937), p. xxvii. Cited in Thomas T. Becker, "Due Process and Child Protective Proceedings: State Intervention in Family Relations on Behalf of Neglected Children," *Cumberland-Samford Law Review* 247 (1971), p. 248.

P. 92. "vain and fickle . . . 'weak and imperfect' . . . 'Poor Helpless Widow.' " Phrases scattered throughout Norton, *Liberty's Daughters*. For a further sense of women's self-perceptions, see pp. 38, 39, 111–21.

P. 93. "prerogative of guardianship." Norton, *Liberty's Daughters*, p. 46.

P. 93. ". . . connected with a Tyrant . . ." Norton, *Liberty's Daughters*, p. 44.

P. 93. Abigail Bailey and Asa and incest. Norton, *Liberty's Daughters*, pp. 49–50.

P. 94. "Robert Frassetto . . . 'qualifying her as a consenting accomplice.' " Personal communication.

P. 95. "to 'hang' her father for her own delinquencies." *People v. Oliver* (1941, Co. Ct.) 25 NYS2d 602, in 74 ALR2d, American Law Reports Annotated, p. 710.

P. 95. "means calculated to overcome it was unnecessary . . ." *Sanders v. State* (1937) 132 *Tex Crim* 25, 102 SW2d 208, in 74 ALR2d, American Law Reports Annotated, pp. 710–11.

Chap. 5. A Little War History (Cont.)

P. 95. Abigail Adams: "she could not prevent the misfortune." Norton, *Liberty's Daughters,* pp. 57–58.

P. 96. ". . . early periods of childhood and youth." Norton, *Liberty's Daughters,* p. 245.

P. 96. ". . . the destiny of a redeemed world . . ." Degler, *At Odds,* pp. 81–82.

P. 96. women as main church attenders. See, e.g., Degler, *At Odds,* pp. 298–99; Cott, *The Bonds of Womanhood,* pp. 126–59.

P. 97. ". . . so strong a hold upon the women or a slighter hold upon the men." Douglas, *The Feminization of American Culture,* p. 119.

P. 98. ". . . abject and helpless of all slaves." Cott, *The Bonds of Womanhood,* p. 159.

P. 98. ". . . feel our obligations." Cott, *The Bonds of Womanhood,* pp. 130–32.

P. 98. boom for science. See Jacques Donzelot, *The Policing of Families* (New York: Pantheon Books, 1979), p. 20. Also Ehrenreich and English, *For Her Own Good,* pp. 33–98.

P. 98. ". . . through true spiritual Christianity." Ehrenreich and English, *For Her Own Good,* p. 199.

P. 98. "doctrine of woman's sphere . . . represented an advance." Cott, *The Bonds of Womanhood,* p. 200.

P. 99. ". . . heaven's blessedness on his head." Jeremy Taylor, cited in Saur, *Maternity,* p. 11.

P. 99. "literature spoke . . . to mothers." Degler, *At Odds,* p. 73.

P. 103. "marital rape . . . 'disappointment and degradation.'" Degler, *At Odds,* pp. 244–45.

P. 105. "reconstituted." Platt, *The Child Savers,* p. 45.

P. 105. "children . . . in mills and factories." For a more detailed picture, see e.g. Anthony F. C. Wallace, *Rockdale: The Growth of an American Village in the Early Industrial Revolution* (New York: W. W. Norton & Co., 1972).

P. 106. "cradled in infamy . . ." Platt, *The Child Savers,* p. 62.

P. 107. "The object of reformatory institutions . . . protection of the individual himself." Cited in Platt, *The Child Savers,* pp. 106–7.

P. 108. *"Ex Parte Crouse."* 4 Wharton 9 (Pa. 1838). See e.g. *Legislative Manual,* p. 5.

P. 108. ". . . extreme cruelty to release her from it." *Legislative Manual,* p. 5.

P. 108. "House of Refuge . . ." Kittrie, *The Right to Be Different,* p. 110.

P. 109. *"parens patriae . . .* Aethelred . . . Edward II." Kittrie, *The Right to Be Different,* p. 9.

Chap. 5. A Little War History (*Cont.*)

P. 109. "children of *property.*" "Developments in the Law, the Constitution and the Family," *Harvard Law Review* 93, no. 6 (April 1980), pp. 1221–22.

P. 109. "The guardianship of the person . . . incapable of taking care of themselves." Kittrie, *The Right to Be Different*, p. 59 (cite omitted).

P. 109. "Universal Landlord." "The King, as the political father and guardian of his kingdom, has the protection of all his subjects, and of their lands and goods; and he is bound, in a more peculiar manner to take care of those who, by reason of their imbecility and want of understanding, are incapable of taking care of themselves." L. Shelford, 1833, cited in Kittrie, *The Right to Be Different*, p. 59.

P. 110. "*honest* guardians." G. G. Coulton, *Medieval Panorama: The English Scene from Conquest to Reformation* (New York: W. W. Norton and Co., 1938), p. 315.

P. 110. ". . . marries the wife purchased by his guardian." Coulton, *Medieval Panorama*, p. 630.

P. 110. Grace, Adam Neville, and his chamberlain Norman. Coulton, *Medieval Panorama*, pp. 630–31.

P. 111. *Wellesly v. Beaufort.* 38 Eng. Rep. 236-Ch. 1827. Cited in Areen, "Intervention Between Parent and Child," p. 898.

P. 111. "I have no doubt about the jurisdiction . . ." *In re Spence* (41 Eng. Rep. 937-Ch. 1847). Cited in Areen, "Intervention Between Parent and Child," p. 898.

P. 112. "The rich . . . left at their own option . . ." Areen, "Intervention Between Parent and Child," p. 899 n. 68.

P. 112. *In re Kottman.* Zainaldin, "The Emergence of a Modern American Family Law," p. 1061.

P. 113. *Mercein v. People ex rel. Barry.* Zainaldin, "The Emergence of a Modern American Family Law," pp. 1065–66.

P. 115. "subsidy system, vested interests flourished." Platt, *The Child Savers*, p. 109.

P. 115. Mrs. Wardner . . . $500. Platt, *The Child Savers*, p. 110.

P. 115. industrial school for girls. Platt, *The Child Savers*, pp. 110–11.

P. 115. "Every female infant . . ." Platt, *The Child Savers*, p. 111.

P. 116. women resent "having the door shut in their face." Platt, *The Child Savers*, p. 78.

P. 116. "like a home without a mother." Platt, *The Child Savers*, p. 79.

P. 116. Daniel O'Connell . . . "Can the state, as parens patriae . . ." E.g., Platt, *The Child Savers*, p. 104.

P. 117. Mary Ellen. The myth and historical version are recounted in Thomas, "Child Abuse and Neglect," pp. 308–9. Version II and the *New York*

Chap. 5. A Little War History (*Cont.*)

Times quote are in "The Children of the State," pp. 5–6. Also see Areen, "Intervention Between Parent and Child," p. 903 n. 92: Since Mary Ellen had been removed, not from her real parents, but from foster parents, "Her case thus reveals more about the neglect of children placed in state custody than about parental neglect. Significantly, at the end of the proceedings so often hailed in social work literature, Mary Ellen was sent off to an institution; she was 'saved'—but only in the sense of being removed from her foster parents, the Connollys. Apparently no one has ever bothered to find out how she fared after she was placed by the state a second time."

P. 119. ". . . cases involved organ grinders . . ." Areen, "Intervention Between Parent and Child," p. 904 n. 94.

P. 120. "Dr. J. D. Scouller . . . contracted with private industry . . ." Platt, *The Child Savers,* p. 105.

P. 121. "The action is not for the trial. . . . No constitutional right is violated." Kittrie, *The Right to Be Different,* p. 112.

P. 121. "Compassion and salvation." Kittrie, *The Right to Be Different,* p. 106.

P. 121. "Has this boy or girl . . ." Kittrie, *The Right to Be Different,* p. 111.

P. 121. Julia Lathrop . . . "This is a legal matter . . ." Platt, *The Child Savers,* p. 131.

P. 122. "Whereases . . ." Platt, *The Child Savers,* p. 131.

P. 122. "You cannot take a boy of tender years . . ." Platt, *The Child Savers,* p. 132.

P. 122. "For the purposes of this Act . . ." *Legislative Manual,* p. 6.

P. 123. Louise Bowen . . . "I happened to know at that time . . ." Platt, *The Child Savers,* p. 133 n. 93.

P. 123. "safeguards . . . for children accused of delinquent behavior." *In re Gault* 387 U.S. 1 (1967). See Kittrie, *The Right to Be Different,* pp. 122, 137–53.

P. 129. ". . . projected lust for his mother." Roland Summit, "Recognition and Treatment of Child Sexual Abuse," to be published in *Providing for the Emotional Health of the Pediatric Patient,* ed. Charles E. Hollingsworth (New York: Spectrum Publishers), ms. p. 35.

6. The Front Lines

P. 133. ". . . cruel and unusual cures . . ." Sanford N. Fox, "Philosophy and the Principle of Punishment in the Juvenile Court," in *The Youngest Minority II,* ed. Sanford N. Katz (American Bar Association Press, 1977), p. 171.

P. 133. ". . . same client population." URSA, Battered Wife Evaluation, 1980, p. 8.

Chap. 6. The Front Lines (*Cont.*)

P. 134. "moral, and religious neglect." Vincent de Francis, J.D., "The Fundamentals of Child Protection: A Statement of Basic Concepts and Principles" (Englewood, Colo.: The American Humane Association, 1978), p. 25. Also see discussion in Sanford N. Katz, *When Parents Fail: The Law's Response to Family Breakdown* (Boston: Beacon Press, 1971), chap. 3, "State Intervention," pp. 52–89.

P. 134. "not . . . empowered to refuse." De Francis, "Fundamentals of Child Protection," p. 7.

P. 134. "A service . . . to the state." Wayne M. Holder, M.S.W., and Cynthia Mohr, Ph.D., eds., "Helping in Child Protective Services" (Englewood, Colo.: The American Humane Association, 1980), p. 5.

P. 135. "By 1963 . . . requiring intervention." De Francis, "Fundamentals of Child Protection," pp. 25–27.

P. 135. "legislation." "Using Kempe's definition of the 'battered child syndrome' individual states began to enact mandatory child abuse reporting statutes in 1964; by 1966, 49 states had enacted this type of legislation.

"In 1974, Congress signed into law the Child Abuse Prevention and Treatment Act (P.L. 93–247) which mandated that all 50 states and territories adopt legislation requiring persons to report suspected cases of abuse to authorities and created a National Center on Child Abuse and Neglect (NCCAN) to issue grants for research projects and demonstration programs, among other duties" (cites omitted). Marian Eskin, "Child Abuse and Neglect: A Literature Review and Selected Bibliography," U.S. Department of Justice, National Institute of Justice, February 1980, p. 5.

P. 135. "Child Protective Services Act." In "The Children of the State," p. 14.

P. 135. "have Central Registries." William S. Hildenbrand, ed., *Child Protective Services Entering the 1980's* (Englewood, Colo.: The American Humane Association, 1979), p. 55.

P. 135. ". . . in need of supervision." Hildenbrand, *Child Protective Services*, p. 97.

P. 136. "or 'other.' " Hildenbrand, *Child Protective Services*, p. 41.

P. 136. ". . . help or not." Hildenbrand, *Child Protective Services*, p. 109.

P. 136. ". . . guilt or blame." Katz, *When Parents Fail*, p. 37.

P. 136. ". . . moral unfitness . . ." Alan Sussman and Martin Guggenheim, *The Rights of Parents,* An American Civil Liberties Union Handbook (New York: Avon, 1980), p. 72.

P. 137. Idaho . . . "objects and other persons." Sussman and Guggenheim, *The Rights of Parents,* p. 78.

P. 137. "spiritual existence as well." Katz, *When Parents Fail*, p. 71.

Chap. 6. The Front Lines (*Cont.*)

P. 137. "aims and outcomes." *Encyclopedia of Social Work*, vol. I, p. 128.

P. 137. ". . . capacity of that material." *Encyclopedia of Social Work*, vol. II, p. 1282.

P. 137. ". . . are Involuntary." De Francis, "Fundamentals of Child Protection," p. 6.

P. 138. ". . . to the limit." De Francis, "Fundamentals," p. 6.

P. 138. ". . . family maladjustments." De Francis, "Fundamentals," p. 6.

P. 138. ". . . hazardous surroundings." De Francis, "Fundamentals," p. 7.

P. 138. ". . . ask the neighbors?" De Francis, "Fundamentals," pp. 21–22.

P. 139. ". . . existence of neglect." De Francis, "Fundamentals," p. 23.

P. 139. "unventilated." De Francis, "Fundamentals," p. 23.

P. 139. ". . . or spiritual neglect." De Francis, "Fundamentals," pp. 25–27.

P. 139. ". . . cooking facilities." De Francis, "Fundamentals," p. 26.

P. 139. ". . . temper tantrums." De Francis, "Fundamentals," p. 26.

P. 139. ". . . at home." De Francis, "Fundamentals," p. 27.

P. 140. ". . . to follow." De Francis, "Fundamentals," p. 27.

P. 140. ". . . or irreligion." De Francis, "Fundamentals," p. 27.

P. 140. ". . . sufficient finances." De Francis, "Fundamentals," pp. 27–28.

P. 140. ". . . to the child?" De Francis, "Fundamentals," pp. 30–31.

P. 140. ". . . for the children." De Francis, "Fundamentals," p. 31.

P. 140. ". . . of evidence." De Francis, "Fundamentals," p. 39.

P. 141. ". . . irrational conduct, intoxication." De Francis, "Fundamentals," p. 42.

P. 141. ". . . necessary and right." Holder and Mohr, "Helping in Child Protective Services," p. 18.

P. 142. ". . . deal with effectively." Holder and Mohr, "Helping," p. 16.

P. 142. ". . . the client's life." Holder and Mohr, "Helping," p. 71.

P. 142. "Your very presence . . . on your non-judgmental judgement." Holder and Mohr, "Helping," p. 71.

P. 142. ". . . and authoritarian." Holder and Mohr, "Helping," p. 74.

P. 143. ". . . big shot." Holder and Mohr, "Helping," p. 77.

P. 143. ". . . see and hear." Holder and Mohr, "Helping," p. 84.

P. 143. ". . . of clarification." Holder and Mohr, "Helping," p. 93.

P. 143. ". . . saw Johnny bleeding?" Holder and Mohr, "Helping," p. 93.

P. 143. ". . . other professionals." Holder and Mohr, "Helping," pp. 16–17.

P. 144. "either verbal or physical." Holder and Mohr, "Helping," p. 17.

P. 144. ". . . they are compatible." Holder and Mohr, "Helping," p. 18.

Chap. 6. The Front Lines (*Cont.*)

P. 144. ". . . invoked humanistically." Holder and Mohr, "Helping," p. 9.

P. 145. ". . . for the child." Holder and Mohr, "Helping," pp. 49–50.

P. 146. ". . . items packed." Holder and Mohr, "Helping," p. 50.

P. 146. ". . . possible solutions." Holder and Mohr, "Helping," p. 20.

P. 146. ". . . all these activities." Holder and Mohr, "Helping," p. 20.

P. 146. ". . . helping relationship." Holder and Mohr, "Helping," pp. 26–27.

P. 147. "You assess the assessments." Holder and Mohr, "Helping," p. 21.

P. 147. ". . . of any profession." Holder and Mohr, "Helping," p. 22.

P. 147. ". . . they must complete." Holder and Mohr, "Helping," p. 24.

P. 147. ". . . of time." Holder and Mohr, "Helping," p. 24.

P. 147. ". . . but you really didn't." Holder and Mohr, "Helping," p. 174.

P. 148. ". . . not yet been extended to dependent-neglect hearings." Dianne M. Faber, "Comment. Dependent-Neglect Proceedings: A Case for Procedural Due Process," *Duquesne Law Review* 9: 627 (1971), p. 656.

7. Taps for Jackie

The main sources used for this chapter are listed below. Since the purpose of changing names in the text would be defeated by using the real names in the citations, these sources will be listed generally, and only facts or judicial holdings page-cited. Sources other than the ones mentioned will be page-cited as usual.

Parham v. J. R. 442 U.S. 584, 61 L. Ed. 2d 101, 99 S. Ct. 2493. *U.S. Supreme Court Reports* 61 L. Ed. 2d, pp. 101–41.

J. L. v. Parham 412 Fed. Supp. 112 (1976), pp. 112–46, and materials supplementary to the trial.

Post-Discovery Memorandum of Plaintiffs.

Defense Supplementary Brief.

Parham v. J. R. and J. L., Minors, Jurisdictional statement on Appeal to Supreme Court, 442 U.S. 584. May 1976.

Brief for Appellees in the Supreme Court of the United States (September 1977).

Brief for Appellants (August 1977).

Appellants Reply Brief (November 1977).

Oral argument before the United States Supreme Court (No. 75–1690).

Chap. 7. Taps for Jackie (*Cont.*)

Personal interviews with David Goren and Debby Goren.

Background news stories, including:
Atlanta Journal, May 5, 1977, p. 2-A.
Gainesville (Ga.) *Times,* December 1, 1977, p. 1-A.
Gainesville *Times,* December 8, 1977, p. 12-A.
Gainesville *Times,* March 12, 1978, p. 10-A.
Macon Telegraph, August 6, 1976, pp. 1-A, 6-A.
Macon Telegraph, February 10, 1977, pp. 1-A–8-A.
Macon Telegraph, February 11, 1977, pp. 1-A, 9-A.

Also, although not specifically cited, see J. Goldstein, A. Freud, and A. Solnit, *Beyond the Best Interests of the Child* (New York: Free Press, 1973); and Goldstein, Freud, and Solnit, *Before the Best Interests of the Child* (New York: Free Press, 1979).

P. 152. ". . . rights of children and youth." 412 Fed. Supp., pp. 22–23.

P. 152. Pennsylvania case. *Bartley v. Kremens,* 402 Fed. Supp. 1039 (1975).

P. 152. "70% of the children at Lakin State Hospital. . ." David Ferlerger (Founder, The Mental Patient Civil Liberties Project) and Harry F. Swanger (National Juvenile Law Center), *Legal Challenges to the "Voluntary" Admission of Children to Mental Institutions,* vols. I and II (Washington, D.C.: Legal Services Corporation), p. 4. See also p. 77: "Petitioner's medical record from both Lakin and Spencer State Hospital carry the diagnosis of 'adjustment reaction of adolescence.' Dr. David Dwight Harshbarger, a licensed psychologist, testified that 'adjustment reaction of adolescence' does not indicate any mental illness or a necessity for full-time institutional care. Randolph R. MacDonald, Director of Children's Services, West Virginia Department of Mental Health, testified that this diagnosis has no meaning to him at all and that petitioners most likely should not have been placed in a mental institution. Thus, petitioner has been institutionalized for the better part of three years without any diagnosis of mental illness."

P. 152. ". . . 456 days . . . 2,035 days . . ." 412 Fed. Supp., p. 120.

P. 153. "(43%) of the 441,429 children . . . in and out of mental institutions . . ." Barbara J. Sowder, Marvin R. Burt, Marilyn J. Rosenstein and Laura J. Milazzo, "Utilization of Psychiatric Facilities by Children and Youth," (Bethesda, Md.: Burt Associates, October 27, 1980).

P. 156. "psychiatrists . . . were Spanish-speaking." Post-Discovery, p. 9.

P. 158. ". . . one-third of the total juvenile/family court proceedings . . ." 'adjudication of wardship.' " Lee E. Teitelbaum and James W. Ellis, "The Liberty Interests of Children: Due Process Rights and Their Application," *Family Law Quarterly* 12, no. 3 (Fall 1978), pp. 162, 173.

P. 158. of 812 Georgia children, 515 by parent, 297 involuntary. 412 Fed. Supp., p. 120.

Chap. 7. Taps for Jackie (*Cont.*)

P. 161. ". . . referred to as 'dumping.' " Plaintiff's petition p. 8, in *In re Lee*, Clearinghouse #6335. *In re Lee*, 68 (JD) 1362 (Cook County Civ. Ct., Juv. Div., Ill., August 24, 1972). Cited in Ferlerger and Swanger, *Legal Challenges*, p. 97.

P. 162. "due process . . . triggers three questions . . ." Teitelbaum and Ellis, "Liberty Interests of Children," p. 156.

P. 163. Supreme Court, 1956. Mr. Justice Frankfurter, in *Greenwood v. United States*, 350 U.S. 366, 375 (1956). Cited in John P. Panneton, "Children, Commitment and Consent: A Constitutional Crisis," in Katz, *The Youngest Minority II* (American Bar Association Press, 1977), p. 58 n.

P. 163. Burger, 1968. Opinion by District of Columbia Circuit Court Judge Burger (now Chief Justice), *Kent v. United States*, 401 F. 2d 408 (1968), p. 4. Cited in Panneton, "Children, Commitment and Consent," p. 50.

P. 163. Burger, 1975. *O'Connor v. Donaldson*, 45 L. Ed. 2d 396, 410 (separate opinions). Cited in Ferlerger and Swanger, *Legal Challenges*, p. 366A.

P. 164. Rosenhan study. David L. Rosenhan, "On Being Sane in Insane Places," *Santa Clara Lawyer* 13 (1973), pp. 379–99. (Originally in *Science* 179 [January 19, 1973], p. 250.)

P. 165. Mrs. Dorothy Packard. See James W. Ellis, "Volunteering Children: Parental Commitment of Minors to Mental Institutions," *California Law Review* 62: 840 (1974), p. 842. Also Nicholas N. Kittrie, *The Right to Be Different: Deviance and Enforced Therapy* (Baltimore: The Johns Hopkins University Press, 1971), p. 65.

P. 166. 1940's and 1950's. Ellis, "Volunteering Children," p. 843.

P. 166. 1975 discharge labels. Mental Health Statistical Note, no. 137 (August 1977), U.S. Department of Health, Education and Welfare, National Institute of Mental Health, table 5, p. 19.

P. 167. *Bartley v. Kremens* labels. Ferlerger and Swanger, *Legal Challenges*, pp. 290A, 291A.

P. 169. hospital costs vs. group homes. 412 Fed. Supp., p. 126.

P. 171. "This case raises . . ." 412 Fed. Supp., p. 136.

P. 171. "Unfortunately . . . there are some parents . . ." 412 Fed. Supp., p. 138.

P. 172. "A child is alleged . . . also emotionally disturbed." 412 Fed. Supp., p. 137, paraphrasing *Gault*.

P. 173. ". . . supporting our predilections." William O. Douglas, *The Court Years, 1939–1975* (New York: Vintage Books, 1981), p. 8.

P. 188. ". . . early Roman father over his children." Teitelbaum and Ellis, "Liberty Interests of Children," p. 168.

P. 192. "Held . . ." *Parham*, 442 U.S. 584 (1979), *U.S. Supreme Court Reports*, p. 107.

P. 192. ". . . requirement would entail." *Parham*, *U.S. Supreme Court Reports*, p. 117.

Chap. 7. Taps for Jackie (*Cont.*)

P. 193. ". . . for additional obligations." *Parham, U.S. Supreme Court Reports,* p. 118.

P. 193. "As with so many . . . American tradition." *Parham, U.S. Supreme Court Reports,* p. 119 (cites omitted).

8. Family Covenant

P. 197. ". . . move into the criminal area." Nicholas Kittrie, personal communication.

P. 197. "Constitutional Argument." Carol Du Bois, ed., *Elizabeth Cady Stanton and Susan B. Anthony, Correspondence, Writings, Speeches* (New York: Schocken Books, 1981), pp. 152–65.

P. 197. ". . . abridge their privileges or immunities." Du Bois, *Stanton and Anthony,* p. 158.

P. 197. ". . . equal rights to all." Du Bois, *Stanton and Anthony,* p. 161.

P. 198. ". . . on the concept of social contract." Nicholas Kittrie, personal communication.

P. 198. ". . . obedience to the criminal law." Charles Rembar, *The Law of the Land: The Evolution of Our Legal System* (New York: Simon and Schuster, 1980), pp. 89–90.

P. 198. ". . . only consequence is a civil liability." Rembar, *The Law of the Land,* p. 41.

P. 199. ". . . speculative therapy." Raymond I. Parnas, "The Relevance of Criminal Law to Inter-Spousal Violence," in *Family Violence: An International and Interdisciplinary Study,* ed. John M. Eekelaar and Sanford N. Katz (Toronto: Butterworths, 1978), p. 191.

P. 200. "prior links." Barbara Basler, *New York Times,* February 25, 1982, p. B-6.

P. 201. ". . . she winds up being punished." Roland Summit, personal communication.

P. 202. ". . . deprivation into help." Bazelon, *Forward, Symposium,* Mental Illness, the Law and Civil Liberties, 13 Santa Clara Law 367 (1973).

P. 203. "children born sinners, with wills that need to be broken." See, e.g., *New York Times,* December 7, 1981, p. A-22: "Until Moral Majority began complaining, a Government booklet entitled, 'Your Child From One to Six,' had been routinely sent out by Senator Richard G. Lugar, Representative of Indiana, to his constituents. For over 60 years various editions of the booklet have proved an evergreen on the Government's self-help pamphlet lists. But back home in Indiana, Greg Dixon, a Moral Majority leader, began denouncing the current edition for counseling parents not to spank their offspring and for implying that children might not be born with strains of evil in them. Mr. Dixon contended this violated Biblical teachings that everyone, Senator Lugar's constituents included, are born sinners."

Chap. 8. Family Covenant (*Cont.*)

P. 203. Section 501 of the Family Protection Act summarized. From *Provisions of S. 1378—Family Protection Act* (New York: National Center on Women and Family Law). See Congressional Record—Senate, June 17, 1981, S6343, p. 22. For an overview of the Family Protection Act and the arguments pro and con, see Douglas Lavine "Congress Nulls Family Fate," *National Law Journal* 3 (July 20, 1981), pp. 1, 30–31.

P. 203. "3,000 establishments . . . 300,000 American kids." "For the Child's Own Good," *NBC News Reports,* February 28, 1980, 10 P.M. E.S.T., produced, written and directed by Robert Rogers, transcript pp. 4–5.

P. 204. ". . . we will go and get you." "For the Child's Own Good," transcript p. 14.

P. 204. war stories about religious institutions. See, e.g., Reginald Stuart, "Home's Ex-Inmates Tell of Beatings," *New York Times,* March 5, 1982, p. A-15.

P. 206. ". . . crimes that threaten our safety and security." Michael P. Rosenthal, "Physical Abuse of Children by Parents: The Criminalization Decision," *American Journal of Criminal Law* 7, no. 2 (July 1979), p. 144.

P. 207. Wisconsin cases. See Dan Allegretti, "Wisconsin Judge's Rape Ruling Angers Residents," *Washington Post,* January 21, 1982, p. A-6.

P. 207. ". . . they won't bother." Jeannine Pirro, personal communication.

P. 208. "law 'has met its match.'" James B. Boskey, "Spousal Abuse in the United States: The Attorney's Role," in Eekelaar and Katz, *Family Violence,* pp. 199–207.

P. 209. ". . . i.e., his liberty." Thomas T. Becker, "Due Process and Child Protective Proceedings, State Intervention in Family Relations on Behalf of Neglected Children," *Cumberland-Samford Law Review* 247 (1971), p. 259.

P. 209. ". . . doubt as to the intention." M. C. J. Olmesdahl, "Paternal Power and Child Abuse: An Historical and Cross-Cultural Study," in Eekelaar and Katz, *Family Violence,* p. 263.

P. 210. M'Naughten rule. Cited in Kittrie, *The Right to Be Different,* p. 23.

P. 210. the horizon effect. Hans Berliner, "Computer Backgammon," *Scientific American* 242, no. 6 (June 1980), p. 64.

Permissions

I acknowledge with thanks permission to quote from the following sources:

The Phil Donahue Show, #19235, of September 23, 1980.

Haven in a Heartless World: The Family Besieged, by Christopher Lasch. Copyright © 1977 by Basic Books, Inc., Publishers, New York.

"Developments in the Law, the Constitution and the Family," vol. 93: 1156, no. 6. Copyright © April, 1980 by the Harvard Law Review Association.

Sexual Suicide, by George Gilder (Quadrangle/New York Times Book Co.). Reprinted by permission of Georges Borchardt, Inc. Copyright © 1973 by George Gilder.

The Mother, Anxiety, and Death: Catastrophic Death Complex, by Joseph C. Rheingold, M.D., Ph.D. Copyright © 1967 by Little, Brown and Company.

Stopping Wife Abuse, by Jennifer Baker Fleming (Doubleday). Copyright © 1979 by Jennifer Baker Fleming.

"Assault Cases That Don't Belong in Criminal Court," letter written by the Honorable Nanette Dembitz, Judge of the Family Court, New York County, to *The New York Times*, published January 19, 1981. Copyright © 1981 by The New York Times Company. Reprinted by permission.

"Fundamentals of Child Protection, a Statement of Basic Concepts and Principles," by Vincent de Francis, J.D. American Humane Association, Englewood, Colorado, 1978.

"Helping in Child Protective Services," ed. Wayne M. Holder and Cynthia Mohr. American Humane Association, 1980.

Power/Knowledge: Selected Interviews and Other Writings, by Michel Foucault, ed. Colin Gordon (Pantheon Books, a Division of Random House, Inc.). Copyright © 1980 by Michel Foucault.

The Policing of Families, by Jacques Donzelot, tr. Robert Hurley (Pantheon Books, a Division of Random House, Inc.). English translation copyright © 1979 by Random House, Inc.

Soul Murder: Persecution in the Family, by Morton Schatzman (Random House). Copyright © 1973 by Morton Schatzman.

"Men and the Victimization of Women," by Judith V. Becker and Gene G. Abel, in *The Victimization of Women*, ed. Jane Roberts Chapman and Margaret Gates. Copyright © 1978 by Sage Publications.

Sex and Power in History, by Amaury de Riencourt (Dell). Copyright © 1974 by Amaury de Riencourt.

Index